STANDARI

Research for Writers

The author

Ann Hoffmann has spent the greater part of her professional life working with or for writers. After a first job in publishing, she travelled widely in Europe and, on returning to England, spent four years as secretary/researcher to the well-known writer, the late Robert Henriques. In 1966 she established a research service for authors. She now devotes the bulk of her time to researching and writing her own books; these include *The Dutch: How They Live and Work*, *Bocking Deanery*, *Lives of the Tudor Age*, and *Majorca*.

In this expanded and revised edition of RESEARCH FOR WRITERS, Miss Hoffmann writes knowledgeably from personal experience on a variety of sources of information, on research methods, on some of the pitfalls to be avoided by the 'novice' researcher, and on the particular problems facing writers of fiction and non-fiction.

Research for Writers

REVISED EDITION

Ann Hoffmann

A & C Black · London

Fourth edition 1992

Being the second edition under the title *Research for Writers*;
first edition published 1986
by A & C Black (Publishers) Limited
35 Bedford Row, London WC1R 4JH

ISBN 0-7136-3584-3

Previously published under the title *Research: a handbook for
writers and journalists*
First edition 1975 Midas Books
Second edition 1979 A & C Black (Publishers) Limited

©1992, 1975, 1979, 1986 Ann Hoffmann

The photograph on the front cover is of the British Museum Reading
Room, reproduced with kind permission by The British Library Board.

Typeset by Florencetype, Kewstoke, Avon
Printed in Great Britain by Biddles Limited, Guildford, Surrey

Contents

Principal Abbreviations used in this Book

AGRA	Association of Genealogists and Record Agents
Aslib	Association for Information Management (formerly called the Association of Special Libraries and Information Bureaux)
BAC	Business Archives Council
BALH	British Association for Local History
BBA	*British Biographical Archive*
BBC	British Broadcasting Corporation
BFI	British Film Institute
BL	British Library
BLAISE	British Library Automated Information Service
BM	British Museum*
BN	Bibliothèque Nationale
BNB	*British National Bibliography*
CD-ROM	Compact Disk-Read Only Memory**
CSO	Central Statistical Office
DNB	*Dictionary of National Biography*
FFHS	Federation of Family History Societies
HMSO	Her Majesty's Stationery Office
ICA	International Council on Archives
IGI	International Genealogical Index
ITC	Independent Television Commission
KIST	*Keyword Index to Serial Titles*

* On 1 July 1973 the former library departments of the British Museum were incorporated in the British Library Reference Division. Scholars and *habitués* of the Reading Room and Department of Manuscripts still use the old affectionate term, 'the BM'. When the Round Reading Room finally closes to readers in 1996 it will no longer be valid and will fall into disuse.
** CD-ROM technology allows the storage of up to 200,000 pages of A-4 paper on one disk. At present it can be accessed from a personal computer only if the latter has a CD-ROM drive. Since it is a 'write-once, read only' medium, the information cannot be accidentally erased or lost.

LA	Library Association
n.d.	no date
N.S.	New Style (dates)
NSA	National Sound Archive
OED	*Oxford English Dictionary*
OPAC	Online Public Access Catalogue
O.S.	Old Style (dates)
PCC	Prerogative Court of Canterbury (wills)
PCY	Prerogative Court of York (wills)
PRO	Public Record Office
SRIS	British Library Science Reference and Information Service

Note: For the sake of brevity and to avoid the clumsy repetition of 'he' and 'she' throughout the book, writers/researchers are referred to by the one pronoun, 'he'. No offence is intended to the female person.

Author's note

When I embarked on this project in 1975 it was with the idea of setting down, for freelance writers faced with the daunting task of researching for publication for the first time, some practical notes on methods and sources that would start them off along the right lines and at the same time help them to avoid some of the pitfalls. Although the book has grown in the process, and this fourth edition enables me to up-date and expand the text still further, it was never intended to be – nor, considering the vast sources available to the modern writer, can it ever be – more than a guide. No one researcher can do more than scratch the surface, let alone compile a comprehensive research manual.

Researching, like writing, is an individual, creative and selective process. It cannot be 'taught'. In his quest for original material – and who does not dream of stumbling upon a cache of hitherto unknown, unpublished papers or the answer to a problem that has baffled scholars for several generations? – the writer never ceases to learn. All the time he is probing, absorbing, adding to his store of knowledge of sources of information largely by trial and error. Either he has a 'nose' for it or he has not. If not, unless he has time on his hands, he would be well advised to use the services of a professional. An elementary grasp of sources can of course be gleaned from a textbook and a few days' intensive study in a good reference library; this has immense value as a springboard. After that he is on his own. Invariably he will find himself, at different stages of his research, thrust into the unaccustomed roles of student, librarian, interviewer, detective and private investigator, and much else besides.

Throughout the compilation of this handbook, therefore, I have had in mind the many time-consuming problems likely to be encountered by a novice writer/researcher, whether he is concerned with fiction or non-fiction. I have dared to suggest, from my own experience, ways in which these problems may be tackled. I have, as it were, laid out on my work bench for fellow craftsmen to pick up, handle and use as they see fit all those tried and trusted reference tools that have served me well during my twenty-odd years as a professional researcher, together with some newer, less tested, aids. They may not be the particular assortment that a colleague would select, being in the main drawn from my own research activities which have concentrated more on the factual, historical and bio-graphical rather than on scientific or technical fields. But to me they have proved loyal and steadfast helpmates, and I am confident that they in turn will help others to solve some of those alarming and often seemingly insoluble conundrums that have the nasty habit of cropping up at the worst possible moment in every writer's working day. Hopefully, too, in the long term, there may result books and features and theses that are not only better researched, but researched with less stress and strain and burning of the midnight oil on the part of their authors.

I should like to take this opportunity to express my gratitude to the many librarians, archivists, curators, press and public relations officers and others who have so efficiently and courteously dealt with my enquiries on a multitude of subjects over the years, and most especially the staff of the British Library. I am also indebted to several fellow writers, research colleagues and librarians who made constructive comments on the first three editions, some of whose suggestions are now incorporated.

Gradually, over the past two decades, we have all become accus-tomed to the new 'information technology'. Terms such as 'data-base', 'on-line'* and 'CD-ROM' are now in everyday use, especially by the younger generation who have grown up with them. No one who has embarked recently on research at a library or archive centre can have failed to make use of the up-to-date microfiche names/titles or subject catalogues or of one of several excellent reprographic facilities currently available. Regular researchers know that if they require lengthy material to be photocopied, microfilm works out cheaper than xerox, especially if it is to be despatched from overseas. Readers at the Public Record Office tap out their document requests with confidence on computer ter-minals, as they will do at the new British Library when it opens in 1993. Increasingly, too, researchers are making use of the computer search services on offer at major libraries.

In previous editions of this book I forecast that the microfilm reader would soon become as normal a piece of equipment in the writer's study as the typewriter then was. I was wrong. Writing now in 1991, it is clear that writers and journalists and researchers

* For an explanation of 'on-line' and related terms, see pages 14–15.

in large droves are investing, not so much in the humble microfilm reader, but in personal computers and word processors. Some individual researchers are even competing with libraries by going 'on-line' in order to have access to the already vast, and rapidly growing, data-bases in this country and overseas.

We writers and researchers of today should count ourselves fortunate to be living in the midst of what the librarians and information scientists call 'the information explosion', in which a computer-generated bonanza of information has become accessible at speed, and at relatively low cost, via 'on-line' retrieval systems worldwide. For all of us this is a bonanza indeed. Never before has so much research material been so instantly accessible.

I also stuck my neck out by predicting that the time was not far off when the writer would do his research without ever setting foot in library or record office, simply by summoning his source material onto a screen at home. That day has not yet come, but we *are* moving in its direction. Already the fortunate computer-owner who is 'on-line' is able to call up onto his personal monitor bibliographical material on any given subject, from international data-bases housing literally millions of references. At present, only those with CD-ROM drives and the appropriate software have access to the vast amount of reference material now being produced on CD-ROM, but it will surely not be long before relatively inexpensive personal computers with this facility, possibly also CD-ROM players with clip-on screens, come on the market. When that happens – perhaps even by the time this edition is published – the writer will be able to read long runs of archives, state papers, newspapers and journals, bibliographies and much else in the comfort and privacy of his own study. (A single CD holds the entire *Encyclopedia Britannica*.) A logical next step will be for *all* printed texts to be fed automatically into the computer at the time of publication. It is unlikely, however, that any attempt will be made to store all texts previously published (a task that would involve going back to the time of Caxton). Thus for the historian and the biographer, for the writer of historical novels – or indeed for any author or journalist who writes about the past – research in the library and archives centre will, for some time yet, still be very much a part of his work routine. Thus, too, the techniques and sources outlined here will remain valid.

As in the earlier editions, books mentioned in the text are listed alphabetically by title at the end of the relevant chapter rather than in one long bibliography at the end. (Listing by title rather than by author runs contrary to recognised bibliographic practice. Its continuance in this edition is, I hope, justified for reasons of quick reference: the works themselves are referred to first by title in the text and users of earlier editions will have become familiar with this method.) Microform editions have been included in a few salient cases only. Publication on film, fiche and CD being such a fast-growing industry, to have attempted more would have been at best incomplete. It would also have added considerably to the bulk (and thus the cost) of this book. A researcher who is 'on the ball' will ask at the library information counter; even if he does not, the competent librarian or archivist will always bring such editions to his attention. Regrettably, it is not possible always to indicate those books which are out of print, as the situation changes constantly and reprints or new editions may become available during the lifetime of this handbook. Most of the out-of-print titles mentioned will be found in the larger public libraries or may be borrowed through the public library lending service; but researchers needing to use such books over a long period are recommended to 'shop around' for them in secondhand and antiquarian bookshops (and even jumble sales), or to ask a book-finding service to try to locate them (see page 41).

Inevitably, with so much new material to hand, some titles have had to be dropped in this edition. The rule of thumb which I have applied here has been to prune and discard what I personally consider to be 'dead wood' (titles that have been superseded by more up-to-date, improved works), but to retain those earlier books that are still among the best on their subject. For example, I doubt very much that a researcher today would want to consult a book about London libraries published as long ago as 1964, whereas a novelist setting his story in England in the early 19th century definitely still needs to know of John Burnett's admirable Pelican *History of the Cost of Living*, so that he can ask for it at the library.

The need to go to press a year before publication makes it impossible to be fully up to date, but readers who follow my guidelines for using library catalogues and bibliographies should have little difficulty in tracing recently published material or new editions of existing works. Addresses and telephone numbers are a different matter, changing as they do, it seems, with unpredictable frequency. (At the time of writing it has just been announced that all London numbers are to be given an extra digit by April 1994.) This means that, depending on the month of publication, even annual guides will be out of date by the time they appear. This aspect – or hazard, if you like – of modern living is one we simply have to learn to accept.

My mail-bag since the appearance of the first edition makes it clear that the handbook has been of use not only to the amateur and student for whom it was intended, and even on occasion to those who make a hobby of entering competitions, but also to the more experienced 'diggers' who – so they tell me – sometimes suffer from extraordinary lapses of memory or mental blocks which may result in their wasting precious time searching for information that in fact is close at hand in their own reference collection or in a local library. To all these people I dedicate this revised edition. In return, the greatest compliment they can pay me will be to *use the book as a working tool, to annotate it profusely, and to up-date it as their research requires*. For this purpose my publishers have again included a few blank pages at the end for personal notes. If, by the time these pages are filled, the book is starting to come apart at the spine through constant usage, hopefully there may be a fifth edition in the pipeline. As before, comments and suggestions for future editions will be most gratefully received.

A.H.
London, 1991

1

The Writer as Researcher

Every writer, unless he is creating a work of pure fantasy, has to do research. The nature and depth of that research will vary enormously, according to the subject of the work, the field of writing (factual article, novel, biography, history, thesis, children's story, etc.) and whether it is intended for the academic, popular or juvenile market. Whereas the scholar may have comparatively unlimited time (and probably also a research grant) which allows him to follow up pretty well every relevant line of enquiry in detail, the journalist's 'copy' must be on the sub-editor's desk at a given hour, and he is always pressed for time. Both texts must be correct, up to date and original – in other words, properly researched and well written.

In the end-product the academic work, with its notes and references, bibliography and index, may look to be the more meticulously researched, but this can be a deception: the thousand-word newspaper or magazine article, in order to present its data in a convincing, accurate and readable way and to show that its author is fully conversant with the latest events and/or published studies on the subject, may well involve as much, and sometimes more, research in proportion to its length. Whatever the field of authorship, the writer has to know a great deal more than he actually puts into words if what he writes is to ring true – and this applies as strictly to fiction writers as to journalists and historians and biographers. Ernest Hemingway, in an interview published in *Paris Review* (Spring 1958), put this very well. 'I always try to write on the principle of the iceberg,' he said. 'There is seven-eighths of it under water for every part that shows. Anything you know you can eliminate and it only strengthens your iceberg. It is the part that doesn't show. If the writer omits something because he does not know it, then there is a hole in the story.'*

---

* The same author, in *Death in the Afternoon*, expounds on this theme at greater length in a memorable passage worthy of framing and hanging above every writer's desk. It will be found at the end of chapter 16; in the paperback edition (Penguin Books, 1973) at pages 181–3.

1

In ideal circumstances an author would write only of what he knows. No one, however, can have first-hand knowledge of every trade or profession in which he wishes to place his characters; few can afford to visit all those far-off lands that they are tempted to use as 'local colour' in their work. In most short stories or novels or plays, therefore, there are bound to be some people, some situations, and some settings that are beyond the personal experience of the writer, and for which he must rely to some extent at least on secondhand material – that is to say, on what others before him have observed and recorded, on printed statistics and factual data, and often on the recollections of third parties. The writer of history or historical fiction has no choice but to rely on documentary sources, either in print or in manuscript. In all these instances the research done must be thorough and, as far as possible, undertaken *in the round* (i.e. from more than one angle, avoiding reliance on any one source), or the result will be cardboard people, cardboard backgrounds and a loss of credibility in what may otherwise be an excellent piece of writing.

The prime importance of researching thoroughly before going into print cannot be over-stressed. Once his reader's confidence has been lost, the author will have an uphill battle to regain it. All too often a disillusioned reader or bright schoolchild will write and tell him where he has gone wrong, or – which is worse – may write and tell his editor or publisher, which in turn destroys their confidence and is likely to influence their attitude to the author's future work.

It is dangerous to rely on only one source for a given piece of information, however authoritative that source may seem to be. Mistakes occur all too frequently in even the most erudite book. They may not be the original author's fault at all, but the result of slipshod proof-reading in the editor's office or a printer's error that occurred at a later stage, such as when the type-setter re-sets a line to incorporate the author's or publisher's corrections. The sad thing is that once they are in print, mistakes are bound to be copied in good faith by someone else, and that person's work in turn may well be used as source material by another, and so on, so that even if a correction is made in subsequent editions of the original work, the misprint in that first edition may be perpetrated *ad infinitum*. By 'misprints' in this context is meant the mis-spelling of a proper name, a mis-quotation or a wrong figure – the sort of error that would not necessarily be spotted by a reader. The other kind of mistake, known as a 'literal' in publishing and printing, which may be a character set up in the wrong fount, or upside down, or two characters transposed, and the more obvious spelling mistake are more likely to be spotted at proof-reading stage.

Such are the hazards of authorship that the writer of non-fiction would do well to keep constantly in his mind's eye as he works the image of future trusting generations of students and researchers relying on his text as an authoritative source.

For most modern writers time is a precious commodity. Gone for ever are those halcyon days when Samuel Johnson could speak of a man turning over half a library to make one book; since his day millions more books have been written and published, and our libraries, archive collections and record repositories now house a bewildering and ever-increasing conglomeration of printed, manu-script, microfilmed and recorded material; they also have access to vast data-bases worldwide. More than ever before has it become essential for the writer/researcher to organize his working hours to the best advantage. He must know where and how to get at the information he requires in the quickest, as well as the most efficient and economical, way. As the great Dr Johnson also said: 'Knowl-edge is of two kinds. We know a subject ourselves, or we know where we can find information upon it.' While the specialist must know his pet subject inside out, there is no question but that for the general writer the knowledge of *where to go* to find what he needs is of the greater value. Quite apart from the fact that no one would want to become a walking encyclopedia, even if it were humanly possible to carry a mass of information on a variety of subjects in one's head all the time, most professional writers would agree that a sound knowledge of available sources (or, failing that, a reliable researcher on whose services they can call) allows them more time to concentrate on the creative activity. Nothing can be more dis-tracting or more paralysing to the flow of ideas and their shaping into words than a nagging worry, 'Where on earth am I going to be able to find out about *that*?'

Seeking information implies curiosity, a characteristic inborn not only in the feline species but in the whole human race. We have all been researchers since we were in the cradle. Long before he can speak or read or write, a baby is obsessed by the desire to find out about the things around him. Attracted by the colour of an un-known object, he reaches out to touch it and, having seized it and found it pleasing to hold, usually puts it into his mouth. What does it feel like? Does it taste good? What is it made of? *What* is it? He has taken the first step along a path of discovery and enchantment that will last a lifetime. From that first childish desire to learn about objects, he progresses to curiosity about himself and his body, and then to other people and animals; from the happenings he observes in his immediate circle to those of history; through history to religion, and then to science and speculation about the future. He

3

will never know it all, but if as he grows older he keeps alive his youthful sense of curiosity he will – especially if he becomes a writer – have endless resources on which to draw, and he will never be bored.

It is a well-known saying that a writer may be angry, disgusted, amused, uplifted or almost anything in between, and his work will be the better for it, but if he is bored it will be reflected in his writing. Robert Louis Stevenson held that life would be only a very dull and ill-directed theatre unless we had some interests in the piece. 'It is in virtue of his own desires and curiosities that any man continues to exist with even patience,' he wrote, 'that he is charmed by the look of things and people, and that he wakens every morning with a renewed appetite for work and pleasure. Desire and curiosity are the two eyes through which he sees the world in the most enchanted colours: it is they that make women beautiful or fossils interesting . . .'*

Because a writer's raw material is derived principally from a study of other human beings, their complex relationships, their strengths and weaknesses and idiosyncrasies, as well as their history, he can probably get away with being more openly curious than any other group of people – provided always that he does not offend by his looking or probing. The arts of observation without seeming to observe and of probing without seeming to probe are skills that can – and should – be acquired.

While most writers are also researchers, not all researchers are talented as writers. The prime function of the researcher is to seek information; that of the writer is more complicated, for his duty is both to impart knowledge and to give pleasure – in other words, to entertain as well as to instruct his reader. And just as a factual book can give pleasure to the reader by the manner in which it is written, so the most absorbing and entertaining of stories can impart knowledge. The one thing a writer must never do, under any circumstances, however, is to distort the truth for the sake of a good story.

Everything that comes within the writer's own experience is grist to the mill and should be stored away, ideally in note form or on tape or computer, for future use. Ideas, an unusual turn of phrase, a gesture, a conversation overheard, brief descriptions of people or places, on-the-spot reports of events, even pain suffered (you think at the time you will always remember how it felt, but you rarely do): these will be of immense value, provided that they are kept in such a way that they can be turned up quickly when required.

---

* From the essay 'El Dorado' in *Virginibus Puerisque*.

(Some practical suggestions for filing and storage are discussed on pages 18–21). Naturally it is not possible to predict years in advance what you are going to need, so that how much or how little is noted and filed must be a decision for the individual writer, but it is a fact of life that once you throw something away, you need it. The Preface to Somerset Maugham's *A Writer's Notebook*, first published in 1949, makes interesting reading on this score, for the author admits that there were many years in which he made no notes at all, that he kept no record of his meetings with famous people. 'I never made a note of anything that I did not think would be useful to me at one time or another in my work,' he states, 'and though, especially in the early notebooks, I jotted down all kinds of thoughts and emotions of a personal nature, it was only with the intention of ascribing them sooner or later to the creatures of my invention. I meant my notebooks to be a storehouse of materials for future use and nothing else.' So spoke the short story writer and novelist. It would be unthinkable for a diarist or biographer to fail to record his meetings with famous people.

In the course of his researching life a writer will be faced with a variety of tasks. These may range from the simple checking of facts (dates, quotations, spellings, statistics) to the tracing of a contemporary account of some historical event, or the more complicated unravelling of someone's ancestry, or an authentic setting for a novel or play. The best-selling author Frederick Forsyth reckons to divide his research into four categories: *geographical* (which necessitates visits to places); *historical* (checkable in source material); *procedural* (which involves contacting and talking to 'inside' people); and *technical* (checkable facts). It will be obvious that there are wide differences, both of skill and approach, between the four, and that some of the categories overlap or merge.

In *factual research* (statistical, historical and technical), the enquirer knows precisely what he is looking for and what he expects to find, so that, provided he knows where to go for the information, he should encounter no great difficulty. Knowing where to go is the key here.

In pure *historical research* the scope is much wider, as regards both the material available and the use that is made of it. As no two writers, given the same plot and the same set of characters, will come up with an identical story, so no two researchers, confronted with the same documentary sources, will use those sources in an identical way. The basic facts – the skeleton – will be similar, of course, but whereas one researcher will explore a certain avenue in more detail than another and quote extensively from a document that in the eyes of his colleague merits no more than a passing reference, the second may be less selective on one aspect of the search but obsessive about detail on another, depending upon the angle from which their respective works are to be written and on the market for which they are intended.

Background research (which includes the geographical and procedural), usually required for a work of fiction, modern or historical, generally demands less discipline but, as a result, may lead the enquirer down some unforeseen channels and possibly end by radically changing the shape or character of his story.

Thus both historical and background research fall into the category of *creative*, as opposed to *factual*, research. In these fields the researcher, not knowing beforehand what he is going to find, must be alive to each and every clue he comes across, any one of which could lead to some vital discovery that could bring his work to life in an exciting and original way.

In general, an article or thesis will require either factual or historical research, or both, whereas most books will demand a mixture of all three types of research, in varying proportions according to their subject and what the writer already knows. In a biography, for example, some factual research will be necessary to substantiate a quotation from a letter or diary of a certain date; historical research to fill in the detail of an event in which the subject of the biography played a leading part; background research to permit the author to describe, say, the environment in which that person grew up. In an historical novel, dates and names and events must be factually correct, while background research will be important in order to bring it to life, to add accurate details of costume, food, manners, etc. of the relevant period. In a modern short story or play, the setting must be authentic and the characters must speak the right language (slang, dialect or technical idiom related to their occupations and age). Some of the problems and pitfalls, as well as the sources of information appropriate to each of these categories of research, are outlined in later sections of this book.

Whatever the subject or nature of the search, the procedure is roughly the same. You may begin with one solid fact or several – this may be a date, or an event, or a name, or just an idea – and you build up your dossier rather like the CID officer tracks his criminal: with patience, persistence and, hopefully, the occasional lucky break. It may take you months to ferret out one vital clue, or you may chance upon it almost immediately; often, however, it is just when you have returned wearily to square one from yet another in a series of blind alleys that you stumble on the missing link (and curse yourself for following up so many red herrings on the way). All researchers know the elation this unexpected discovery produces, and it is nowhere more aptly described than by the university professor quoted in Dr A.L. Rowse's *A Cornish Childhood* as saying, '. . . I felt that curious thrill, the authentic sensation of the researcher . . . It is as if you were to sit down and find you have sat on the cat. The thing comes alive in your hand . . .' Peter Fleming, discussing the art of research with the late Joan St George Saunders of Writers' and Speakers' Research, the first professional research service in this country (there are several others now), likened it to fox hunting: 'The horns sound, one races for the first covert – then a halt while the hounds snuffle around in the undergrowth. Here the cunning hunter circles around the wood and knows instinctively which way the hounds will break. Off you go again and by the end of the day you are still there – perhaps to be blooded with success!'*

One of the researcher's greatest problems lies in deciding when to call it a day. It is always possible – and tempting – to go on delving just a little further – provided, of course, that time and adequate funds are available. But he must keep in mind the terms of reference of his work and discipline himself accordingly. Only experience will enable him to acquire the 'feel' of the job, to know when he should follow his hunch and go off at a tangent, when to replace the reference books on the shelf and pick up his pen. The temptation will nearly always be there to continue researching 'for a little while longer'. All too easily the writer can slip into the comfortable routine of a perpetual student.

It is a bad thing to postpone indefinitely the real creative process. Indeed, to prolong researching unduly is regarded by some historians as an indication of a fear of the actual writing. Therefore once a certain stage in the research has been reached, it is best to press on with a first draft. A modest amount of further research will almost certainly be necessary, and possible, at a later stage, when you will know more precisely what you need or in order to up-date, to fill in any gaps or to explore aspects of your subject which you may have ignored at the outset but now wish to include. Very often an editor or agent, after a first reading of the author's typescript, will suggest modifications or additions; in the case of a book, it will be the copy editor who will query with the author certain spellings or statements, some of which may involve extra research.

* Letter to the author from Mrs St George Saunders, 15 August 1975. Quoted by kind permission of Sir Alan Urwick.

Modern society is constantly on the move, new studies appear every week, and since it now takes an average of between nine and twelve months from delivery of manuscript to the date of publication of a book, unless a writer is submitting an article of topical interest for almost instant publication in a newspaper or journal, it will be impossible for his work to be fully up to date. Modern typesetting procedures and the current practice of going straight into page proofs instead of first into galleys and then into page have made it prohibitively expensive for any but the most essential corrections and up-datings to be incorporated at his stage – apart, of course, from printer's errors and 'literals'. You should not allow this to worry you unduly: it is the same for everyone, and a well-researched, well-written work will always achieve recognition as such.

In the fulfilment of his work, whether it be long or short, fiction or non-fiction, the author will surely have experienced the deep sense of satisfaction that is the reward of a thorough job of research. If it has not been altogether too traumatic an exercise, he may even go along with the view of the poet Robert Herrick:

> Attempt the end, and never stand to doubt;
> Nothing's so hard, but search will find it out.

2

Organization and Method

The writer's first task, when embarking on a new project, is to survey and organize the material already in his possession. By the time he has done this, he will have a pretty good idea of how much additional research needs to be done. Then, and only then – and always bearing in mind the intended length and complexity of the end-product, as well as the time and funds available – is he ready to move on to tap other sources.

At this stage he should make a preliminary list of everything he needs to find out and where he thinks he will have to go to get it. The key here is to *plan ahead*. Books you want may be in use by other readers, so that you will have to wait a few weeks for them; the people you hope to interview may be busy or away; information you send for may take longer than you anticipate to arrive. You will be surprised also at how much time and money you will save by taking the trouble to write down all those people and places you envisage having to visit: with the aid of a good map and gazetteer you can plan itineraries that take in several assignments on each trip.

Just as it is false economy to skip the amount of time necessary for a thorough study of basic material and sources, so it is foolish to neglect to give proper thought to setting up a system for the storage and easy retrieval of that material, remembering always to make suitable provision for material still to be acquired. Since both these operations cost money as well as time (time = money being a constant theme throughout this book), this is an appropriate place in which to outline some of the financial aspects of research.

Costs of Research

The first thing to remember is that it is always going to cost more than you expect. Leaving aside the question of working time, outgoings will include stationery and equipment, travelling and motor expenses, search fees (charged by some private libraries and by clergy in the case of parish registers), the purchase of books, periodicals and newspapers, photocopying, photography, telephone and postal expenses (these can be unexpectedly heavy). Meals away from home when researching can be expensive, and you should not forget the lighting, heating and cleaning of a room used as office or study, since over the years this too can mount up – and if you are making an income from writing most of such outgoings can be included as legitimate expenses to set against tax. The fees of a professional researcher, if employed, will be another major item, as will those of an indexer, and, at the end of the day, unless you are a good typist, you should allow for the cost of producing the final typescript in two or more copies. Computer-owners should remember to include the cost of the print-out from disk.

It is an excellent idea to make a list of every conceivable expense you think you are going to incur – and then double it. Costs are rising all the time, and if a book takes four years to complete instead of the eighteen months you envisaged at the outset, this will play havoc with your budget. However, you will not have to fork out the total amount in one go, but as you proceed.

If you are fortunate enough to have a book or article commissioned, explain to the publisher or editor before you negotiate the contract or settle the fee just how much research expenditure is likely to be involved, and, in the case of a book, try to negotiate an adequate advance against royalties; this will probably be payable in instalments. Journalists may be able to arrange their assignments on an expenses-paid basis. In all cases, it is wise to keep a record of every item of expenditure, from a packet of paper clips to the hotel bill, and to ask for receipts for all major payments: you may not be a published writer when you start out, but if you end up as the author of a bestseller or even a writer with a modest regular income from his work, you will need to justify your expenses to the tax inspector.

It is always dangerous to state prices in print, especially in these days of inflation. As a guideline to the uninitiated, however, it should be borne in mind that at the time of going to press (autumn 1991) freelance researchers and record agents are charging between £8 and £15 an hour, depending on the special skills involved. Typing costs vary according to the service you require: most agencies and home typists now offer a word-processing facility, with either daisy-wheel or laser printing (consult list on back page of *The Author*). A ream of good quality A-4 bond typing paper retails at approximately £8.50, bank typing paper (for copies) at £6.00;

carbon film (the best for smudge-free copies) costs up to £12.00 per hundred sheets, typewriter ribbons around £2.00 for the older type of manual machine, more for electronic machines. (If you are a member of the Society of Authors you will be able to order supplies through their fringe benefit scheme – provided you can collect the goods from their office – or by shopping around locally you may find a supplier selling stationery at a discount.) Servicing a typewriter will run into at least £50 a year.

Photocopying varies from as little as 10p to 25p a sheet, plus VAT, depending on size (the cheapest being those you make yourself on coin-operated machines), to as much as £1 plus VAT per A-3/A-2 sheet for copies of newspaper pages. Bear in mind that applications by post will be subject both to a minimum charge and to a handling fee. Some libraries offer an express service at additional cost. Genealogists and family historians constantly bemoan the fact that photocopies of birth, marriage and death certificates now cost £5.50 apiece if applied for in person or between £12.00 and £15.00 when ordered by post (see chapter 7, pages 121–2).

One major expense so often overlooked by a writer is the cost of quoting from copyright material: fees are liable to be charged for anything more than a few lines, although in practice some agents and publishers will be content, in the case of a short passage, with a suitable acknowledgment or possibly a free copy of the book. Reproduction fees for illustrative material, on the other hand, vary according to the size of the reproduction and the nature of the rights sought (i.e. British Commonwealth rights, world rights, etc.), but are normally not payable until the date of publication. Sometimes a publisher is willing to bear all or part of such expenses, and an author wishing to quote extensively from copyright material or to use pictures from private photographers, picture agencies or libraries would be well advised to ascertain the costs in advance and to discuss the financial division of responsibilities prior to the contract being drawn up for signature.

'Hidden' expenses will include the number of free copies an author is expected to hand out. Normally he will receive six free copies of his book and may buy additional copies at a substantial discount. It is courteous to give signed copies to those who have helped to prepare the book for the press, such as the professional researcher, translator, indexer or proof-reader (where these are not taken care of by the publisher), and to the typist; copies should also be presented to anyone who has provided a substantial amount of material or given the author access to private papers. The publisher is responsible for sending out review copies.

Equipment

No one would dream of taking up a sports or leisure activity without the proper equipment; nor should a writer or journalist embark on his researches lacking the few essential tools of the trade. It is true that pen and paper, the rudiments of shorthand or speed-writing, access to a good library, and an unlimited amount of time were once all that was needed, and although one might still 'get by' with these, today, when time is money (a recurrent theme of this book, for which I make no apology), it is both sensible and practical to make full use of all that modern technology provides to help us obtain the information we seek as speedily and as inexpensively as possible.

The basic equipment required can be divided into three groups: 1) equipment for use in the writer's study; 2) the tools he takes with him in briefcase or car when researching outside the home; and 3) equipment that is 'desirable' (i.e. where funds permit) or for special assignments.

The suggested items are (excluding normal stationery):

For the study
Typewriter/word processor
Good desk lamp
Tape recorder (or transcribing system) with foot pedal
Filing cabinet or other storage system
Card index system
Large magnifying glass
Stapler/punch (better than paper clips for fastening papers)
Paper guillotine (for trimming notes and enabling you to use all blank scraps)
Letter scales (will save a lot of time queuing at post office, especially if you keep a supply of stamps of varying denominations)
Highlighter pens in different colours (marvellous for marking up press cuttings/photocopies/notes)
Soft pencils (for writing on backs of photographs)

To take out 'on the job'
Briefcase and/or shoulder bag
Personal computer
Mini tape recorder/pocket memo/electronic note-taker, with plenty of spare cassettes and batteries
Larger tape recorder, with detachable microphone (for interviews

Camera and plenty of film, flashbulbs, spare battery (if job requires it; Polaroid or disc camera would be adequate if pictures needed only for research purposes, but a good SLR at least is essential if illustrating own work)

Clipboard (useful for writing on as you walk around or when interviewing)

Pocket magnifier

Mini-stapler

Phonecard (useful for making calls from phone boxes)

Plenty of biros *and* pencils (local record offices and most MSS departments of libraries permit note-taking only in pencil)

Pencil sharpener

Ruler

Map of area to be visited

Local bus/rail time-tables

Small cash book (for noting all expenses)

Spare pair of reading glasses (if used)

Torch

Cash (coins), for cloakroom lockers and self-operated photocopying machines (also useful for tea and coffee vending machines)

For security reasons nowadays many libraries and record offices require visitors to deposit briefcases before entering the search rooms. (Ladies have an advantage here, with the kind of briefcase that doubles as a handbag!) Be sure, therefore, to keep all papers securely fastened or in envelope-type folders so that you do not drop loose sheets on the way.

N.B. Ladies should be aware of the practicality of wearing slacks or jeans for climbing up and down tall library ladders.

For professional researchers or those with special assignments:

A more sophisticated tape recorder, such as those widely used by radio reporters (a 'must' if recordings are to be broadcast)

Telephone answering machine (to answer calls when you are out on the job)

Video recorder or clock radio/cassette recorder

Telephone charge clock (worth its weight in gold if you are on expenses, as you can read off costs of all calls instantly)

and, finally, for those who can afford them

Word processor or computer with appropriate software, floppy and hard disks, and daisy-wheel or laser printer

Microfilm/microfiche reader
Photocopier

Computers

It does not fall within the scope of this book to discuss the pros and cons of word processing for writers. Nor is there space to discuss either the hundreds of books on computing now on the market or the software currently available. The best advice I can give potential buyers is to do their research very thoroughly indeed before comitting themselves to the purchase of expensive equipment, so that they are absolutely sure to make the correct choice for their particular needs. Readers toying with the acquisition of a word processor should first read the article on the subject in the current *Writers' & Artists' Yearbook*; also recommended is the Society of Authors' *Quick Guide*, 'Buying a Word Processor'. Ray Hammond's *The Writer and the Word Processor*, although published in 1984, is still compulsive reading and will almost certainly convince you that you need one. (He will even tell you how to run it on a shoestring!) Gordon Wells' *Low Cost Word Processing* is a useful handbook.

What *is* relevant here – and of paramount importance to the modern researcher – is the use of the personal computer not only for the storage and retrieval of research material, but also for 'on-line' access to outside data-bases.

Storage of information on computer can be effected in one of three ways. The cheapest is to use an ordinary audio cassette recorder, but the recall of material thus stored is painfully slow by comparison to the 'floppy' or 'hard' disk systems. A floppy disk system (preferably one with a second disk drive) will probably be adequate for the average writer/researcher; but the writer or professional researcher embarking on a major research programme or wishing to establish his own data-bank of source material will sooner rather than later find it worthwhile to switch to a hard disk (also known as a 'Winchester') system, which is capable of storing up to a hundred times the amount of data and which will produce the information required on screen ten times faster. It is, of course, more expensive.

Going 'on-line' makes it possible for you, through your personal computer, to communicate with other computers and so to extract information from data-bases and data-banks all over the world. The only additional equipment that this involves is a 'modem' (which is plugged into the telephone) and some communications software; you then subscribe to one or more data-bases and on top of this you pay only for the time you are linked to the relevant database. (Charges levied for entering and searching a data-base differ from one producer to another.) Since the transmission of data via telecommunication channels is considerably cheaper than the cost of voice transmission (telephone calls) from one side of the globe to another, 'on-line' retrieval will cost you very much less than you might imagine. This is not to say, of course, that it is cheap. But it is only when you relate the cost to the vast wealth of material to which you have virtually instant access, and compare this with the amount of research that would be necessary, in terms of time = money, to give approximately the same result, that you come to appreciate its tremendous value and potential.

While it is unlikely that any but the established, prolific writer or the professional researcher will contemplate going 'on-line' at present, it should not be forgotten that access to many data-bases is available to individual members of the public through various library computer search services. (For more details see chapter 3, pages 38–9.) Whether or not an individual should go 'on-line' depends (a) on how much research he does and (b) on the value he puts on his personal working time. Most readers of this handbook will find it sufficient to use the library computer search service from time to time. For those who wish to know more about the subject, the following titles are recommended: *Going Online* by Terry Hanson, the *Keyguide to Information Sources in Online and CD-ROM Database Searching* by John Cox, *Online Bibliographic Databases* by James L. Hall and the Aslib *UK Online Search Services*. (Aslib also publishes a number of books on specialised on-line data-bases.)

Microform readers

It may not be many years before the microform (microfilm and microfiche) reader becomes as normal a piece of equipment in the writer's study as the typewriter and personal computer/word processor are today: one has only to consider the dramatic increase in filmed and recorded material in recent years, and the space-saving advantages the storage of such material has over printed and bound books, to see that this is a real possibility. Until the day comes when we are borrowing almost as many microfilms and CDs as books from the library, however, it will scarely be economic to purchase such a machine for private use. The writer needing to study micro-films at home on a short-term basis may be able to find a firm who will hire him a machine for this purpose (consult the yellow pages of your local telephone directory, or write to one of the big photo graphic firms such as Agfa, Bell & Howell, Canon or Kodak; alternatively you can ask the Electronic and Business Equipment Association, 8 Leicester Street, London WC2H 7BN (tel. 071–437 0678).

Photocopiers

Unless a writer does a great deal of photocopying, it is hardly worthwhile purchasing a machine. Some of the cheaper desk-top models will copy only from loose sheets and on special (expensive) paper, and not all those that will take bound books give satisfactory results, especially if the volume to be copied is thick and tightly bound. Although eager salesmen may promise copies at a fraction of the commercial cost, which can be tempting, when one takes into account the cost of materials, electricity, servicing charges, annual depreciation of the machine and operating time – valuable working time – there is not that much saving. The prime value of having a photocopier at hand is the *convenience* of being able to run off copies instantly, without making a special trip to town.

Organization of Material

There are few hard and fast rules in research, but it is wise to establish at the outset, and adhere to, some systematic method of note-taking and storage of data. There is little point in accumulating a mass of notes, press cuttings and other material unless a system is devised whereby you are able to pull out reasonably quickly what you want when you want it in the course of writing. It is equally important that you should replace that material after use in such a way that you can put your hands on it instantly at a later date.

Methods may differ according to individual circumstances and taste, and according to the type of documentation to be handled. The researcher who is already geared to a computer will feed his research into his personal data-bank, either on 'floppy' or 'hard' disk. The rest of us fall into two camps – those who favour a card index system, and those who prefer notebooks, pads or sheets of paper, with a cabinet large enough to house them.

Card index system

The great advantage of a card index is its flexibility. It need not be expensive if slips of paper cut to the correct size are used instead of cards (a local printer will often supply these, using offcuts from other jobs, at a very low cost) and, for further economy, old envelope cartons, shoe boxes, cereal packets or similar containers can be cut down and converted into temporary filing receptacles, suitably labelled, and using stiff card to make alphabetical or other guide cards for the necessary divisions. For more permanent use the commercially manufactured metal or plastic index boxes or drawers are recommended; guide cards with plastic tabs are the most hard-wearing, and record cards will stand up to continual handling better than the flimsier slips. (For real economy, the researcher can always do what some professional indexers do, and once a particular job is finished, re-use the cards or slips by writing on the other side – preferably using a different coloured biro so that there is no danger of confusion should the odd one be accidentally turned over.)

Cards or slips may be carried to and from the reference library or other place of research, as required, either in envelopes (clearly marked in subjects or whatever divisions best fit the job in hand) or in small packs secured by rubber bands. They can be sorted into alphabetical, subject or chronological order, either in one continuous series or per chapter and, if necessary, re-grouped as the work proceeds; coloured cards and coloured stickers (available in various shapes) may be used to denote different subjects or periods within each main division, and slips bearing brief cross-references can be inserted as appropriate. The value of such a system is that its permutations are so great.

Loose sheets and notebooks

Many writers prefer to make their notes on larger sheets of paper. For them the shorthand reporter type of notebook is to be recommended, or there are various sizes of ruled pads, with or without punched holes for fitting into loose-leaf ring binders or spring binders. Keeping notes in exercise books is not a good idea, unless a separate book is used for each section of the research, and even then it is advisable to number the pages and make a simple index in the front of the book, otherwise it may be difficult to locate the exact subject-matter when it is required.

For filing purposes it is best, when using sheets of paper rather than cards or slips, to note each item on a separate sheet or at least to leave a good gap between each item so that the notes can be cut up at home and each one slotted individually into its right folder or envelope. Although this may sound extravagant, writing on both sides of the sheet, unless it is on the same subject and clearly indicated by a bold 'PTO' or arrow at the bottom right-hand corner of the first side, is false economy – much valuable material has been 'lost' in this way. It is all too easy to gather up notes and file them without checking to see what is written on the back; nothing is more frustrating to the writer than to *know* that he has made a note of some vital fact or quotation or source – but *where*? It is also a good plan to get into the habit of putting material away as soon as possible after returning from the library, or after use. Otherwise the telephone may ring, there is nothing else handy on which to jot down a message, so the sheets lying on the desk are turned over, scribbled on – inevitably, sooner or later, something will go astray.

Working chronologies

Some writers engaged on an historical study or biography find it helpful to make themselves a working chronology to keep at their elbow while they work. This can be a straightforward listing of events or, in the case of a biography, may consist of a loose-leaf ring binder with the sheets arranged so that when the book is open the left-hand page lists the happenings in the life of the biographee and his family, while the right-hand page lists outside events of approximately the same date. Ample space should be left between dates for subsequent insertions as research proceeds, to avoid the necessity of retyping pages. The time spent on the preparation of this simple working tool will be amply repaid by the ease with which the writer will be able to see his subject in perspective as he works.

Another useful system for the non-fiction writer is a small card index containing, on separate cards, a brief note of all the important points that must be covered, chapter by chapter. Before planning each chapter the writer can cast his eye over the cards and re-group them in the order in which he intends to deal with them, and when that chapter is finished anything that needs to be mentioned again later can be transferred on to the relevant section, so that he will not lose sight of it when the time comes.

Filing

If the documentation is not vast, the most convenient form of storage may be in large manila envelopes, clear plastic or multi-coloured document wallets, numbered or clearly marked as to subject or content; some researchers prefer the 'concertina' type of file or the folders secured with elastic that have up to nine divisions. For all but the simplest research collections, however, a steel filing cabinet will be a worthwhile investment. There are some small trolley-type cabinets on castors, which will suit the writer who likes to have his material at his elbow, at desk or armchair, wherever he works; otherwise the single- or multi-drawer cabinet, with or without suspension filing, is the best buy. As each book or writing project is completed, the material can be cleared out, parcelled up and stored elsewhere to make space for the next assignment.

So far as the storage of used material is concerned, the cardboard cartons obtainable free from wine shops and supermarkets are most useful; but photographs and manuscripts are best kept dust-free and flat in the boxes usually supplied with most good-quality typing papers. For the perfectionist, or the writer who envisages the need to have quick access to his old material, there are on the market excellent lightweight storage containers, ranging from collapsible box files to the more rigid corrugated board storage cabinet complete with drawers. It is worth remembering that cardboard allows documents to 'breathe', whereas metal does not; valuable archive material (e.g. original letters) should not be kept for any length of time in a closed filing cabinet.

Whatever system is adopted, and it will vary according to individual needs (and pockets), there are two essentials that will prove their worth over and over again: the establishment of a key for quick reference, and a system of clear labelling. Notebooks with alphabetical divisions or the most compact of desk-top card indexes are adequate for the former, a supply of labels and felt marker pens in various colours for the latter. The card index, which may be kept in a box or in a rotary filing unit, should be as simple as possible, containing just sufficient information – either names and telephone numbers, or titles of books and periodicals, with page references and/or dates, or any suitable code of reference numbers – to send the user directly to the required source material.

A word of advice now to those who are setting up a new filing system – THINK BIG! As work progresses, you are bound to accumulate at least twice as much material as you planned for, and you should bear in mind, too, that a four-drawer filing cabinet takes up no more floor space than the single-drawer model. Few writers will be like the well-known historian and biographer who has admitted to having taken four years to decide to buy a proper filing cabinet and another four years to fill it – but those who do find themselves with empty drawers at the outset can always put them to good use. (Think of the peace of mind it will give you when you go away to research or on holiday to know that the one and only copy of your unfinished manuscript is securely stowed away, comparatively fireproof and out of the reach of vandals!)

The same goes for original material loaned to the writer. This is a big responsibility, and it is advisable always to make a point of photocopying or taking notes of what you need and returning the originals to their owners without delay. If this is absolutely not possible, at least keep the material in a safe place. Newspaper cuttings will go brown if kept in the daylight for any length of time, photographs can be easily damaged and rendered unsuitable for reproduction if left lying around on the desk, and some picture agencies require the borrower to pay substantial costs for the loss or damage of negatives or transparencies.

Books should always be treated with special care, whether they are loaned by private individuals or borrowed from the library. If they are to be handled a great deal, it is a good idea to cover them with plastic film or brown paper. *Never* write in the margins or turn down corners to mark a reference (unless of course the book belongs to you and you regard it as a working copy); and be very careful when photocopying that you do not bend it in such a way as to damage the binding.

Take special care to write on the backs of photographs only with a very soft pencil; anything else can do irreparable damage. It is best to keep all illustrative material in a separate drawer, box file or filing tray, with each print inside a plastic folder or stiffened envelope. Elementary advice, maybe, but it is a fact that many photographs suffer through being left lying about unprotected; even if they are stacked underneath other papers they may sometimes inadvertently be scribbled on, and once that kind of damage is done it cannot be undone.

For those who are interested, there is an excellent British Library booklet, *Caring for Books and Documents* by A. D. Baynes-Cope. Researchers who handle original documents are also recommended to read 'Notes on the Use of Private Papers for Historical Research' in the *Bulletin of the Institute of Historical Research*, November 1966 (reprints of this useful article are available from the Royal Commission on Historical Manuscripts, Quality House, Quality Court, Chancery Lane, London WC2A 1HP).

Three final tips:

1 Having set up the system that suits you and your project, do make an effort to keep the filing up to date, or the whole purpose will be defeated. If it is not possible to slot material away as it comes in, it is a good idea to keep some kind of 'pending' box or file, or a nest of filing baskets, into which you can put it until you have the time.

2 Remember that every good filing system has a 'Miscellaneous' file, and get into the habit of looking there for anything you cannot find instantly. As the 'Miscellaneous' file grows – and it is wise to allow plenty of space for it – new subject headings will

suggest themselves and the appropriate material can be extracted and filed separately.
3 NEVER THROW AWAY ANY NOTES without keeping a record of the sources.

Research Methods

Having established his storage system, the writer is ready to go out and seek the additional material he needs.

Use of libraries

Finding your way round the library or libraries where you intend to do the bulk of your research is half the battle for the writer. The first thing to remember is that the librarian's job is to guide the researcher or reader to the right books; he is not paid to do original research for you. It is nevertheless astonishing how much a cooperative, interested librarian *will* do, and it is always politic to take him into your confidence about the scope of your research and what you are writing. Similarly, it is advisable to contact the librarian of a special library, either by telephone or letter, before making a first visit; provided he is given due notice of your interest, the librarian or one of his assistants will usually then prepare a preliminary selection of titles, and work can begin without delay. If you do not do this, you may find that the librarians are tied up with other readers when you arrive, and you can easily waste half a day of valuable researching time.

In public libraries, the reference departments of most public libraries and the majority of special and private subscription libraries, the reader has access to the stacks and will be free to browse among the books arranged on the shelves related to his subject; where this is not the case, he should ask a library assistant to explain how the catalogue or subject index is arranged and how to order books. At the major copyright and university libraries a certain number of reference works are on what is known as 'open access', that is to say on shelves where they may be consulted by the reader or from which they may be taken to the reader's desk (but not of course out of the reading room); all other titles must be applied for either on the library requisition slips or, in the case of the new British Library, on the computer terminals provided; this involves looking up the relevant shelf-marks in the general catalogue. As it may be anything up to two hours before the books are delivered to the reader's desk, it is essential to order what is needed at the earliest moment, if not a day or two in advance, and to fill in the waiting period by using works that are on the open shelves or by looking up shelf-marks of books that you are going to need in the next phase of your research. Because of lack of space, many libraries today 'out-house' selected classes of books; for example, at the time of writing some British Library titles are kept in a depository at Woolwich and may take twenty-four hours or more to arrive at the Bloomsbury reading room. This will be greatly improved when the new Library is fully operational.

Researchers wishing to use the British Library or other copyright libraries, those of the Imperial War Museum, National Maritime Museum, Royal Botanic Gardens and most university and museum libraries must obtain a reader's ticket, and it is advisable to do so in advance of your first visit – although temporary day tickets will usually be issued on demand. Applications have to be countersigned by someone of authority (a JP, doctor or person of recognised professional status) who will vouch for you as a responsible person; you will also be asked to state the nature of your research. Except at the Bodleian Library in Oxford, which now makes a charge to readers, tickets are free and once obtained are normally renewable, but intending readers are required to state in the first instance that they cannot undertake their particular research in other libraries. Write to the Admissions Office of the relevant library for full details and application forms.

On your first visit to a library, you will need to devote a little time to familiarising yourself with the layout and cataloguing system. Ask one of the library assistants to explain any unusual features, and how to look up anonymous works, yearbooks and directories, or the proceedings of learned societies. Some major libraries display a map showing the layout, or there may be a printed leaflet available. Most have separate card indexes arranged under authors and subjects, but occasionally one comes across a 'dictionary' type of catalogue which combines author, subject and title in one alphabetical listing. Nowadays the catalogue after a certain date is most likely to be on microfiche; the updating of these by computer is a godsend to researchers, as it keeps the listings constantly up to date. You should be meticulous in replacing all microfiches in their correct numerical sequence after use, for the sake of subsequent researchers (and long-suffering librarians).

In smaller libraries the catalogue is usually cumulative, but in others there may be separate drawers or cabinets containing cards for acquisitions within a stated period. This 'Recent Acquisitions'

section should not be overlooked. The trap here for the inexperienced lies in the word 'acquisitions', for although this section of
the catalogue will comprise mainly new titles, it will also include
books that have been purchased or otherwise acquired recently –
some of which may have been published a number of years ago.
When you fail to find the book you are looking for in the general
catalogue, therefore, always turn to this section.

The majority of libraries in the United Kingdom have adopted
the Dewey Decimal Classification, which divides human knowledge
into ten classes, each sub-divided to accommodate subjects within
each class. Try to memorise the main divisions, as follows:

000 General Works
100 Philosophy
200 Religion
300 Social Sciences
400 Languages
500 Science
600 Technology
700 The Arts and Recreations
800 Literature
900 Geography, Biography and History

The *British National Bibliography* (*BNB*) also uses the Dewey
classification, and if you are seeking a published work on a certain
subject, and do not know the author or precise title, you should go
straight to the relevant class listing, as you would do in the library.

A word of advice here for the uninitiated who find themselves
confronted by an on-line or CD-ROM catalogue and an unfamiliar
array of 'new technology' equipment. DO NOT PANIC! Firstly,
there is bound to be an instruction manual – probably very dog-
eared as a result of frantic searching by other users in need of
assistance, and usually pretty incomprehensible to the lay person!
This manual will tell you which keys to press and in what order.
Secondly, once you have pressed the first key, step-by-step instructions will appear on screen to guide you through the next phase,
and if you do something wrong a message will appear instantly on
screen to that effect, with instructions on how to remedy the error.
Thirdly, you can put yourself in the hands of a trained library
assistant, who will do it all for you the first time. (In my experience, far from resenting such demands on their time, librarians are
only too pleased to show off their newly acquired skills and to play
with their 'new toys'; but this attitude will not last for ever. Watch
very carefully: you will not be popular if you have to ask a second
time.)

Note-taking

There are three 'golden rules' of researching:

1 *Copy accurately*
   Care must be taken to retain original spellings in quoted matter, using an editorial *sic* in square brackets if necessary. It is a good idea to get into the habit of double-checking all figures and proper names immediately they are written or typed. For example, the date '1943' can so easily be copied as '1934' when one is tired (or more easily, because one's mind is on the current year, '1929' as '1992'!), and whereas it takes only a few seconds to verify the figure at the time, such a mistake can take hours to correct later – or may not be discovered until the work is in print. Writing unusual proper names and place names in block capitals in the researcher's notes also helps to avoid error and will save a lot of trouble if, several weeks later, the writer is unable to decipher his own hurried scribbles.

2 *Check, double-check and, if in doubt, triple-check all facts*
   Primarily where verbal recollections are given to the researcher by private individuals, but whenever and wherever possible in all other cases, especially if any doubts are entertained as to the accuracy of facts (even if printed facts), these should be verified in another source. Where confirmation of a fact or figure cannot be obtained and the writer remains in doubt, it is best either to avoid using it or, if you must, to state the source or sources relied on. The problem of 'conflicting authorities' is discussed in chapter 4 (page 70).

3 *Keep a note of all sources*
   The importance of keeping full reference notes cannot be over-stressed. Valuable time may be wasted if, for example, when his first draft is written, the writer wishes to examine a particular source in more detail but cannot turn up instantly a note of the author, title, date and relevant page number, and preferably also the shelf-mark of the library where he originally saw it. Even more time will be wasted if he has omitted to follow the recommendation under (1) above to check his page references at the time and, failing to find what he is looking for at, say, page 241, he has to thumb through a hefty tome, possibly without the help of an index, only to discover the right passage at page 421. (Whenever this happens, the short cut is to try first all the permutations for the number originally writen down.) Making brief cards or slips for each reference as you go along will halve the work when it comes to compiling a 'notes and references' section or the bibliography (see chapter 10, 'Preparation for the Press',

pages 158–66). Press cuttings and photocopies should be clearly marked with the book title, newspaper or periodical, plus volume number, date, publisher and page number where appropriate. Remember to do this before you hand in the volume or microfilm or replace it on the shelf.

What should you do when you come across an incorrect date or figure in a library book, perhaps a wrong page entry in an index? In the interest of future users, the temptation is to amend the text – in pencil, of course – but is it worth the risk of being expelled from the premises for life? The duty librarian is probably too busy to take much heed. My opinion is that if it is a modern title, provided you have the time and the inclination, you should write to the publisher asking him to make the correction in any reprint or new edition. If it is an old book, sadly there is nothing to be done.

Photocopying

All reference libraries and most other libraries and record offices operate a photocopy service, subject to the usual copyright restrictions and a ban on old or rare editions that might be damaged in the process. Microfilms and the type of photocopy suitable for reproduction can usually be obtained only from major libraries and record offices, and may take several weeks, but the electrostatic print or 'rapid copy' or 'xerox' as it is sometimes called, which is the most useful to the researcher, is often available while you wait or within twenty-four hours. Some libraries have installed coin-operated machines and expect you to make your own copies.

With material that is out of copyright there is no problem, but unless the copyright owner has given permission in writing, copying of all other printed matter is restricted to one article from any one issue of a newspaper or periodical, at any one time; or to a total of one-tenth of any one book in copyright. In all cases the applicant will be required to sign a statement that he has not before obtained a photocopy of the same extract, that he requires the copy purely for the purposes of research or private study and that he will not use it for any other purpose without the permission of the copyright holder. The cost is modest when one considers the amount of time it takes to copy a text by hand. Another factor to be borne in mind is that the photocopy is an *accurate* copy. When ordering photocopies from a library, it is essential to keep a note of the author, title, date of publication and edition of the source material, since these will not always appear on the photocopied sheets and the originals may not be returned to you; write these on the photocopies before storing.

Commercial photocopying services abound in every city and major town these days, with self-operating machines at some railway stations, department stores and supermarkets. The quality of copies varies considerably, as does the cost; some places offer a substantial discount for a large number of copies made at any one time. These 'copy shops' are not usually worried about copyright and will often copy a complete book without demur, although in so doing both they and the purchaser are breaking the law. Anyone planning to copy a large amount of text still in copyright should first apply for permission to the publisher.

Infringement of copyright by reprography is an international problem. The British Copyright Council's recent booklet *Photocopying from Books and Journals* clarifies the present law.

Copyright

A new statute, the Copyright, Designs and Patents Act 1988, came into force in the United Kingdom on 1 August 1989. It replaces all previous copyright statutes and seeks to re-state the law of copyright in this country. This new Act forbids 'unfair dealing' in all works still in copyright, i.e. during the author's lifetime and for fifty years after his death. It also confers certain moral rights on the copyright owner. In practice this means that anyone wishing to quote substantially from a work in copyright must obtain permission from the owner of that copyright, normally the writer of the work in question, if he is still alive, or, after his death, his heirs and/or literary executor or anyone to whom he may have assigned the copyright. It sometimes takes quite a while to trace the copyright owner, and it is prudent therefore to make application to use such material in good time, through the original publisher of the relevant work. Biographers and historians should remember that although a letter *belongs* to the recipient, the copyright in it is vested in the writer of the letter and, after his death, to his estate; this applies also to letters published in the press.

British copyright law is immensely complicated. While the quotation of short passages for the purposes of criticism or review is deemed to be 'fair dealing', in all other cases involving more than a short phrase or a couple of lines of poetry it is advisable to seek permission. Some publishers hold that quotations totalling less than four hundred words from any one work do not require special clearance, provided that acknowledgment is made to the author, title and publisher; but most literary agents and the Society of

Authors recommend formal clearance. A fee will sometimes be payable, the amount depending on the length of the passage or passages it is intended to quote and on the nature of the rights sought (i.e. British only, or British Commonwealth or world rights). Foreign rights are frequently controlled by publishers or literary agents abroad, but the UK publisher should be able to provide a name and address to write to. It is most important to allow adequate time for the clearance of all such requests before going to press.

International copyright is safeguarded by two separate conventions: the Berne Convention and the Universal Copyright Convention, to which different countries adhere.* For details of these and of the new Copyright Statute of the United States, which came into force in January 1978, see the articles on British and US copyright in the current *Writers' & Artists' Yearbook*.

So far as the United Kingdom is concerned, the Society of Authors' *Quick Guides*, 'Copyright and Moral Rights' and 'Copyright in Artistic Works, incl. Photographs', set out the present position very clearly. Another recommended title is Eric Thorn's *Understanding Copyright*.

Use of typewriters, tape recorders and personal computers

Most major libraries have special typing rooms for students or set aside a portion of one search room for those who wish to bring typewriters or personal computers. This is a useful facility where there is a long delay in photocopying, as the researcher can take home with him at the end of the day everything he has copied. The number of microfilm, cassette or microfiche readers is often limited, and if you know in advance that the records to be consulted are on film or tape or fiche it is wise to enquire whether advance notice should be given of an intended visit. Portable tape recorders are not usually permissible, except by special arrangement with the librarian – this will depend on whether or not a private room can be made available so that other readers are not disturbed. Dictating into a tape recorder undoubtedly saves time and fatigue, in the library, but can create problems of transcription unless proper names are spelled out and punctuation indicated; nothing at all will be saved if, at the end of the day, it proves necessary to go back to the original to check a quotation. The researcher will find a small tape recorder of real value, however, where a good deal of inter-

* Stop press (February 1992): the EC has proposed a new directive increasing the duration of copyright in member states to seventy years; this may well become law during the lifetime of this edition.

viewing or travelling has to be done: even if there are objections to using such a device during an interview, a quick dash to the car or hotel afterwards to record one's impressions while all is fresh in one's mind is very worthwhile, and so is a recorded on-the-spot description of buildings and scenes to be portrayed in a writer's work. For this purpose the small battery-operated type of machine known as a 'pocket memo' or 'electronic note-taker' is ideal, as it is hand-held. A larger machine with separate microphone and facility for longer-playing tapes is more suitable for interviewing or sound recording, and here it is best to choose a model which will run both on batteries and on mains. The latter will probably have a socket for plugging in a foot pedal (essential for tape transcription); if you intend to transcribe much of the material on your mini- or micro-cassettes, then you will need a transcriber (again with foot pedal).

Using a modern clock radio-cum-cassette recorder or television video recorder it is possible to record programmes from radio or TV while you are away from home, and this too can be of value to the researcher who must be elsewhere when such programmes are on air or screen.

It may be opportune here to pass on a few hints on the use of microfilm readers. The machines do vary slightly, and it is wise in the first instance to ask a library assistant to show you how to operate one. It is very important never to touch the film with greasy fingers or to get it twisted, and always to re-wind the film onto the original spool before returning it to the issue desk. (Nothing is more exasperating to the next user than to discover that the spool must be re-wound!). In libraries where there are a number of machines installed, there is bound to be a good deal of noise as users wind and re-wind, and some people find they cannot do more than an hour or two's work on microfilm at a time, partly because of the noise and partly due to eyestrain. Some professional researchers surmount these difficulties with the aid of ear plugs and/or tinted glasses.

Interviewing

Interviewing people, and getting the maximum information out of them, is a skill that is acquired with practice. There are no hard and fast rules, but here are a few tips from personal experience:

Always write or telephone in advance, stating clearly who you are, why you need the information, and precisely what it is you seek.

If time permits, take 'two bites at the cherry'. People are naturally on the defensive at a first interview, but when you go back a second time they already know you and will welcome you as a 'friend'.

Don't ask a crucial or controversial question right at the start. If necessary, put the person being interviewed at ease, make some social small talk first. It can be quite productive sometimes to bring out your 'key' question almost at the end of the interview, as though it were an afterthought and not all that important – the interviewee will be relaxed by that time and much more expansive.

Don't assume that you can use a tape recorder. A lot of people are nervous of being recorded and will 'freeze' if you insist. A good plan is to have your machine tucked away in your briefcase and then, when the interview is well under way, you can say something like, 'This is tremendously good stuff, I can't get it all down accurately in my rusty shorthand . . . would you mind very much if I switched on my recorder?'

Always offer to let interviewees see anything you are going to quote in print, and ask them how they would wish to be acknowledged. And never fail to write afterwards to thank them for sparing the time to talk to you.

The question of how far to trust information given to you from personal recollection is dealt with in the chapter on Biography (see pages 110–11.)

A useful booklet, prepared primarily for the guidance of genealogists, or those compiling family or local histories, is Eve McLaughlin's *Interviewing Elderly Relatives*. The only other titles I have found on 'creative' interviewing (creative as opposed to personnel) are both published in the United States, but should be available in some libraries here: *The Craft of Interviewing*, by John Brady, and *Creative Interviewing: The Writer's Guide to Gathering Information by Asking Questions*, by Ken Metzler.

In the last decade modern technology has totally transformed the researcher's job, firstly by giving him access to source material in greater quantity and faster than ever before, and secondly by liberating him from the more irksome manual tasks that used to take up so much of his working time. Other technological 'miracles', some of which are already in the pipeline, will undoubtedly follow during the lifetime of this book. It will be up to the writers and researchers of the future to take full advantage of these innovations and to harness them to their particular needs as they arrive. Meanwhile the writer/researcher is still going to garner the bulk of his source material in the library or archives centre; the techniques of note-taking and interviewing, as described above, will continue to be practised; and the proper storage of research material will always be of special importance.

There are many ways of researching. One method will be right for some writers and quite wrong for others. Ultimately you adopt that which best suits you and your work and, inevitably, your pocket. While in this book I have constantly at the forefront of my mind the needs of fiction writers, biographers and family historians, it is my hope that the more academic writers also may pick up some snippets of value here. Students preparing theses and writers of research reports or other academic works will get additional help from Eileen Kane's *Doing Your Own Research*.

The Author, quarterly journal of the Society of Authors, free to members, £4.50 per issue to non-members

'Buying a Word Processor', *Quick Guide* no. 3, rev. ed., Society of Authors, London, 1990*

Caring for Books and Documents, by A. D. Baynes-Cope, 2nd ed., British Library, London, 1989

'Copyright and Moral Rights', *Quick Guide* no. 1, rev. ed., Society of Authors, London, 1989*

'Copyright in Artistic Works, incl. Photographs', *Quick Guide* no. 11, Society of Authors, London, 1990*

The Craft of Interviewing, by John Brady, Random House, New York, 1977

Creative Interviewing: The Writer's Guide to Gathering Information by Asking Questions, by Ken Metzler, 2nd ed., Prentice-Hall, Englewood Cliffs, N.J. (USA), 1989

Dictionary of Information Technology, by Tony Gunton, Penguin, Harmondsworth, 1992

Doing Your Own Research, by Eileen Kane, Marion Boyars, London, 1985

Going Online, by Terry Hanson, 8th ed., Aslib, London, 1991

Interviewing Elderly Relatives, by Eve McLaughlin, 2nd ed., Federation of Family History Societies (FFHS), 1987, available through local family history societies or FFHS, c/o Benson Room, Birmingham & Midland Institute, Margaret Street, Birmingham B3 3BS

Keyguide to Information Sources in Online and CD-ROM Database Searching, by John Cox, Mansell, London, 1991

* The *Quick Guides* published by the Society of Authors are free to members or otherwise obtainable at £1.50 each, post free, from the Publications Department, Society of Authors, 84 Drayton Gardens, London SW10 9SB.

Low-Cost Word Processing, by Gordon Wells, Allison & Busby, London, 1986

'Notes on the Use of Private Papers for Historical Research', reprinted from the *Bulletin of the Institute of Historical Research*, November 1966, available free from the Royal Commission on Historical Manuscripts, Quality House, Quality Court, Chancery Lane, London WC2A 1HP

Online Bibliographic Databases, by James L. Hall, 4th ed., Aslib, London, 1986

The Online Manual, by J. Cousins and L. Robinson, Blackwell, Oxford, 1991

Photocopying from Books and Journals: A Guide for All Users of Copyright Literary Works, by Charles Clark, British Copyright Council, London, 1990

UK Online Search Services, 4th ed., Aslib, London, 1989

The Writer and the Word Processor, by Ray Hammond, Coronet Books, Hodder & Stoughton, London, 1984

Writers' & Artists' Yearbook, published annually by A & C Black, London; articles on British and US copyright and on word processing

3

Basic Sources of Information and their Location

A writer's raw material will normally be derived from a combination of the following sources: personal knowledge, experience and observation; printed, microfilmed or computer-stored material (books, newspapers, periodicals, etc.); unpublished documentary, recorded or filmed sources (manuscripts, family papers, theses, archive collections, tapes, photographs, etc.); and other people's knowledge, experience and observation. Of these the most important must be the first-mentioned, since it is a writer's own viewpoint, drawn from his personal knowledge, experience and observation, that above all else puts a stamp of originality upon his work and distinguishes it from the work of every other writer.

Except where the work in hand is one of pure reminiscence – and even then certain statements will probably need to be substantiated by fact – it is however not enough to rely solely upon your own knowledge. As soon as your original material has been studied and sorted according to the shape of the projected piece of writing, you must consider what are the other sources of information to be tapped.

The last few years have brought an upsurge in electronic publishing. Firms such as Bowker-Saur, Chadwyck-Healey of Cambridge, Research Publications of Reading and University Microfilms International lead the field with most of the British and US national bibliographies, library catalogues, long runs of newspapers and periodicals, state papers, indexes and an ever-increasing number of essential reference tools now marketed in microfiche, microfilm or CD-ROM (Compact Disk-Read Only Memory) form.

Unfortunately these new tools cost money. This, coupled with the need for equipment on which to read them, virtually rules out their purchase by the individual researcher at the present time. However, as more libraries/archive centres throughout the country increase their holdings on fiche and film and CD, the easier – and quicker – it will be for everyone, especially for those who live in the provinces, to get at the information they seek.

Printed Sources

Books

Printed books and information about books are obtainable primarily from bookshops, publishers and libraries. When you are engaged on a specific project, you will always find it worthwhile to acquire copies of the standard works on your subject, which you can keep at your elbow and either annotate in the margins or interleave with narrow strips of paper or markers on which you write some basic headings or other indications. It goes without saying that library books and books belonging to other people should *never* be marked in any way; but 'working copies' are a writer's essential reference tools and should be used to the best advantage.

New books may be purchased from booksellers or, in case of difficulty, direct from the publishers. A good bookseller will be aware of what has been published recently on a particular subject and, through *The Bookseller* and other trade papers, and his contact with publishers' representatives, of what is forthcoming. He will look up titles for a customer in the current *Whitaker's Books in Print* or *Books of the Month* and *Books to Come*, as well as in individual publishers' catalogues. If the title is not in stock, however, delivery may take a couple of weeks or more, depending on the publisher, and it is sometimes quicker to telephone one of the larger bookshops in London or one of the big provincial cities rather than wait for your local shop to obtain a copy.

A most useful and inexpensive publication for the book-buyer is Peter Marcan's *Directory of Specialist Bookdealers in the United Kingdom*, which lists bookshops under subject headings and contains a great deal of other relevant, practical information. Those who live in the south-east will find Roger Lascelles' *Bookshops of Greater London* invaluable: as well as general and specialist booksellers, it includes details of antiquarian and secondhand dealers (with a subject index).

The bulk of the books you will need for your research are likely to come from libraries, and even recently published titles can be obtained reasonably quickly through the public library service if an application card is filled in at the time you see a book announced, or a review; there is a small fee for reservation, and normally such new books may not be renewed after the initial three-to-four-week borrowing period, if they are reserved by another reader. However, three weeks should be sufficient for you to make any notes you require, or to decide whether or not you need to purchase the book.

Provided you are not in a hurry, you should be able to obtain most of the books you need through the public library service, thanks to the inter-library lending scheme and the services of the British Library Document Supply Centre at Boston Spa, West Yorkshire. Application to the Centre must be made either through the British Library or your local public library, not direct. Film, fiche and other types of documentation are also available on loan.

If you are unwilling to wait – and so often material is required for one chapter or section of your work before you can proceed to the next – it may be worth your while to travel to London or your nearest centre for a day or two's research in one of the copyright, university or other major reference libraries. It should be remembered, however, that new titles are not instantly available in such libraries: the acquisition and cataloguing processes may take up to a few months.

Copyright and reference libraries

Under the provisions of various Copyright Acts that have been passed since 1709, certain libraries are entitled to receive one free copy of every book published in the United Kingdom. These are: the British Library (London); the Bodleian Library (Oxford); the Cambridge University Library (Cambridge); the National Library of Wales (Aberystwyth); the National Library of Scotland (Edinburgh); and Trinity College Library (Dublin).

In all these libraries the researcher can be confident of finding everything he needs that has been published from the 18th century onwards, and also much earlier material (collections that have been bequeathed or titles purchased over the years in the saleroom). A small percentage of stock may have been destroyed during the last war or otherwise mislaid.

Graduates and other *bona fide* researchers and students are able to use the various well-stocked university libraries, of which the University of London Library, the John Rylands University Library of Manchester and the Sydney Jones Library of Liverpool University are excellent examples. Other libraries include those of the major museums, such as (in London) the Imperial War Museum, the National Maritime Museum, the Natural History Museum, the Science Museum and the Royal Botanic Gardens at Kew.

Major reference libraries open to the general public include the Central Reference Library just behind Trafalgar Square, London; Birmingham Central Reference Library; and Newcastle-upon-Tyne Central Library. A visit to the nearest of these and to other reference libraries in the provinces may well fulfil your needs and save you from the expense of travelling farther afield.

The British Library is currently in the throes of moving to its new, purpose-built premises – the biggest move in library history, involving some eleven million items. By 1996 all the major London collections, with the exception of the Newspaper Library and the National Sound Archive, will be brought together under one roof at St Pancras, London (between Euston and King's Cross stations). Although for some time to come the hard core of established readers are sure to continue to bemoan the demise of the historic Round Reading Room in Bloomsbury, conditions in the new building are a vast improvement, not only for readers but also for staff and – most importantly – for the preservation of the collections.

Admission to the British Library and to most other copyright and major libraries is free. (The Bodleian Library, Oxford, recently introduced a charge to readers.) Readers' tickets, valid for one or more years, are issued on personal application and are for research which cannot be done elsewhere (the subject of research must be stated and the form signed by a university tutor, a member of the legal profession or some other person of authority who will vouch for you as a responsible person). At the new British Library a higher-level pass will be issued to readers wishing to use manuscripts or certain rare books. Tickets must be shown each time you enter the library; temporary tickets, valid for one or two days, will usually be issued on the spot without formality. Allow a little extra time on your first visit for this purpose: some libraries nowadays insist on taking an instant photograph for incorporation into the reader's ticket.

Holders of public library tickets in their home town may use them to gain admission to the special reference collections of all London public libraries and to borrow books from the lending branches. Tickets may also be used at other libraries by arrangement with the librarian.

Many libraries are open late on certain evenings in the week. At the British Library, the Reading Room does not close until 9 p.m. on Tuesdays, Wednesdays and Thursdays; the Central Reference Library in Westminster is open until 7 p.m. from Monday to Friday. If you have to travel some distance, you would do well to plan your schedule to make the maximum use of the longest possible working day. Books usually have to be handed in half-an-hour before closing time, and photocopying orders will not be accepted after a certain time, so that it is important not only to allow for any necessary last-minute note-taking, but also for ordering, and paying for, photocopies.

For those who can afford it, a subscription to the London Library, 14 St James's Square, London SW1Y 4LG (tel. 071–930

7705), will prove very worthwhile. Members may take out ten books at a time (fifteen for country members, who may also borrow by post but have to pay the postage in both directions). Subscribers have access to the stacks and the use of a comfortable reading room, and may purchase the printed author catalogue and subject index volumes (a boon to those who live in remote areas and wish to order by post or telephone). The annual subscription, currently £80, may be set against a professional writer's tax; short-term subscriptions are available, with or without borrowing facilities (apply to the Librarian for details).

Another London subscription library is the Highgate Literary and Scientific Institution Library, 11 South Grove, Highgate Village, London N6 6BS (tel. 081–340 3343); the subscription there is £26 for one person, £40 for a family. Among the few surviving provincial subscription libraries are those of Birmingham, Exeter, Leeds, Newcastle-upon-Tyne and Plymouth (see Appendix I, page 180).

Special libraries

The use of libraries in general has been discussed in the previous chapter. The questions that now arise concern location: how to find out about the special libraries that are likely to help you in your particular field, and how to locate in those libraries the particular books you need.

The first place to look is in the *Aslib Directory of Information Sources in the United Kingdom*. This gives a comprehensive listing of practically every library and source of information in this country; it contains a subject index, details such as opening hours and the facilities available; it is brought up to date regularly, and all libraries possess the latest edition – ask for it at the enquiry desk. The Library Association's *Libraries in the United Kingdom and the Republic of Ireland* is a handy annual paperback which lists addresses, telephone numbers and names of librarians. Other useful sources are the *Guide to Libraries and Information Units*, published by the British Library Science Reference and Information Service (SRIS), which has both an organization and a subject index, the *Museums Year Book*, and the *Directory of London Public Libraries*, published by the Association of London Chief Librarians.

The best international guides to libraries and research institutions are *The World of Learning*, H. Lengenfelder's *The World Guide to Libraries* and *The World Guide to Special Libraries*, and a new publication, *Guide to Libraries in Western Europe*.

Regrettably, space does not permit the mention in this handbook of more than a few individual libraries, named in the text under the various subjects of research discussed. A selective list of UK libraries is printed in Appendix I and of foreign libraries under the relevant country in chapter 9, 'Information from and about Foreign Countries'.

Catalogues and guides

Every library has a catalogue of some kind, either an author index or a subject or title index, or all three, on cards or microfiche or electronic access ('on-line' or CD-ROM); some of the larger libraries have printed catalogues and guides to their collections, and these are usually available on the open shelves of the reference library. For the British Library, for example, there is the 360-volume *General Catalogue of Printed Books to 1975* with supplements (on microfiche) to 1991. (The Catalogue to 1975 is also on microfiche and CD-ROM.) At the new Library readers use the Online Public Access Catalogue (OPAC) to search for any item they require under author, title, pressmark, classmark or keyword. Linked to an automated book request system (ABRS) which enables the reader to request or reserve any catalogued item, and swiftly informs him should that item be unavailable. Readers will also find useful R.C. Alston's recent *Handlist of Unpublished Finding Aids to the London Collections of the British Library*. The Library's *Subject Catalogue of Printed Books: 1975–1985* is on microfiche.

It often happens, however, that you need information at the library on a subject about which you know very little, let alone the names of authors or titles of authoritative works, and here without the OPAC keyword search facility a subject index will not be of much help, as it will list only the relevant titles that are on the shelves of that particular library; nor will it evaluate them. There are several ways round this problem: to ask the reference librarian for the 'standard work' and for any recent studies, and evaluate them yourself (a glance at the index and bibliography will give a pretty good idea of how thoroughly an author has gone into his subject and how up to date the book is); to consult Walford's *Guide to Reference Material* or its US equivalent, Sheehy's *Guide to Reference Books*, published by the Library Association and the American Library Association respectively, the latter title being more international in outlook (both have excellent subject indexes); to read up the subject initially in a modern encyclopedia and use the short bibliography normally given there as a starting point for further research; or to use a more comprehensive bibliography where one exists. *Printed Reference Material and Related*

Information Sources, written for librarians, is highly recommended as a bibliography and evaluation of reference books for research.

Bibliographies

The best way to find out if there is a bibliography on a certain subject is to consult the *World Bibliography of Bibliographies* and the cumulative *Bibliographic Index*, both of which should be available in most major libraries. Among special subject bibliographies likely to be of most use to the British writer/researcher are the *Bibliography of British Literary Bibliographies*; the *London Bibliography of the Social Sciences*, which since 1990 has been incorporated in the *International Bibliography of the Social Sciences*; and the *New Cambridge Bibliography of English Literature*. Recent UK titles can be traced in the *British National Bibliography* (*BNB*), which has been published weekly since 1950, with regular cumulations and author, title and subject indexes. The bibliographies of other countries are listed in volume 3 of the *Guide to Reference Material* mentioned above, under 'National Bibliographies'. The *World Bibliographical Series* launched in 1977 by Clio Press aims to provide a uniform collection of bibliographies covering every country in the world, at the rate of about fifteen volumes per year.

The Library Association, 7 Ridgmount Street, London WC1E 7AE (tel. 071–636 7543) has published bibliographies on a variety of subjects over the years, and these will be found in most reference libraries or in the Association's own library. It is also always worth enquiring from the Book Trust (formerly National Book League), Book House, 45 East Hill, Wandsworth, London SW18 2QZ (tel. 081–870 9055) whether they have a book list on a particular subject.

Readers unfamiliar with bibliographic practice should remember that the numbers given in the index are entry numbers, *not* page numbers.

Electronic and other book information services

The use of electronic equipment for access to bibliographical information has transformed the researcher's routine dramatically. Nevertheless some members of the older – pre-computer – generation are baffled, even frightened, by the new technology and its jargon. They need not be. Wherever such a facility exists, be it an on-line open access catalogue or a data-base search service, help is at hand. OPAC users receive step-by-step instruction on screen, and trained library assistants are on duty to guide others through the complexities of computer searching.

A computer search is always done by a qualified member of staff after consultation with, and preferably in the presence of, the reader. It will be charged according to staff time, the time connected to the computer and the cost of printing out the material retrieved. An estimate will always be given beforehand. Print-outs are normally available within a couple of days.

The British Library Automated Information Service (BLAISE), to which other libraries and institutions subscribe, was launched in December 1977. It operates in two fields: bibliographic records, chiefly in the humanities and social sciences (BLAISE-LINE) and medical information (BLAISE-LINK).

BLAISE-LINE provides access to some forty million records worldwide. Files include the *British Library General Catalogue*, the *British National Bibliography* from 1950 (BNB MARC), the *Library of Congress Catalog* from 1968 (LC MARC), *Fifteenth Century Printing* (ISTC), the *Eighteenth Century Short Title Catalogue* (ESTC), *Audiovisual Materials* (AVMARC), *Conference Proceedings*, *Cartographic Materials*, *Music*, *European 'Grey' Literature** (SIGLE) and *Whitaker's Current Books*. The holdings of the major British university libraries and American research libraries can be searched, as well as the vast US data-base, the Online Computer Library Center (OCLC), which contains over twenty-four million entries. At the British Library Science Reference and Information Service (SRIS) you will be offered access to different data-bases.

Space does not permit anything like a complete list of the numerous other data-bases in the United Kingdom, Europe and the United States to which access is on offer. DIALOG, the world's largest, based in California, naturally has a strong bias towards US material. CELEX is the official data-base of European Community law. There are many others.

Researchers interested in a computer search should ask at the British Library or other reference library for an up-to-date information leaflet/price list and discuss their requirements with a member of staff. It should be borne in mind that the time and cost of such a search are minimal compared to that of a similar search by manual means.

On a totally different level, the Book Trust (Book House, 45 East Hill, Wandsworth, London SW18 2QZ; tel. 081–870 9055) operates a Book Information Service for members and non-members. A simple single query will be answered free of charge (send a stamped addressed envelope), but additional queries are charged (currently

---

* Literature not normally available through bookselling channels and thus difficult for the lay person to find.

at £10 per hour plus VAT for members, £20 per hour plus VAT for non-members).

Tracing books

Often you want to trace a particular book whose exact title and author you do not remember. Provided you have a vague idea of these, or the approximate date of publication, it is not difficult. In other cases it used to involve a lengthy search, but if you can use the OPAC mentioned on page 37 you will probably be able to trace the item instantly by its keyword.

The earliest listing in this country is the *London Catalogue of Books*, covering the period 1700–1855. The *English Catalogue of Books*, volume 1 of which covers the period 1801–36 and later volumes (variously at three- and five-year intervals), continues until 1968. *Whitaker's Cumulative Book List* (from 1924) used to be published quarterly, with annual and five-year cumulations; since 1984 it has appeared annually and is now called *Whitaker's Book List*. As mentioned above, there is a Whitaker file available for on-line searching in BLAISE-LINE, updated regularly by the firm. There are also *Whitaker's Books in Print*, *Children's Books in Print* and *Religious Books in Print*, all annuals. Most libraries and booksellers today subscribe to the microfiche edition of 'Whitaker's'; this is now updated weekly as well as monthly.

For US titles the *National Union Catalog* (on open access at the British Library) is especially useful as it gives authors' dates. There are also the annual *American Books in Print*, the cumulative volumes of the *American Book Publishing Record*, and the *Cumulative Book Index*. Bowker's *Subject Guide to Books in Print* is another valuable source, published annually and listing US non-fiction titles under some 66,000 subject headings.

It is worth remembering that the weekly trade paper, *The Bookseller*, publishes bumper spring and autumn issues (available as a separate subscription) containing details of forthcoming books for the next six months. Another tip, if you wish to keep fully up to date, is to put yourself on the mailing lists of those firms who publish in your particular field or fields of interest. And keep an eagle eye open for reviews and advertisements in the national press. It goes without saying that you will be an avid browser in your local bookshop!

Obtaining out-of-print books

If you want to acquire titles that are out of print, either for your own reference collection or for work on a specific project, you should make a point of informing your local antiquarian or second-hand bookseller of your special interest. He will then not only let you know when suitable books come in, but will also advertise for them through the trade, probably in *Bookdealer*; there is no charge for this service and no obligation to buy when a quotation is forthcoming, subject to the book or books remaining unsold in the meantime; but the process may take several weeks. *Cole's Register of British Antiquarian and Secondhand Bookdealers* and *Sheppard's Book Dealers in the British Isles* are the handbooks most used by the trade; another recommended title is the *Skoob Directory of Secondhand Bookshops in the British Isles*.

The best way to obtain an out-of-print title is to use a specialist bookfinding service. Leading UK booksellers who offer customers this service include Blackwell's (Oxford), Hatchard's (Cambridge) and Heywood Hill, Maggs Bros. and Waterstone's (London). Reputable bookfinding specialists include Bookfinders (Moor Lane, Westfield, East Sussex TN35 4QU; tel. 0424 754291); Len Foulkes (13 Pantbach Road, Birchgrove, Cardiff CF4 1TU; tel. 0222 627703); Melrose Books (35 Dornden Drive, Langton Green, Tunbridge Wells, Kent TN3 0AE; tel. 089 286 2078); and Twiggers (108 Reedley Road, Stoke Bishop, Bristol BS9 1BE; tel. 0272 682155). The latter firm offers an ordinary search for up to four titles free of charge and, at modest cost, an extended, specialist or American search. It must be said, however, that obtaining out-of-print books from abroad is not 100% satisfactory: by the time your dealer has received a quotation and passed it on to you with his commission added on, even before you effect a bank transfer, the books may well have been sold to another customer. (See chapter 9, page 141, for further information on firms importing foreign titles.)

The *Books on Demand* programme of paper facsimile reproductions marketed by University Microfilms International (White Swan House, Godstone, Surrey RH9 8LW; tel. 0883 744123) includes some 100,000 out-of-print titles (over 20,000 of which have only recently been declared out of print) and over 50 subject bibliographies, some on microfilm. Approximately 4,000 new titles are added each year.

Newspapers and Periodicals

The major holding in this country of national and foreign papers and periodicals is at the British Library Reference Division, Department of Printed Books: newspapers and weeklies at the

British Library Newspaper Library, Colindale Avenue, London NW9 5HE (tel. 071-323 7353), opposite Colindale Underground Station; all other periodicals at the main Library. The major exceptions to this broad division are the pre-1801 London newspapers (the Burney and Thomason collections respectively), which used to be at Bloomsbury, the Oriental collection formerly at Store Street and the South Asian collection at the India Office Library. All these will be brought to the new St Pancras building by 1996. British Library ticket holders are admitted to the Newspaper Library without formality; for others short-term tickets will be issued on application in person to the Superintendent in the search room, subject to proof of identity.

There is a card-index catalogue at Colindale (with a duplicate at St Pancras) listing alphabetically by title all the papers held, with dates. The researcher using this index should remember that where there are several papers or magazines of the same title, the cards are arranged within the title alphabetically under the place of publication. An eight-volume printed *Catalogue of the Newspaper Library, Colindale*, was published in 1975.

The British Library Newspaper Library is currently in the process of an extensive programme of microfilming, with a view to relieving pressure on the handling of the original newsprint. For some years now most current foreign papers have been purchased only on microfilm and since 1986 all UK newspapers are microfilmed on receipt. This is a great convenience both to the reader and to the library staff, as in many cases up to a year's run of a paper or journal can be housed on one spool, thus eliminating the handling of bulky volumes and conserving storage space. Microfilms of newspapers and journals are currently on sale (prices on application). Photographic or electrostatic enlargements may be obtained from microfilm, and photocopies (a whole page or double spread, according to size, slightly reduced) may be ordered at £1 an A3/A2 sheet plus VAT, subject to the usual copyright regulations (only one article from any one issue of a paper or periodical at any one time). Where photocopies are ordered by post, there is a minimum charge and the Library also levies a handling charge. An express service is available at extra cost.

Tracing newspapers and periodicals

The researcher wishing to trace an early English-language newspaper will find all those published in Great Britain and Ireland in the period up to 1900 listed in the *British Library General Catalogue of Printed Books*. Another very useful source for early newspapers is G. A. Cranfield's *Handlist of English Provincial Newspapers and Periodicals, 1700–1760*. *Willing's Press Guide*, first published in 1871 as *Frederick May's London Press Directory*, and now issued annually, is one of the best quick reference guides to modern newspapers and periodicals in the United Kingdom; recent editions also cover publications overseas. A complete set of *Willing's*, and also the earlier *European Press Guide*, is on the open shelves at Colindale; it contains an A–Z list, a list of publications under subjects, and (until recently) a list under English counties and towns. The *Tercentenary Handlist of English and Welsh Newspapers, Magazines and Reviews*, in two parts (I, London; II, Provincial), lists papers and journals under the date on which they were first issued (useful if you want to know what was published in a particular period); there is also a title list. *The Newspaper Press in Britain*, an annotated bibliography edited by David Linton and Ray Boston, contains a useful chronology of British newspaper history 1476–1986 and a location listing of papers and other archives. The British Library's own *Bibliography of British Newspapers* is in progress.

So far as foreign newspapers are concerned, the *Europa World Year Book* gives details of the press of each country; and volume 3 of the *Guide to Reference Material* lists the various national source books under each country in both the 'Newspapers' and 'Periodicals' sections.

Benn's Media Directory (formerly *Benn's Press Directory*) covers the whole world and is the oldest-established media guide: now in three volumes and published annually, it is directly descended from *Mitchell's Newspaper Press Directory*, which was first published in 1846. It covers newspapers, periodicals, house journals and much other related information on embassies and high commissions, news agencies, broadcasting and all aspects of the media including cable and satellite. Subscribers are entitled to use a unique information service – Benn's Media Information Service (BEMIS) – which will answer spot queries on UK or overseas media free of charge; should any enquiry need extensive research, this is costed individually before the work is undertaken. The *Directory* is not cheap, and is probably beyond the pocket of individual researchers, but the local library is almost certainly a subscriber and enquiries may be channelled through them. Write or telephone to the Editor, BEMIS, Benn Business Information Services Ltd, PO Box 20, Sovereign Way, Tonbridge, Kent TN9 IRQ (tel. 0732 362666).

In the general catalogue at the British Library periodicals are entered in a series of volumes filed under 'P' and headed 'Periodical Publications'; the titles are arranged alphabetically under the place of publication. The transactions or proceedings of most learned societies are not here, but catalogued under the name of the society. It is necessary, therefore, first to look in the general catalogue under the title of the periodical, which will give either a finding reference to 'Periodical Publications' (i.e. the place of publication) or to the name of the relevant society, which may be catalogued under a particular country, town or university. This sounds more complicated than it is in practice, and you will very quickly get into the swing of it. Periodicals which are not catalogued may be at the British Library Document Supply Centre; ask at the enquiry desk how to obtain them.

Most reference libraries will either have a bound copy of the latest edition of *Ulrich's International Periodicals Directory* or subscribe to the quarterly-updated microfiche. Now in its thirtieth edition, this is the best source of information on periodicals, irregular serials and annuals published throughout the world. (N.B. It can also be searched 'on-line' via DIALOG.)

So far as British newspapers and periodicals are concerned, *Serials in the British Library*, which has replaced the earlier *British Union-Catalogue*, is the standard guide. Another useful reference tool is *Periodical Title Abbreviations*. Walford's *Guide to Current British Periodicals* promises to be as useful to the researcher as the same compiler's *Guide to Reference Material*, referred to several times in this handbook. Cynthia L. White's *Women's Magazines 1693–1968* is a first-class survey of that field and will enable you to find out which magazines were in circulation at a particular date and what they contained. Finally, use should be made of the microfiche *Keyword Index to Serial Titles* (*KIST*), which lists all significant words in titles in British Library collections.

Now that *The Times* is on microfilm, you should have no difficulty in finding a library in your region where you may have access to the complete run, starting with the first issue of 1 January 1785. Other papers may not be so easy to find in the provinces, but a list of newspapers (worldwide) that are available on film or CD-ROM may be obtained from Research Publications Ltd, P.O. Box 45, Reading RG1 8HF (tel. 0734 583247), should you wish to purchase them for private use. *The Guardian* (from 1990) is available on CD-ROM from Chadwyck-Healey Ltd, Cambridge Place, Cambridge CB2 1NR (tel. 0223 311479).

Indexes to newspapers

The most valuable of British newspaper indexes to the researcher is the *Index to The Times*. The official index has been published since

1906, and an earlier, slightly less accurate version, known as *Palmer's Index to The Times*, from 1790 to June 1941. The *Index* is now published monthly, with annual cumulations; since 1973 it has included references to the *Sunday Times, Times Literary Supplement, Educational Supplement* and *Higher Education Supplement*. The *Index* is useful not only for verifying reports in *The Times* itself, but as a guide to the dates of reports to be found elsewhere. Other newspapers in the United Kingdom which publish or have at one time published indexes are the *Financial Times* (May 1912–20, and more recently from 1981), the *Glasgow Herald* (annually from 1907) and *The Guardian* (from 1986). These indexes are on the open shelves at Colindale and many reference libraries, together with indexes to several American papers such as the *New York Times, Washington Post, Chicago Tribune* and *Los Angeles Times*, and indexes to a few Commonwealth and foreign newspapers. Microfilms of indexes to a number of British and continental newspapers are published by Research Publications of Reading. Since 1991 the same firm has marketed a *British Newspaper Index* on CD-ROM which includes all those papers included in the *Times Index* plus the *Financial Times, The Independent* and *The Independent on Sunday*. University Microfilms International offer *Newspaper Abstracts* on CD-ROM, covering the major US newspapers.

Indexes to periodicals

The earliest index to periodicals is *Poole's Index to Periodical Literature*, which covers the period 1802–1906; it has a comparatively recent author index which is extremely useful. There are also the *'Review of Reviews' Index* to periodicals in the years 1890–1902 and the *Wellesley Index to Victorian Periodicals, 1824–1900*, among others. The *Reader's Guide to Periodical Literature* is an American publication that has been issued since 1900; its English equivalent, the *Subject Index to Periodicals*, first published in 1915, changed its name in 1962 to the *British Humanities Index*, and is now published quarterly, with annual cumulations. Other more specialised periodicals indexes include the *Current Technology Index* (which has replaced the *British Technology Index*), the *British Education Index* and a series published by H. W. Wilson of New York, of which the *Art Index*, the *Biography Index*, the *Business Periodicals Index*, the *Humanities Index*, the *Index to Legal Periodicals* and the *Social Sciences Index* (the last two formerly published as one index 1965–74, and before that date as the

International Index) are the most likely to be of interest to the UK writer/researcher.

Among the indexes to particular magazines which are of immense value to researchers are those to the *Gentleman's Magazine*: the printed index volumes cover the period 1731–1819, with separate indexes to the biographical and obituary notices. *Notes & Queries* carries indexes to each volume and cumulated indexes for every twelve volumes. Both of these publications are excellent sources of information on a variety of subjects. Among recent indexing projects has been the index compiled by Geraldine Beare to the *Strand Magazine* 1891–1950, also of great value.

The majority of modern periodicals carry volume indexes, and these are a great help in tracing material quickly. Where there are no such printed indexes, it is necessary to skim through the contents page of each issue to find a particular paper or feature, or the researcher can apply to the editorial office of the publication concerned, if this is still in existence, where a card index may be held.

Most public libraries keep long runs of local newspapers, county magazines and publications of their local historical and archaeological societies; these will also be found on the shelves of county record offices.

The British Library Science Reference and Information Service houses a vast number of scientific and technical periodicals, including those formerly at the Patent Office Library.

The researcher wishing to trace a medical paper should do so in the *Index Medicus*, to which most medical libraries subscribe.

Press cuttings

Mention of press cuttings was absent from the first two editions of this handbook, and I was taken to task for the omission. The reason for it was a personal one, since in my experience artificial collections of this nature are not to be regarded as reliable source-material: they are reliable and comprehensive only in so far as the person assembling the cuttings was reliable and conscientious. However, they do have a value – as a starting-point in research – and should not have been dismissed out of hand. The best advice to be given here is: use them, but use with care, and never as a substitute for original research.

The major exception to this has to be the admirable press cuttings library of the Royal Institute of International Affairs at Chatham House, which contains much material of value to researchers on foreign and Commonwealth matters. The collection prior to 1940 is on microfilm, that of the period 1940–70 has been transferred to the British Library Newspaper Library at Colindale (indexes at Chatham House), and the present library collection runs from 1971.

Many newspapers, libraries, trade associations and other professional bodies maintain cuttings collections, and it is always worth asking what they have and having a look at them: you may well pick up leads for further research in this way.

Official Publications

Research in the field of government and official publications is complex and beyond the scope of this handbook. Two excellent guides are Frank Rodgers' *Guide to British Government Publications* and Stephen Richards' *Directory of British Official Publications*. There is also the CD-ROM *Catalogue of United Kingdom Official Publications*. Her Majesty's Stationery Office issues *Sectional Lists* which carry details of departmental publications; these are revised regularly and are available free of charge from HMSO and from booksellers who are HMSO agents. The most useful of these to the researcher is Sectional List no. 60, *History in Print*. Another free leaflet of interest is *Government Statistics: A Brief Guide to Sources*, produced by the Central Statistical Office and published by HMSO. Publications of some four hundred British official organizations are listed in the *Catalogue of British Official Publications Not Published by HMSO*.

Most British official publications are available at the main reference libraries and public libraries. The British Library Reference Division Official Publications Collection houses government publications of all countries, publications of the European Commission, the United Nations and other international and intergovernmental bodies. British Parliamentary papers, complete sets of *Hansard* and the *London Gazette*, current UK electoral registers and all the main statistical yearbooks are among a large number of reference books on the open shelves.

Researchers seeking information on the United Nations and its specialised agencies may use the library of the United Nations Information Centre, Ship House, 20 Buckingham Gate, London SW1E 6LB (tel. 071–630 1981).

On Europe the best source-book is Ian Thomson's *The Documentation of the European Communities*. Researchers may also use the Library and Information Unit at the European Commission, Jean Monnet House, 8 Storey's Gate, London SW1P 3AT (tel. 071–973 1992).

Miscellaneous

The *Essay and General Literature Index*, covering work published since 1900, is the best place to look for miscellaneous articles, reviews, etc.; now issued twice a year, with monthly previews and regularly cumulated volumes, it is normally available in the larger reference libraries.

To check quotations it is best to look first in the 'standard' works of which there are very many, in various editions far too numerous to list here, but available in every reference library. Some of the more recent compilations will be found in Appendix II, 'Reference Books for the Writer', page 195. Use should also be made of concordances to the Bible, to Shakespeare, Tennyson and many other major writers; people tend to forget just how time-saving these can be when one is reasonably sure of the author and when one has a major word or phrase to go on. *Granger's Index to Poetry*, with its title, first line, author and subject indexes, is indispensable. The *Song Index* and its supplement are useful sources for songs up to 1934, and there is also the *Song Catalogue* section of the *BBC Music Library Catalogue of Holdings*; the *Popular Song Index* and its supplements bring the catalogues up to the present time. For music bibliographies and catalogues of printed music – outside the scope of this handbook – see volume 3 of the *Guide to Reference Material*, under 'Music', and the *British Catalogue of Music*.

If you need to check on any particular kind of literature or printed matter – for example, hymns or nursery rhymes – you should always look in the subject index of the reference library first, to find out the standard work.

Translations

The best source is the *Index Translationum*, which has been published since 1932; it is now issued annually by UNESCO, and most reference libraries subscribe to it.

Street and telephone directories

The Guildhall Library in London has a collection of street directories from the late 18th century, and so has the Westminster History Collection of Westminster City Libraries, at 158–160 Buckingham Palace Road, London SW1W 9UD. P. J. Atkins' *The Directories of London 1677–1977* is a comprehensive bibliography. Most county record offices have sets of their local directories. These are extremely useful for checking addresses and names of neighbours, in biographical and family history research, as are the court guides (for the aristocracy) which also date from the late 18th century. The yellow pages of modern telephone directories will help you if you want to contact experts in a particular field.

Maps

The Map Library of the British Library will be transferred to St Pancras by 1996. There is a printed *Public Services Guide* to the collections. The Public Record Office, most local record offices and some libraries, such as Birmingham Central Reference Library, also hold special historical collections. Volume 3 of the *Catalogue of the National Maritime Museum Library* is another good source-guide.

Stanford's, at 12–14 Long Acre, London WC2E 2LP (tel. 071–836 1321), sells antique and modern maps and atlases covering the world. The first edition of the Ordnance Survey has been reprinted, and the historical series is still available; the modern editions, in various scales, may be purchased from HMSO or their main agents, the London Map Centre, 22–24 Caxton Street, London SW1H 0QU (tel. 071–222 2466), or ordered from most booksellers.

Unpublished Sources
Manuscripts and private papers

The major source of manuscripts in England is the Department of Manuscripts at the British Library. The collection currently housed at the British Museum will be transferred to St Pancras in 1996. Access to the MSS search room requires the 'higher level' type of reader's ticket. There is a ten-volume *Index of Manuscripts in the British Library*, listing in one alphabetical sequence the holdings to 1950; more recent acquisitions, catalogued as Add. MSS, will be found in a series of volumes on open access. There are a number of printed British Library catalogues, and a good quick reference guide to these is M.A.E. Nickson's *The British Library: Guide to the Catalogues and Indexes of the Department of Manuscripts*. This useful booklet also lists the reference books on open access in the MSS search room and the catalogues available there of MSS holdings in other libraries.

(N.B. During the transition to St Pancras, intending visitors to the Department of Manuscripts should contact the British Library in advance for up-to-date information.)

If you wish to trace the location of other MSS or to ascertain whether any private papers exist, or to find out if such papers have been deposited or registered, you should first get in touch with the Royal Commission on Historical Manuscripts, Quality House, Quality Court, Chancery Lane, London WC2A 1HP. The Commission maintains a National Register of Archives, consisting of thousands of unpublished reports on privately owned records and those held in repositories other than the Public Record Office. Publications of the Commission include a most useful *Guide to Sources for British History* series, of which eight volumes have been published to date: 1, *Papers of British Cabinet Ministers 1782–1900*; 2, *The Manuscript Papers of British Scientists 1600–1940*; 3, *Guide to the Location of Collections described in the Reports and Calendars Series 1870–1980*; 4, *Private Papers of British Diplomats 1782–1900*; 5, *Private Papers of British Colonial Governors 1782–1900*; 6, *Papers of British Churchmen 1780–1940*; 7, *Papers of British Politicians 1782–1900*; 8, *Records of British Business and Industry 1760–1914*.

The search room of the Commission is open to the public, and enquiries may be made in person or in writing (addressed to the Registrar), but not by telephone. Visitors obtain file numbers on computer.

So far as literary manuscripts are concerned, searchers should contact the Location Register of English Literary Manuscripts and Letters at the University of Reading. This valuable project will eventually include papers from 1700 to the present day; the first phase has resulted in the 2-volume printed *Location Register of Twentieth Century English Manuscripts and Letters*. Another project in progress is the *Index of English Literary Manuscripts*, at present covering the period 1450–1900.

An excellent finding aid to unpublished material is the Chadwyck-Healey *National Inventory of Documentary Sources in the United Kingdom*, on microfiche, updated eight times a year and also on CD-ROM. Most major libraries subscribe, and there are useful leaflets explaining how to use the inventory. *British Archives: A Guide to Archive Resources in the United Kingdom and Ireland*, by Janet Foster and Julia Sheppard, is another indispensable reference tool, listing archive collections by town, by county and alphabetically; the introduction contains useful advice to the first-time user of archival material. David Iredale's *Enjoying Archives* is both practical and entertaining.

Public records

The Public Record Office holds archives going back to the 11th century; nowadays all official records are automatically deposited within thirty years and (with certain exceptions) are open to the public thirty years after their creation. The bulk of the records were moved in 1976 from the old building in Chancery Lane to a modern one in Kew, but a few classes of records have been retained in central London for the time being; a list of these is available from the PRO, or intending researchers may write or telephone for information, either to Ruskin Avenue, Kew, Richmond, Surrey TW9 4DU (tel. 081–876 3444) or to Chancery Lane, London WC2A 1LR (same tel. no.). Readers' tickets (valid for several years) or temporary tickets for short periods are obtainable at both places. For security reasons, you are required to deposit your handbag and briefcase, and you will need a £1 coin to operate your locker.

At the PRO documents are ordered by computer, and readers are issued with bleepers which let them know when they can collect from the issue desk. Qualified staff are on hand to deal with enquiries and to explain how to operate the computer terminals. There is a large typing room at Kew, and in both buildings good facilities for ordering photocopies and microfilms. Documents are classified by Department or Ministry rather than by subject, so that it is necessary to know first of all (or to find out) to which class the documents you need belong. You then look up the class lists of the relevant date, in order to find the piece numbers (files) you have to order. It is not as complicated as it sounds, and the PRO issues a number of excellent information leaflets on various subjects which are of much help to the novice.

Parliamentary records from 1497 are at the House of Lords Record Office, and records of British rule in India to 1947 at the British Library Oriental and India Office Collections, 197 Blackfriars Road, London SE1 8NG. The Imperial War Museum, Lambeth Road, London SE1 6HZ, houses documentary and illustrative material on the two World Wars, and the Churchill Archives Centre at Churchill College, Cambridge CB3 0DS, is collecting papers of 20th-century politicians, scientists and both military and naval commanders; however not all of these are yet open to the public.

At the Guildhall Library in London you will find records relating to the City from medieval times, including those of many of the City livery companies (although some of these perished in the Great Fire of 1666). Consult the *Guide to Archives and Manuscripts at Guildhall Library.*

The National Library of Scotland possesses a priceless collection of manuscripts, ranging from early monastic writings to modern political papers; there are printed and manuscript indexes. There is also the National Register of Archives (Scotland), a branch of the Scottish Record Office, General Register House, Edinburgh EH1 3YY. M. Livingstone's *Guide to the Public Records of Scotland*, although published as long ago as 1905, is still a useful work of reference, and the two-volume *List of Gifts and Deposits in the Scottish Record Office* describes briefly the family muniments and business records that make up this collection.

If you seek Irish records, contact the Public Record Office of Northern Ireland, 66 Balmoral Avenue, Belfast BT9 6NY. When the old Public Record Office in Dublin was destroyed in 1922 most, but not all, of the records perished. The National Library of Ireland, Kildare Street, Dublin, and Trinity College Library in the same city both possess fine collections of historical manuscripts.

HMSO *Sectional List* no. 60, *History in Print*, lists publications available from HMSO, including those of the Public Record Office, the Public Record Office of Northern Ireland, the Scottish Record Office and the House of Lords Record Office.

Theses

It is always worthwhile checking on dissertations, as these can be a most valuable source of information. Aslib has since 1950 published an *Index to Theses accepted for Higher Degrees in the Universities of Great Britain and Ireland*; it is now a quarterly publication produced in collaboration with Learned Information Ltd, under the title *Index to Theses with Abstracts*. The universities of Oxford, Cambridge and London publish separate annual lists. There are *Abstracts of Dissertations* for Oxford and Cambridge going back to 1925, and lists for London in the University Calendar 1930–40, as well as *Subjects of Dissertations, Theses etc. for Higher Degrees* covering 1937–51. The Institute of Historical Research has published annual lists of history theses since 1901. Issued in May each year, they consist of two parts: 'Theses completed' and 'Theses in progress'.

For American theses, the *Comprehensive Dissertation Index* is the main source, covering all doctoral dissertations accepted in North America since 1861. As well as the annual, five- and ten-year cumulative volumes, it is available on microfiche and may be accessed through DIALOG. A wide range of dissertations submitted to North American universities may be obtained on microfilm from University Microfilms International, White Swan House, Godstone, Surrey RH9 8LW; catalogues on a variety of subjects are available on request.

Indexes to foreign theses are printed in *Guide to Reference Material*, volume 3, under 'Theses'. See also a most useful hand-book, D. H. Borchardt and J. D. Thawley's *Guide to Availability of Theses*.

Broadcast and televised material

As a result of the new Broadcasting Act which came into force in 1991 there are very many far-reaching changes in progress in the worlds of radio and television. While these do not affect the re-searcher into historical material, anyone seeking current infor-mation should first contact the relevant radio or television company direct. The *Guide to the BBC*, published annually, lists the tele-phone numbers of the various BBC information offices (currently 071–580 4468 for radio, 081–743 8000 for television). To date no publications are forthcoming from the recently established Independent Television Commission; the Radio Authority issues a *Pocket Book* and the occasional newsletter. Addresses and tele-phone numbers of all BBC, independent and local radio and tele-vision companies are listed in the current *Writers' & Artists' Yearbook* and *The Writers' Handbook*.

BBC Enterprises Data Enquiry Service (Room 7, 1 Portland Place, London W1A 1AA; tel. 071–927 5998) offers a fast and efficient research service to members of the public on a fee-paying basis, using BBC and external sources. You may also use the BBC Written Archives Centre (Caversham Park, Reading RG4 8TZ; tel. 0734 472742), which is open to *bona fide* researchers; or staff will undertake research, if required, at an hourly rate. Enquiries should be made in the first instance by letter, not by telephone. The BBC Sound Archives are not open to the public but may be accessed through the British Library National Sound Archive.

Most sizeable reference libraries possess the Chadwyck-Healey microfiche editions of *BBC Radio: Author and Title Catalogues of Transmitted Drama, Poetry and Features, 1929–1975* and *BBC Television: Author and Title Catalogues of Transmitted Drama and Features, 1936–1975 (with Chronological List of Transmitted Plays)*. Also available on microfiche are the *Radio Times*, from 1923, *The Listener*, from 1929, and the *BBC Home Service: Nine O'Clock News 1939–1945* (60,000 pages of newsreaders' typescripts).

Two useful paperbacks that will help with all media contacts are Denis MacShane's *Using the Media* and Jane Drinkwater's *Get It On Radio and Television*. Also recommended are the *Professional Publishing Media Directory* and the *Professional TV and Radio*

Media Directory. Most radio and television writers will be familiar with Norman Longmate's *Writing for the BBC*.

The National Sound Archive (NSA) is at 29 Exhibition Road, South Kensington, London SW7 2AS (tel. 071–589 6603). It will *not* be moving to the new British Library premises at St Pancras.

The NSA Library is on open access, and there are no formalities except that anyone wishing to use the viewing or listening facilities must make a prior appointment. Those who live in the north may make use of the listening service at the British Library Document Supply Centre at Boston Spa, West Yorkshire; there is a similar (but charged) service at the North Devon Library Services Headquarters, Barnstable, Devon.

One of the largest sound archive collections in the world, the NSA currently intakes some 50,000 items per year, many of them unique unpublished recordings. It also acts as a point of contact between the public and the BBC Sound Archive, from which any requested items are fetched to Kensington free of charge. Apart from outside recordings, the NSA makes its own of productions of the Royal Shakespeare Company, the Royal National Theatre and the Royal Court, and of a number of poetry readings.

Filmed and recorded material

The researcher interested in filmed material and the history of the cinema should contact the British Film Institute at 21 Stephen Street, London W1P 1PL (tel. 071–255 1444). The library is open to non-members as a separate subscription or daily rate (for details see Appendix I, page 183). The National Film Archive, a division of the BFI, has its headquarters at the same address but the films themselves are stored at Berkhamsted. Among other collections there are the British Pathé News Film Library at Pinewood Studios (tel. 0753 651700) and the Visnews Television News Library at Cumberland Avenue, London NW10 7EA (tel. 081–965 7733); the latter holds old cinema newsreels going back to 1910.

There is a wealth of printed works. *Halliwell's Film Guide* is the standard reference source. Also recommended is a three-volume paperback set, the *International Dictionary of Film and Filmmakers*. In progress are the Saur *International Film Index*, of which the first volume, *Titles and Directors 1895–1990*, is available, and the *Aurum Film Encyclopedia*, two volumes to date. But by far the most comprehensive source so far, for the early period, is the mammoth *History of the Cinema 1895–1940*, a collection of 3,900 microfiches plus a printed guide and index, from Chadwyck-Healey.

Oral history collections

Although the term 'oral history' is a fairly recent one, in fact this was the very first kind of history, as Paul Thompson has pointed out in *The Voice of the Past*. The growth of oral history study groups today reflects an interest in and awareness of the value of this field of research, which demands quite different skills from those of the historian who handles only documentation.

Researchers interested in the subject would do well to subscribe to *Oral History*, the journal of the Oral History Society. (Contact the Society either through the National Sound Archive, mentioned above, or at the Department of Sociology, University of Essex, Wivenhoe Park, Colchester, Essex CO4 3SQ; tel. 0206 873333.) The best reference sources are the *Directory of Recorded Sound Resources in the United Kingdom* and *Oral History: An Annotated Bibliography 1945–1989*. In the United States, where there is also much activity and interest in this field, there are a number of guides and the Oral History Association journal, *Oral History Review*.

The *National Life Story Collection*, a National Sound Archive project currently in progress, is bringing together recordings of 20th-century people from all walks of life; this is bound to prove a valuable source for researchers.

It is a sobering thought that by the year 2000 only some 50% of all records may be on paper, as opposed to film, tape and computer storage systems. Future researchers will therefore spend an increasingly greater proportion of their working time looking and listening instead of poring over the printed or handwritten page in library and record office, and no doubt there will soon be many more facilities of this nature. Like it or not, the revolution is under way, and we are going to have to get used to it, so the sensible thing to do is to prepare ourselves by acquiring the necessary new skills.

Abstracts of Dissertations approved for the PhD, MSc and MLitt Degrees 1925/6–1956/7, Cambridge University Press, 1927–59

Abstracts of Dissertations for the Degree of Doctor of Philosophy 1925–40, Oxford University Press, 12 vols, 1928–47 (BLitt and BSc theses are included in vols 10 and 12)

American Book Publishing Record, published weekly and monthly, with annual and 5-year cumulative volumes, by Bowker, New Providence, N.J. There are sets of cumulative volumes covering the period 1950–84 and an earlier volume for the years 1876–1949.

Art Index, published quarterly since 1929 by H. W. Wilson, New York

Aslib Directory of Information Sources in the UK, published by Aslib, London and brought up-to-date regularly; available for purchase by non-members; latest edition (6th), ed. Ellen Codlin, 2 vols, 1990

Aurum Film Encyclopedia, ed. Phil Hardy, in progress; first 2 vols, Aurum Press, London, 1991

BBC Home Service: Nine O'Clock News, 1939–1945, Chadwyck-Healey microfiche

BBC Radio: Author and Title Catalogues of Transmitted Drama, Poetry and Features, 1929–1975, Chadwyck-Healey microfiche

BBC Television: Author and Title Catalogues of Transmitted Drama and Features, 1936–1975, with Chronological List of Transmitted Plays, Chadwyck-Healey microfiche

Benn's Media Directory (formerly *Benn's Press Directory*), published annually by Benn Business Information Services Ltd., Tonbridge, Kent, 3 vols

Bibliographic Index, published since 1938 by H. W. Wilson, New York; now twice a year in paperback with annual cumulation volumes; on-line from November 1984

Bibliography of British Literary Bibliographies, ed. T. H. Howard-Hill, Oxford University Press, Oxford, 1969– , in progress

Bibliography of British Newspapers, British Library, London, 1982– , in progress (6 vols to date, by county)

Biography Index, published since 1946 by H. W. Wilson, New York; now quarterly with annual cumulations, also on-line and CD-ROM from July 1984

Bookdealer, published weekly since 1971 by Werner Shaw, London

Books in Print (American), published annually by Bowker, New Providence, N.J.; now also *Books in Print Plus*, updated bi-monthly, and available for MS-DOS/Mackintosh

Books of the Month and *Books to Come*, published monthly by Whitaker, London

The Bookseller, published weekly by Whitaker, London; special spring and autumn issues

Bookshops of Greater London, compiled and published by Roger Lascelles, Brentford, 6th ed., 1990

British Archives: A Guide to Archive Resources in the United Kingdom, by Janet Foster and Julia Sheppard, 2nd ed., Macmillan, London, 1989

British Catalogue of Music, published annually by British Library, London, since 1963; cumulative vol. 1957–85, Chadwyck-Healey, 1988

British Library General Catalogue of Printed Books: original ed. to

1975 out of print; reprinted, 360 vols + 6 supplementary vols, Saur, Munich, 1980–88; CD-ROM by Saztec Europe, distributed in UK by Chadwyck-Healey. Supplements 1976–89, reprinted by Saur, 1983–91; microfiche ed., updated regularly, British Library, London, 1986–   ; also on-line via BLAISE-LINE.

The British Library: Guide to the Catalogues and Indexes of the Department of Manuscripts, by M. A. E. Nickson, 2nd ed., British Library, London, 1982

British National Bibliography (BNB), weekly since 1950, with cumulative monthly, annual and some 5-yearly volumes; now published by British Library, London; also available on microfiche, CD-ROM and on-line via BLAISE-LINE

British Union-Catalogue of Periodicals, originally published in 4 vols by Butterworth, London, 1955–58, with supplement, 1962; also supplementary vols of *New Periodical Titles* and *Scientific Periodicals*. Replaced in 1981 by *Serials in the British Library, q.v.*

Catalogue of British Official Publications Not Published by HMSO, published in 6 bi-monthly issues with annual cumulations and separate *Keyword Index*, Chadwyck-Healey, Cambridge

Catalogue of United Kingdom Official Publications, on CD-ROM, Chadwyck-Healey, Cambridge, retrospective to 1980, and updated and cumulated quarterly

Catalogue of the National Maritime Museum Library, vol. 3, *Atlases and Cartography*, HMSO, London, 1971

Catalogue of the Newspaper Library, Colindale, compiled by P. E. Allen, 8 vols, British Library, London, 1975

Children's Books in Print, published annually since 1969 by Whitaker, London

Cole's Register of British Antiquarian and Secondhand Bookdealers, published by Michael Cole, 7 Pulleyn Drive, York YO2 2DY, latest ed., 1991

Comprehensive Dissertation Index 1861–1972, 37 vols; annually since 1973, with 5- and 10-year cumulations, also on microfiche, University Microfilms International (for UK distributor see note at end of list); also on-line via DIALOG

Cumulative Book Index, published annually since 1928 by H. W. Wilson, New York; now monthly, with quarterly cumulations and annual volumes, and on CD-ROM from 1982

Current Technology Index (formerly *British Technology Index*), published since 1962; previously by Library Association, now bi-monthly by Bowker-Saur, London

The Directories of London 1677–1977, by P. J. Atkins, Cassell, London, 1990

Directory of British Official Publications: A Guide to Sources, by Stephen Richards, 2nd ed., Mansell, London, 1984

Directory of London Public Libraries, published by the Association of London Chief Librarians, updated irregularly; latest ed., 1990

Directory of Recorded Sound Resources in the United Kingdom, ed. L. Weerasinghe and J. Silver, British Library, London, 1989

Directory of Specialist Bookdealers in the United Kingdom, 4th ed., Peter Marcan, High Wycombe, 1988

The Documentation of the European Communities, by Ian Thomson, Mansell, London, 1989

The English Catalogue of Books: first vol. 1801–36 and subsequent 3- and 5-year cumulations; discontinued (last vol. published 1969)

Enjoying Archives, by David Iredale, Phillimore, Chichester, 1985

The Europa World Year Book, 2 vols, published annually by Europa, London

Financial Times Index, from 1981, available on monthly subscription, with annual cumulative volumes, from Research Publications, Reading

Gentleman's Magazine: General Index to the first 56 volumes (1731–86), 2 vols; *General Index ... 1787–1819, Index to the Biographical and Obituary Notices, 1731–1780 and 1781–1819*, 2 vols: 1st vol., British Record Society, London; 2nd vol., Garland, New York and London

Get It On Radio and Television, by Jane Drinkwater, Pluto, London, 1984

Glasgow Herald Index, published annually since 1907 by Outram, Glasgow

Government Statistics: A Brief Guide to Sources, prepared annually by Central Statistical Office and published by HMSO, London (gratis)

Granger's Index to Poetry, first published 1904, 8th ed., ed. W. E. Bernhardt, Columbia University Press, New York, 1986

Guardian Index, from 1986, available on monthly subscription with annual cumulative volume, from University Microfilms International

Guide to Archives and Manuscripts at Guildhall Library, Guildhall Library, London, 1989

Guide to Availability of Theses, by D. H. Borchardt and J. D. Thawley, Saur, Munich, 1981

Guide to the BBC, published annually by British Broadcasting Corporation, London

Guide to British Government Publications, by Frank Rodgers, H. W. Wilson, New York, 1980

Guide to the Contents of the Public Record Office, 3 vols, 1963, 1968, is out of print, but still available at the enquiry desks in the reference rooms. There also is the current main guide, updated regularly, which will lead the searcher to the relevant class lists. Part II of the current Guide, and the Index, are available on microfiche.

Guide to Current British Periodicals in the Humanities and Social Sciences, ed. A. J. Walford, Library Association, London, 1985

Guide to Libraries and Information Units, 29th ed., ed. Peter Dale, British Library Key Resource series, London, 1990

Guide to Libraries in Western Europe, ed. Peter Dale, British Library Key Resource series, London, 1991

Guide to the Public Records of Scotland, by M. Livingstone, HMSO, London, 1905

Guide to Reference Material, ed. A. J. Walford, 5th ed., 3 vols: vol. 1, *Science and Technology*, 1989; vol. 2, *Social and Historical Sciences, Philosophy and Religion*, 1990; vol. 3, *Generalities, Languages, the Arts and Literature*, 1991; *Concise Edition*, 1981 (new ed. in preparation), Library Association, London

Guide to Reference Books, ed. Eugene P. Sheehy, American Library Association, Chicago, 9th ed., 1992

Guide to Sources for British History: based on the National Register of Archives: 1, *Papers of British Cabinet Ministers 1792–1900*: 2, *Manuscript Papers of British Scientists 1600–1940*; 3, *Guide to the Location of Collections described in the Reports and Calendars Series 1870–1980*; 4, *Private Papers of British Diplomats 1782–1900*; 5, *Private Papers of British Colonial Governors 1782–1900*; 6, *Papers of British Churchmen 1780–1940*; 7, *Papers of British Politicians 1782–1900*; 8, *Records of British Business and Industry 1760–1914*, Royal Commission on Historical Manuscripts, HMSO, London, in progress, 1982–

Halliwell's Film Guide, ed. Leslie Halliwell, 7th ed., Paladin, London, 1990

Handlist of English Provincial Newspapers and Periodicals, 1700–1760, by G. A. Cranfield, Cambridge University Press, Cambridge, 1961

Handlist of Unpublished Finding Aids to the London Collections of the British Library, by R. C. Alston, British Library, London, 1991

Hansard: Parliamentary Debates, 1803 onwards; now published daily during sessions by HMSO, London. Chadwyck-Healey,

Cambridge, publishes various series of Parliamentary Papers from 1715, on microfilm and microfiche.

History in Print, Sectional List no. 60, HMSO, London, updated regularly (gratis)

History Theses, 2 vols to date, Institute of Historical Research, London, 1976, 1984

Humanities Index, formerly *International Index* and *Social Sciences and Humanities Index*, published since 1974 by H. W. Wilson, New York; now quarterly with annual cumulative volumes, also available on-line and on CD-ROM

Index of English Literary Manuscripts, covering the period 1450– 1900, 4 vols, Mansell, London, 1991

Index of Manuscripts in the British Library, 10 vols, Chadwyck-Healey, Cambridge, 1985

Index Medicus, published monthly since 1960 by National Library of Medicine, Washington

Index to Theses with Abstracts, continuing series of *Index to Theses* published since 1950, now quarterly by Aslib/Learned Information Ltd, London and Oxford

Index Translationum, published quarterly 1932–40, and annually since 1949, by UNESCO, Paris

International Bibliography of the Social Sciences, first published in 1952 by UNESCO, Paris; now by Routledge, London

International Books in Print, 2 vols, Bowker, New Providence, N.J., updated regularly; latest ed. (10th), 1991

International Dictionary of Film and Filmmakers, ed. Christopher Lyon, 3 vols, Macmillan, London, 1987–91

International Film Index, vol. 1, *Titles and Directors 1895–1990*, Saur, Munich, 1991

Keyword Index to Serial Titles (KIST), on microfiche, British Library, London, 1987, updated regularly

Libraries in the United Kingdom and the Republic of Ireland, published annually by the Library Association, London; 18th ed., ed. Ann Harrold, 1991

List of Gifts and Deposits in the Scottish Record Office, 2 vols, HMSO, London, 1971, 1976

The Listener, weekly, London; on microfilm 1929–79, microfiche from 1980, both Chadwyck-Healey, Cambridge

Location Register of Twentieth-Century English Literary Manuscripts and Letters, 2 vols, British Library, London, 1988

London Bibliography of the Social Sciences, published annually, with supplements, from 1974 by British Library of Political and Economic Science, London; final vol. (24th supplement), 1989; from 1990 incorporated into *International Bibliography of the*

Social Sciences, q.v.

London Catalogue of Books, series of overlapping catalogues covering the years 1700–1855 (first vol. published by Bent, 1773)

London Gazette, published since 1665; now daily, Monday to Friday, by HMSO, London

Mitchell's Newspaper Press Directory, first published 1846; now *Benn's Media Directory, q.v.*

Museums Year Book, published annually by the Museums Association, London

National Inventory of Documentary Sources in the United Kingdom and Ireland, by subscription (8 units per year) from Chadwyck-Healey, Cambridge; also on CD-ROM

National Life Story Collection, in progress at National Sound Archive, London

National Union Catalog (US), Library of Congress, Washington: series of pre-1956 author lists, 754 vols, main series 1956–82; on microfiche from 1983. Includes author, title, subject and series indexes.

Newspaper Abstracts, major United States newspapers covered from 1985/7, on CD-ROM from University Microfilms International

The Newspaper Press in Britain: An Annotated Bibliography, ed. D. Linton and R. Boston, Mansell, London, 1987

Notes & Queries, published since 1849 by Oxford University Press, Oxford, with various volume indexes and cumulated indexes; now quarterly

Oral History, journal of the Oral History Society, 1971– , now published twice a year

Oral History: An Annotated Bibliography, compiled by Robert Perks, British Library, London, 1990

Periodical Title Abbreviations, 2nd ed., ed. L. G. Alkire, Gale Research, Detroit, 1977

Poole's Index to Periodical Literature, 1802–1906, Boston, Mass., reprinted 1938 and 1969; *Cumulative Author Index*, Pierian Press, Ann Arbor, Michigan, 1971

Popular Song Index, by Patricia P. Havlice, Scarecrow Press, Metuchen, N.J., 1975; supplements, 1978, 1984, 1989

Printed Reference Material and Related Information Sources, ed. Gavin L. Higgens, Library Association, London, 3rd ed., 1990

Professional Publishing Media Directory and *Professional TV and Radio Media Directory*, both twice a year since 1986, Professional Books, Abingdon

Radio Authority Pocket Book, first published June 1991, Radio Authority, London; to be updated regularly

Radio Times, weekly, BBC Enterprises, London; on microfilm 1923–79, microfiche from 1980, both Chadwyck-Healey, Cambridge

Reader's Guide to Periodical Literature, published since 1900 by H. W. Wilson, New York, now 17 issues per year (including quarterly cumulations) and annual cumulation; available on-line and CD-ROM from 1983

Religious Books in Print, published annually since 1984 by Whitaker, London

'*Review of Reviews' Index to Periodicals 1890–1902*, London, 13 vols, 1891–1903

Serials in the British Library, quarterly with annual cumulations, microfiche, British Library, London, since 1981; *Serials in the British Library 1976–1986*, microfiche cumulation, 1988

Sheppard's Book Dealers in the British Isles, now published by Richard Joseph Publishers, Farnham; latest ed., 1991–92

Skoob Directory of Secondhand Bookshops in the British Isles, 3rd ed., Skoob, London, 1989

Social Sciences Index, published since 1974 quarterly with annual cumulations, H. W. Wilson, New York; available on-line and CD-ROM from 1983

Song Catalogue, in *BBC Music Library Catalogue of Holdings*, BBC, London, 4 vols, 1966

Song Index, by M. E. Sears and P. Crawford, H. W. Wilson, New York, 1926; supplement, 1934

Strand Magazine: Index 1891–1950, by G. Beare, Greenwood, Westport, Conn/London, 1982

Subject Catalogue of Printed Books: 1975–1985, on microfiche, British Library, London, 1985

Subject Guide to Books in Print, published annually since 1957 by Bowker, New Providence, N.J.

Subject Index to Periodicals, published annually 1915–53, then quarterly, with annual cumulations, 1954–61; now the *British Humanities Index*, q.v.

Subjects of Dissertations, Theses and Published Work presented by Successful Candidates at Examinations for Higher Degrees, covering 1937–51, University of London Library, London

Tercentenary Handlist of English and Welsh Newspapers, Magazines and Reviews, The Times, London, 1920

The Times, microfilm edition 1785 to present day, Research Publications, Reading

The Times Index, 1795 to present day, currently 12 monthly issues plus annual cumulative volume, Research Publications, Reading; available on microfilm for years 1906–76. Also *Palmer's Index to The Times, 1790–June 1941* (out of print).

Ulrich's International Periodicals Directory, 3 vols, Bowker, New Providence, N.J., 1991, with free quarterly update to subscribers; also on microfiche, on-line and CD-ROM

Using the Media, by Denis MacShane, Pluto, London, 1979

The Voice of the Past, by Paul Thompson, Oxford University Press, 2nd ed., 1988

Wellesley Index to Victorian Periodicals, 1824–1900, ed. W. E. Houghton, University of Toronto Press/Routledge, London, 3 vols, 1966–79

Whitaker's Book List (formerly *Cumulative Book List*), published since 1924 by Whitaker, London, annually since 1984; also *Bookbank* monthly, bi-monthly or annually on CD-ROM

Whitaker's Books in Print, published annually by Whitaker, London

Willing's Press Guide (first published 1871 as *Frederick May's London Press Directory*), now annually by Reed Information Services Ltd, East Grinstead, 2 vols

Women's Magazines 1693–1968, by Cynthia L. White, Michael Joseph, London, 1970

World Bibliographical Series, Clio Press, Oxford, in progress, 1977–

World Bibliography of Bibliographies, 4th ed. by T. Besterman, Lausanne, 4 vols and index, 1965–66; *Supplement 1964–1974*, ed. A. F. Toomey, 2 vols, Rowman & Littlefield, Totowa, N.J., 1977

World Guide to Libraries, by Helga Lengenfelder, 10th ed., Saur, Munich, 1991

World Guide to Special Libraries, by Helga Lengenfelder, 2nd ed., 2 vols, Saur, Munich, 1990–91

The World of Learning, now published annually by Europa, London

Writers' & Artists' Year Book, published annually by A & C Black, London

The Writers' Handbook, ed. Barry Turner, published annually by Macmillan, London

Writing for the BBC, by Norman Longmate, 8th ed., BBC, London, 1988

Note: Bowker and Saur titles are distributed in the UK by Bowker-Saur Ltd., Borough Green, Sevenoaks, Kent TN15 8PH (tel. 0732 884567); Scarecrow Press titles by Shelwing Ltd., 127 Sandgate Road, Folkestone, Kent CT20 2BL (tel. 0303 850501); H. W. Wilson titles by Thompson Henry Ltd., London Road,

Sunningdale, Berks SL5 0EP (tel. 0344 24615). University Microfilms International is represented in Europe by Information Publications International Ltd., White Swan House, Godstone, Surrey RH9 8LW (tel. 0883 744123).

4

Factual and Historical Research

The more research you undertake, the more you learn about sources. If you keep a careful note of every reliable source used (a card index filed under subjects is the best for easy reference), you can build up for yourself not only a unique and valuable research tool, but one that will save you hours of searching whenever a similar problem crops up in your work. It will prove its worth time and time again.

So much is in print these days that there can be scarcely any subject from, say, animated cartoons to Zimbabwe, on which you are not going to find some 'standard' work or encyclopedia; nor a trade or profession from archery to zoology for which there is no recognised association, biographical dictionary or 'Who's Who' – all essential sources for the researcher. Obviously it is impossible in one short chapter to deal exhaustively with particular sources. Some starting points only are suggested here, therefore, under the two headings 'Factual' and 'Historical' research, together with a warning of some of the pitfalls that lie in the path of the unwary. In all research you have to begin by consulting first one authoritative source, which leads you to the next, and that in turn to another, and so on, until you have satisfied yourself that you have found out all that you need to know. Patience and persistence are the essential qualities. Remember, too, that a negative result in research may have value.

Factual Research

The major difficulty here is that topical facts and figures are frequently out of date by the time they are published. The same applies to all writing on modern society, for the world is continually changing, developing faster with every day that passes. The best way round this problem is to rely on the latest printed information or data otherwise obtained at the time of submitting your typescript, but to indicate to your editor or publisher that you intend (or expect) to up-date specific points, either in the text or by means of an explanatory note, at proof stage. Then just before finally going to press you can telephone to the organization from which the original information came and ask for the most recent facts and figures available. All such up-datings must be kept to the absolute minimum, as author's corrections on proofs are very costly.

Another problem is that the bases used for the calculation of statistics vary from one subject to another, and from one organization to another, so that comparison can be, at worst, highly dangerous, and at best, misleading; often, also, you may find it impossible to obtain the precise breakdown you seek. Without expert help and knowledge it is unwise to meddle with statistics: where these do not exactly fit the context, the best solution is to quote them as they are presented and to add a footnote to this effect.

Sources of factual information

Mention has been made in earlier chapters of the computer search services that are now available. Although their use will undoubtedly become more widespread within the next few years, it is unlikely that they will be within the reach of all freelance writers for some time to come. Therefore most factual research will continue, for the time being, to be drawn from printed sources and from personal contact with authoritative experts in the field or with press and public relations officers.

Encyclopedias provide an excellent starting point, but they should always be supplemented by reference to the latest yearbooks. You can find out what yearbooks exist on a given subject by consulting *Current British Directories*, with its subject index and most useful abbreviations index, or the *Bowker International Serials Database Update* (formerly *Irregular Serials and Annuals*), which is the quarterly supplement to *Ulrich's International Periodicals Directory*. Among general publications most useful to the English writer for quick reference are *Whitaker's Almanack, The Statesman's Year Book, Britain: An Official Handbook, The Annual Register of World Events*, and the *Europa World Year Book*.

The Times newspaper is the best source for recent events; its *Index* is now published monthly, with annual cumulations. *Keesing's Record of World Events*, which started in July 1931 as a weekly publication, *Keesing's Contemporary Archives*, is now published ten times a year, with an annual index and annual bound volume; it has an excellent reputation, and most reference libraries subscribe to it. You can also rely on its US equivalent, *The Weekly World News Digest.*

So far as UK statistics are concerned, you have at one end of the scale a free booklet published annually by HMSO, *Government Statistics: A Brief Guide to Sources* and, at the other, the comprehensive *Reviews of UK Statistical Sources* series, sponsored by the Royal Statistical Society and the Social Science Research Council. There is also a *Guide to Official Statistics*, published by the Central Statistical Office; the CSO also issues a *Monthly Digest* and an *Annual Abstract of Statistics*. For Europe there is *Statistics Europe*; for the United States the *American Statistical Index*, which is held in London in the Official Publications Collection of the British Library.

On facts in general there are two very handy paperbacks: *Facts in Focus* and *Chambers' Quick Facts*. Also worth looking at are the titles in the new *Chambers' Compact Reference* series; translated from the French, this series covers a wide range of modern and historical subjects. The *Guinness Book of Records* and the *Shell Book of Firsts* are surprisingly useful source-books. There are many more.

How to trace books using bibliographies, concordances and books of quotations has been discussed in the previous chapter. There have been some good general guides to factual research, as recommended in earlier editions of this book, but most are now out of print. A new title is *Finding Facts Fast*.

The Information Bureau (51 The Business Centre, 103 Lavender Hill, London SW11 5QL; tel. 071–924 4414), formerly the *Daily Telegraph* Information Bureau, offers a general research and information service on a subscription basis, using printed and on-line resources, a vast press cuttings collection, and business and media contacts built up over many years. For non-account holders requiring one-off quick checking of dates, facts and figures, or names to contact in associations, there is a minimum charge (valid autumn 1991) of £5 + VAT (hourly rate £60 + VAT).

The Science Reference and Information Service of the British Library (SRIS) offers both a free enquiry service and a priced research service in the fields of science, technology and business information. Resources used include the unique SRIS collections backed up by those of the whole British Library. N.B. Currently split between reading rooms at 25 Southampton Buildings, London, WC2A 1AW, Chancery House (opposite 25 Southampton Buildings) and 9 Kean Street, London WC2B 4AT, SRIS will be moving to the new British Library at St Pancras in 1993. In the meantime the following telephone numbers apply: Business

Information Service, quick enquiries 071–323 7454; research service 071–323 7457; Science and Technology Information Service, enquiries 071–323 7288/7494; priced research service, 071–323 7477. The enquiry number at St Pancras is 071–323 7915.

A free leaflet outlining the services of the SRIS is available on request, also a free short guide, *Using the Business Collection*. Rather more detailed are the *Guide to Directories at the Science Reference and Information Service* and *Scientific Abstracting and Indexing Periodicals in the British Library: A Guide to SRIS Holdings and their Use*. Other recommended titles in this field are *How to Find Information in Science and Technology*; *Libraries, Information Centers and Databases in Science and Technology*; and *Reference Books for the Historian of Science*.

Getting hold of experts

You may often find yourself at a loss as to how to get in touch with experts on particular subjects when there is no one in your immediate circle who can help. Here the best advice to be given is, 'Do not be shy. Go straight to the horse's mouth' – in other words, look up the professional or trade association concerned (or it may be an international company, a bank, or almost any other kind of group), and either write or telephone to the general secretary, press or public relations officer. Remember that all these people have a vested interest in being portrayed correctly, and also that the expert is always flattered to be consulted. If the person you approach is too busy or unable for some other reason to give you what you want, he will usually be able to suggest an alternative contact.

The best way to find out if there is a relevant association is to look in an up-to-date *Directory of British Associations and Associations in Ireland* or the equivalent volumes for Europe, the *Directory of European Industrial and Trade Associations* and the *Directory of European Professional and Learned Societies*. Another goldmine of information of this nature, and fully up to date, is the *Hollis Press & Public Relations Annual*, which lists an enormous number of press contacts (with addresses and telephone numbers) in virtually every field of professional, industrial and commercial life, as well as official and public information sources, PR consultancies and much other invaluable data. The same firm now publishes a similar directory for Europe, *Hollis Europe*. There is also a list of societies and institutions in *Whitaker's Almanack*, but this is not so informative, nor is it as comprehensive as the two publications mentioned above. Lastly, do not overlook your local 'yellow pages' directory, in case there is some contact on your own doorstep.

The *NUJ Freelance Directory* is a computerised catalogue of freelance journalists in Britain and Ireland (and some overseas), listed alphabetically, geographically and by subject speciality. It is available at modest cost to non-members and has a useful role to play in the finding of local contacts.

Historical Research

Recommended studies of English historical sources are J.J. Bagley's *Historical Interpretations*, covering the period from 1066 to the present day, and the comprehensive *English Historical Documents* series, from *c.* 500 to 1914. *Sources in British Political History 1900–1951* is a good guide to 20th-century historical archives, while the excellent Macmillan *Historical Facts* and *Political Facts* series (volume details at end of chapter) are invaluable for quick reference.

For the researcher who wishes to delve more deeply there are some excellent bibliographies: the *Bibliography of British History* series consists of separate volumes for each period from the earliest times to 1914, while the rather more selective, but no less useful, *Bibliographical Handbooks* published by Cambridge University Press for the Conference on British Studies cover the period 1066–1970.

As far as general histories are concerned, *The Cambridge Ancient History, The Cambridge Medieval History* and *The New Cambridge Modern History* are standard works. William W. Langer's *An Encyclopedia of World History* is a superb one-volume work of reference, chronologically arranged from prehistory to the modern period.

The Oxford History of England is the authoritative work on English history, while a reliable and inexpensive paperback series handy to keep at your elbow while working is the nine-volume *Pelican History of England*; also useful is Winston S. Churchill's *History of the English-Speaking Peoples*. A more recent publication, *The Cambridge Historical Encyclopedia of Great Britain and Ireland*, with contributions from sixty major historians in a single volume, is an essential reference tool for all historical researchers: it consists of seven chronological sections, each followed by interpretative articles written by specialists, with useful marginal notes and cross-references, plus a biographical Who's Who and an index. At the other end of the scale, as a quick reminder of the dates

69

of kings and queens, and the salient points of each reign, you cannot better Ronald Hamilton's *Now I Remember*.

Space does not permit the inclusion here of historical sources of other countries, but the reader is referred to chapter 9, 'Information from and about Foreign Countries' (pages 141–57) and also to volume 3 of the *Guide to Reference Material*, under 'Ancient History', 'Medieval and Modern History' and the appropriate area of the world (or individual countries).

Conflicting authorities

One of the main problems that you must be prepared to encounter in historical research is that of conflicting authorities. Inevitably at some stage in your work you will come across two, if not three, or more, different dates or interpretations of the same event. How do you know which one to trust?

Wherever possible, you should yourself go back to the original, contemporary source. If this is not feasible, you have the choice of either weighing up the theories advanced by the various historians and coming down firmly on one side – and sticking to it – or, if you have the space and the inclination, of giving an account of the conflicting views and your reasons for preferring one to all others.

Dates

The different reckonings of dates in historical documents often confuse the beginner. Under the Julian calendar, which was in universal use throughout the Middle Ages and in some countries, such as England and Russia, until as late as the 18th and early 20th centuries respectively, the year began on 25 March. The Gregorian calendar, in which 1 January was reckoned as the beginning of each year, was introduced on the Continent in 1582, when ten days were cut out of that year in order to take care of accumulated errors of reckoning. This new calendar was not adopted in England until 1752, although for some years prior to that date a double indication was normally given in official documents (and in some private papers) for dates falling between 1 January and 24 March, as, for example, '24 February 1655/6'. The trap is that during the period 1582–1752 a traveller could leave, say, Italy, on one date and arrive in England several days earlier, because of the discrepancy in the calendar. From the end of the 16th century most English official correspondence with foreign powers carries either both dates, i.e. '12/22 December 1635', or an indication of the reckoning used, i.e. 'O.S.' (Old Style) or 'N.S.' (New Style).

The practice followed by most modern historians is to take the beginning of the historical year as 1 January. All dates between 1 January and 24 March are thus written as, for example, '22 February 1559' rather than '22 February 1558/9', except in quoted matter, where the date should always be copied faithfully as in the original text and an explanatory 'O.S.' or 'N.S.' added in square brackets if necessary. For a full discussion of this whole question, see C. R. Cheney's *Handbook of Dates for Students of English History*. This useful book contains, among other information, tables of regnal years, Easter days and calendars for all possible dates of Easter from AD 500 to the year 2000, which will enable the researcher to avoid the most common errors of dating in historical work. Another standard reference work on the subject is the *Handbook of British Chronology*. *Whitaker's Almanack* contains an 'Easy Reference Calendar' from 1770 to the present.

Dates in private papers sometimes cause the researcher a headache. Letter-writers not infrequently give an incomplete date or omit it altogether, and another trap to watch out for is that at the new year people through the ages have tended to forget, writing, for example, '5 January 1888' when they meant '5 January 1889'. Where neither contents nor letterheading provide the answer, and the date does not become clear as research progresses, you will have to choose between doing without that particular document and hazarding an intelligent guess – in which case you should make it clear that the original is undated.

The use of periodicals in historical research

Periodicals of interest to the historical researcher include *Historical Research*, formerly the *Bulletin of the Institute of Historical Research*, the *English Historical Review*, the Historical Association's *History*, and *History Today*, all of which should be checked for recent studies relevant to the job in hand. Women's magazines and newspapers are an excellent source for fashion, prices and entertainments at a particular date, and papers such as *The Tatler & Bystander* and *Illustrated London News* provide useful background information on the social scene. Advertisements sometimes yield as much information as textual material.

American Statistical Index, published monthly, with annual and cumulative indexes and abstract vols, by the Congressional Information Service, Washington

Annual Abstracts of Statistics, Central Statistical Office, HMSO, London

Annual Register of World Events, now published by Longman, London

Bibliographical Handbooks series, published by Cambridge University Press for the Conference on British Studies: *Anglo-Norman England 1066–1154*, ed. M. Altschul; *The High Middle Ages in England 1154–1377*, ed. B. Wilkinson; *Late-Medieval England 1377–1485*, ed. D. J. Guth; *Tudor England 1485–1603*, ed. M. Levine; *The Seventeenth Century*, ed. D. Berkowitz; *Restoration England 1660–1689*, ed. W. L. Sachse; *Late Georgian and Regency England 1760–1837*, ed. R. A. Smith; *Victorian England 1837–1901*, ed. J. L. Altholz; *Modern England 1901–1970*, ed. A. F. Havighurst

Bibliography of British History, 6 vols to date, regularly brought up to date, published by Oxford University Press: *English History to 1485*, ed. E. B. Graves; *Tudor Period, 1485–1603*, ed. Conyers Read; *Stuart Period, 1603–1714*, ed. M. F. Keeler; *The Eighteenth Century, 1714–1789*, ed. S. Pargellis and D. J. Medley; *British History 1789–1851*, ed. L. M. Brown and I. R. Christie; *British History 1851–1914*, ed. H. J. Hanham

Bowker International Series Database Update (formerly the *Irregular Serials and Annuals*, quarterly supplement to *Ulrich's International Periodicals Directory*), published by Bowker, New Providence, N.J., from 1985

Britain: an Official Handbook, HMSO, London, annually

The Cambridge Ancient History, 12 vols of text, 5 vols of plates (some vols now revised), first published by Cambridge University Press, 1923–39

The Cambridge Historical Encyclopedia of Great Britain and Ireland, ed. Christopher Haigh, Cambridge University Press, 1985

The Cambridge Medieval History, 8 vols, plus portfolios of maps (some vols now revised), first published by Cambridge University Press, 1911–36

Chambers' Compact Reference series, in progress, 8 vols to date (8 further vols to come 1992), Chambers, Edinburgh

Chambers' Quick Facts, published by Chambers, Edinburgh, 1991

Current British Directories, published by CBD Research, Beckenham; regularly updated (11th ed., 1988)

Directory of British Associations & Associations in Ireland, published by CBD Research, Beckenham, 10th ed., 1990

Directory of European Industrial & Trade Associations, published by CBD Research, Beckenham, 5th ed., 1991

Directory of European Professional & Learned Societies, published by CBD Research, Beckenham, 4th ed., 1989

An Encyclopedia of World History, 5th, ed., by William L. Langer,
   Harrap, London, 1975 (out of print)
English Historical Documents, ed. D. C. Douglas, 12 vols, in
   progress, Eyre Methuen, London
English Historical Review published quarterly since 1886 by
   Longman, Harlow
The Europa World Year Book, 2 vols, published annually by
   Europa Publications, London
Facts in Focus, Central Statistical Office, Penguin Books in associ-
   ation with HMSO, Harmondsworth, 5th ed., 1980
Finding Facts Fast, by A. Todd and C. Loder, Penguin,
   Harmondsworth, 1990
Government Statistics: A Brief Guide to Sources, published
   annually by HMSO, London (gratis)
Guide to Official Statistics, 5th ed., HMSO, London, 1990
Guide to Reference Material, ed. A.J. Walford; vol. 3, *Generalities,
   Languages, the Arts and Literature*, 5th ed., Library Association,
   London, 1991
Guinness Book of Records, published by Guinness, Enfield; regu-
   larly updated (38th ed., 1991)
Handbook of British Chronology, ed. E. B. Fryde *et al*, Royal
   Historical Society, London, 3rd ed., 1985
Handbook of Dates for Students of English History, by C. R.
   Cheney, Royal Historical Society, London, 1978; reprinted 1982
Historical Facts series, published by Macmillan, London: 6 vols to
   date, covering 1485–1985 (first 2 vols entitled *English Historical
   Facts*, subsequent vols *British Historical Facts*), 1975–88
Historical Interpretations, by J. J. Bagley, 2 vols: 1, *Sources of English
   Medieval History, 1066–1540*; 2, *Sources of English History, 1540
   to the Present Day*, David & Charles, Newton Abbot, 1972
Historical Research (formerly the *Bulletin of the Institute of
   Historical Research*), since 1987 published three times a year by
   Blackwell, Oxford, for the IHR
History, published three times a year by the Historical Association,
   London
The History of the English-Speaking Peoples, by W. S. Churchill, 4
   vols, Cassell, London, 1956–58
History Today, published monthly since 1951, London
Hollis Press & Public Relations Annual, published by Hollis
   Directories, Sunbury-on-Thames, Middx
Hollis Europe, published annually by Hollis Directories
   Sunbury-on-Thames, Middx
Illustrated London News, weekly from May 1842; now monthly,
   London

Keesing's Record of World Events (formerly *Keesing's Contemporary Archives*), published since 1931; now ten issues per year, with annual index and annual bound vol., Longman, Harlow

Monthly Digest of Statistics, Central Statistical Office, HMSO, London

The New Cambridge Modern History, 14 vols, first published by Cambridge University Press, 1957–74 (some vols now revised)

Now I Remember, rev. ed., by Ronald Hamilton, Chatto & Windus, London, 1983; paperback, Hogarth Press, 1984

NUJ Freelance Directory, National Union of Journalists, London, updated regularly

The Oxford History of England, 15 vols, Clarendon Press, Oxford 1936–65

The Pelican History of England, 9 vols, Penguin Books, Harmondswoth, 1950–65

Political Facts series, published by Macmillan, London: *British Political Facts*, 1900–85, ed. D. Butler and G. Butler, 6th ed., 1986; *European Political Facts*, 4 vols, covering period 1648–1990, eds. C. Cook, J. Paxton *et al*, 1978–91

Reference Books for the Historian of Science, by S. Jayawardene, Science Museum, London, 1982

Reviews of United Kingdom Statistical Sources, 13 vols, Heinemann/Pergamon, London, 1974–80

Shell Book of Firsts, ed. Patrick Robertson, 2nd rev. ed., Michael Joseph, London, 1984

Sources in British Political History, 1900–1951, ed. Chris Cook, 6 vols, Macmillan, London, 1985

Statesman's Year Book, published annually by Macmillan, London

Statistics Europe, published by CBD Research, Beckenham, 5th ed., 1987

The Tatler & Bystander, first published 1709, now monthly, London

The Times Index, 1795 to present day, current subscription (12 monthly issues plus annual cumulative volume), Research Publications, Reading; available on microfilm for years 1906–76. Also *Palmer's Index to The Times, 1790–June 1941* (out of print).

Weekly World News Digest, published weekly, with cumulative indexing, by Facts on File, Oxford; also on CD-ROM from 1980. *News Digest 5 Year Indexes*, 8 vols, covering period 1946–85; also (with *Yearbooks* 1941–87) available on microfiche.

Whitaker's Almanack, published annually by Whitaker, London

5

Research for Fiction Writers and Dramatists

The amount and depth of research to be undertaken by the writer of fiction will depend upon his choice for the story's setting and the extent of his own knowledge of that setting, and also upon his acquaintance with the kind of people he is writing about. Basically, the research will be concerned with creating an authentic background to the plot and with writing dialogue in the correct idiom. As the problems which face the writer of modern fiction and drama are rather different from those of the writer of historical fiction and drama, they are here examined separately. All that is said about the novel applies equally to the short story and to drama.

The Modern Novel

Background

There is no substitute for a personal visit to every place in which your story, or scene of a story, is to be set. Only through first-hand experience will you absorb the atmosphere of a place, find out exactly how long it will take your character to get from A to B and what buildings or other landmarks he will pass on the way; by using your eyes and ears and nose, by travelling on the local bus, and by spending a few evenings at the pub, you can learn pretty well everything you need to know about the way the locals live, behave and talk. And if you make a point of attending at least once each kind of event that is going to crop up in your story or play – whether it is a boxing match, a race meeting, a sale at Sotheby's, a ballet performance, a court hearing, or anything else – there will probably be little further research that you need to do, beyond the seeking of a few facts and figures to supplement your personal observation.

Inevitably, sometimes, a personal visit is out of the question, and then you have no choice but to rely on secondhand sources. If this is the case, first of all equip yourself with a good, large-scale map or two – preferably a street map of each town in which the action of your story is to take place, as well as a map of the whole district. You can obtain much free information of this nature from town halls or tourist offices.

Travel brochures are always a helpful source, and there are any number of excellent general topographical guides to various regions of the United Kingdom. (How to obtain information on places abroad is dealt with in chapter 9, 'Information from and about Foreign Countries', pages 141–57.) *Whitaker's Almanack* and *Britain: An Official Handbook* each contain a surprising amount of data which will be invaluable for the story or drama set in this country. AA publications such as the *Great Britain Road Atlas* and the *Book of British Towns* are useful for quick reference, while the researcher wishing to find out more about the origin and meaning of place-names should consult the *Concise Oxford Dictionary of Place-Names* and the volumes (by county) published by the English Place-Name Society.

If you need to describe particular buildings you will find Nikolaus Pevsner's *Buildings of England* series, also one per county, enormously helpful; also the new *Guide to Country Houses* series. In addition, all stately homes and castles open to the public produce their own guidebooks, some more comprehensive and informative than others. Two annual publications, the AA's *Stately Homes, Museums, Castles and Gardens* and the less expensive *Historic Houses, Castles and Gardens in Great Britain and Ireland* carry brief details of all such properties. The curators of these historic houses are usually well informed, but may be too busy to talk to you on days when the public is admitted; a telephone call or preliminary letter beforehand may well lead to a special appointment and personally guided tour, with much additional information.

Other essential reference tools are railway and bus time-tables of the area you are describing: these will (or should) save you from making an elementary mistake such as putting a character on the train at the wrong London terminus or misjudging the time taken for a particular journey. A writer setting his tale on board a cruise ship or private yacht will find the *World Cruising Handbook* a mine of information on harbour regulations, ports of call, and much else.

An excellent way to get the 'feel' of a place, when it is not possible for you to visit it, is to take out a subscription to the local newspaper and county magazine; you will find lists of these, under towns, in both *Benn's Media Directory* and *Willing's Press Guide* (see chapter 3, 'Basic Sources of Information', page 43).

People

Often the background to a story or play will concern a particular profession or industry, and here too the best method of research is to mix as much as possible with people in the field. The secretary of the relevant professional or trade association (check names and addresses in the current *Directory of British Associations and Associations in Ireland*, in *Trade Associations and Professional Bodies of the United Kingdom*, in the *Hollis Press & Public Relations Annual*, or in *Whitaker's Almanack* – see chapter 4, pages 68–9) will usually be very helpful if you do not have any personal contacts, and most large corporations or companies have a press and public relations department or member of staff who will assist you. You should not feel diffident about approaching such people; it is rare for a genuine request for information to be refused point blank, and very often the enquirer will be invited to visit a factory or training establishment or to attend as an observer one or two meetings of the relevant society – all this is grist to the mill. Nevertheless, it is unfair to impinge too much on someone else's time or expertise – even if this is being paid for by his company – and so a luncheon or dinner invitation is a nice gesture. An incredible amount can be learned from an hour's conversation face to face.

Much of what has been said about background research also applies to finding out about people, for there is nothing better than to spend time with whatever age, regional, or occupational group the writer wishes to bring into his story. It is essential to observe at first hand how people behave, talk and dress. Every writer should try, therefore, to cultivate a wide circle of friends in all walks of life, and the fiction writer especially will do well to get to know a psychologist with whom he can discuss the actions and reactions of his characters, as well as a doctor with whom he can verify medical symptoms and treatments. The crime writer ought to be on friendly terms with at least one member of the police force who is willing to put him right on procedures and jargon; only as a last resort should he telephone or write to New Scotland Yard (where, however, if he has a genuine problem an information officer will usually help). For all writers of crime and detective fiction access to copies of *Moriarty's Police Law*, or the more recent *Butterworth's Police Law*, and Keith Simpson's *Forensic Medicine* is indispensable.

When reliance must be placed on documentary sources, a careers pamphlet or training manual for the relevant trade or profession will yield a good deal of information. The memoirs and diaries of eminent people in that trade or profession should be looked at, and also the appropriate in-house or trade journals, for these will all provide up-to-date material and jargon, and sometimes also historical detail.

So far as the behaviour of your characters is concerned, personal observation may be supplemented by a simple textbook on psychology or behavioural study, such as those published by Penguin Books. Desmond Morris has written two fascinating studies, *Manwatching* and *Gestures*, illustrating all kinds of gestures, signals and actions that people make and their interpretation, which are of interest to all writers.

Two useful sources of information on nicknames (both modern and historical) are the *Handbook of Pseudonyms and Personal Nicknames* compiled by H. Sharp, and the *Pseudonyms and Nicknames Dictionary* published by Gale Research of Detroit, USA. A more recent work is Carl Sifakis's *Dictionary of Historic Nicknames*.

On names in general, look first at the *Penguin Dictionary of Proper Names* and the *Penguin Dictionary of Surnames*. Oxford University Press's *Dictionary of First Names* and *Dictionary of Surnames* are rather more comprehensive and international in scope. For recommendations on literary pseudonyms and names of characters in published fiction, see the final paragraph of this chapter, page 88. More academic genealogical studies are mentioned in chapter 7, 'Family and Local History', pages 117–35.

Language

It is highly dangerous for the writer who is unfamiliar with a foreign language, local dialect or occupational slang to dabble in these fields, but if he must do so he should always try to get what he has written verified by an expert. So far as English is concerned, your first step should be to consult the National Sound Archive (29 Exhibition Road, London SW7 2AS; tel. 071–589 6603); an appointment will be arranged for you to listen to relevant recordings. (This can be in London, in Yorkshire or in Devon, see page 54.) Among printed works Peter Trudgill's recently published *The Dialects of England* is first class. Most reference libraries will also have the four-volume *Survey of English Dialects* by H. Orton and E. Dieth, and the *English Dialect Dictionary* by J. Wright.

There are a number of so-called 'slang dictionaries', and these have their uses. However, since it is necessary first to know the word or expression whose meaning you wish to look up in them, their value must be limited. Happily there is now *The Thesaurus of Slang*, a splendid compilation containing an alphabetical list of 12,000 standard English words for which you can look up some 150,000 slang terms, common idioms and colloquialisms. Less comprehensive, but useful for quick reference is Jonathan Green's *Slang Thesaurus*. The late Eric Partridge's *Slang Today and Yesterday*, with its separate sections dealing with slang spoken in chronological periods and in various occupational groups, is still valid historically. Mr Partridge also compiled a *Dictionary of the Underworld, British and American*, which will serve the crime writer well (although this too is arranged as a dictionary), and also a fascinating *Dictionary of Catch Phrases* (British and American) from the 16th century to the present day. An up-to-date work is Jonathan Green's *Newspeak: A Dictionary of Jargon*. Among other valuable books on the subject, *Sea Slang of the 20th Century* by W. Granville covers the language of yachtsmen, fishermen, bargemen and all naval personnel, but is now rather dated.

Quite often a writer is at a loss to know how one of his characters would address another, perhaps someone in an elevated position. Here either *Debbrett's Correct Form* or *Titles and Forms of Address* will provide the answer, supplying as a bonus a guide to practically every situation likely to arise, socially and professionally, including American usage. These books will also be invaluable for the researcher wishing to know how to write or talk to titled or official persons whom he needs to contact for information.

The Historical Novel

The writer of an historical novel must be thoroughly familiar with the period in which his story is set, and especially knowledgeable about the manners, customs and daily life of the people concerned. He must also be accurate about major events and prominent people. This will not present any great difficulty so long as he keeps at his elbow as he works a general bibliography and authoritative history of the period, as well as a good biographical dictionary (suggested titles are mentioned in chapter 4, 'Historical Research' (pages 65–74) and chapter 6, 'Biography' (pages 96–116)). A trap that inexperienced writers sometimes fall into is one of anachronisms: that is, the mention of, say, ice cream or zip fasteners at a period before these came on the scene. You can avoid such errors by checking in an encyclopedic dictionary or *The Shell Book of Firsts*.

In recent years a number of gifted historians, notably the French writers Fernand Braudel, Georges Duby and Roy Ladurie (all now translated into English) have added a new dimension to social history, for which we humble researchers, seeking ever more detail on the private lives of people through the ages, must be enormously grateful. For reasons of space I have had to be ruthlessly selective in considering which titles to recommend here. By pruning some of what may now be considered rather 'dead wood' in English and purely regional works from the earlier editions, I have been able to introduce some newer studies that are European in scope and written with the benefit of contemporary research. Readers who have read and absorbed my chapters 3 and 4 should be more than adequately equipped to ferret out other titles on more specific subjects.

It is of the utmost importance to use contemporary sources wherever possible, and you should make good use of the *English Historical Documents* series. Also recommended are the *They Saw It Happen* and the *Human Documents* series; some of these are now out of print, but they will be found in most reference libraries. G. M. Trevelyan's *English Social History* remains one of the best general accounts of life in this country through the ages, while a more recent study is Asa Briggs' *A Social History of England*. Two admirable multi-volume works are Fernand Braudel's *Civilization and Capitalism 1400–1800* and *A History of Private Life*, edited by P. Ariès and G. Duby. The lifestyle of the upper classes is admirably portrayed in Mark Girouard's *Life in the English Country House*. R. Graves and A. Hodge's *The Long Week-End* is very evocative of the years between the two world wars. The *Penguin Social History of Britain*, the first volume of which appeared in 1982, is also worth collecting. In addition, there are a number of excellent encyclopedias and social histories devoted to particular periods – Madeleine S. and J. Lane Miller's *Encyclopedia of Bible Life*, for example, or, on English life, studies such as E. N. Williams' *Life in Georgian England*, Dorothy Marshall's *English People in the 18th Century*, J. H. Plumb's *Georgian Delights,* John Fisher's *The World of the Forsytes*, the *How We Used to Live* series from A & C Black (early Victorian times to the present), and Norman Longmate's *How We Lived Then: A History of Everyday Life during the Second World War*, to mention but a few. G. D. H. Cole and R. Postgate's *The Common People 1746–1938* has become a standard work; see also *The Common People: A History from the Norman Conquest to the Present*, by J. F. C. Harrison, and two studies by E.P. Thompson,

Customs in Common and *The Making of the English Working Class*. *British Trials 1660–1900* contains first-hand accounts of thousands of trials. In lighter vein, but very informative, are C. L. Graves' *Mr Punch's History of Modern England*, covering the years from 1841 to 1914, and Leslie Baily's *BBC Scrapbooks 1896–1939*. Rona Randall's *The Model Wife* is a well-illustrated mine of information about marriage and the role of a wife in the 19th-century household. For the present century it is worth looking at the recent *Portrait of a Decade* series.

Autobiographies and diaries are extremely useful as source-material for the historical novelist in that they provide absolutely authentic accounts of day-to-day life and thought of the period, written in the contemporary idiom. *British Autobiographies*, compiled by William Matthews, is an annotated bibliography of material printed or published before 1951. John Burnett has made two useful studies of working-class material, the three-volume *Autobiography of the Working Class*, covering the period 1790–1945, and a paperback, *Useful Toil: Autobiographies of Working People from the 1820s to the 1970s*.

William Matthews' *British Diaries 1442–1942* and John Stuart Batts' *British Manuscript Diaries of the 19th Century* are standard works, both listing the diaries under the year in which they commence, which enables the researcher to ascertain what material exists for a particular period. Matthews also compiled an annotated bibliography of *American Diaries* written prior to 1861 and *American Diaries in Manuscript 1580–1954*. His work has been updated, expanded and continued by another American bibliographer, Patricia Pate Havlice, in an invaluable volume, *And So To Bed: A Bibliography of Diaries published in English*; this contains an index to Matthews' listings and also a general index of authors, editors, titles and subjects. Also worth consulting are *English Family Life 1576–1716: An Anthology of Diaries*, edited by Ralph Houlbrooke, and *Women's Diaries, Journals and Letters: An Annotated Bibliography*, compiled by Cheryl Cline.

Most public libraries have a local collection, and you should always ask if there is a book dealing with a particular region, town, industry or local family, in the period about which you are writing. (For further suggestions, see chapter 7, 'Family and Local History' pages 117–35.)

One good method of keeping the story of an historical novel or play in line with world or national events is to refer constantly to a published chronology. There are a number to choose from, such as the series published originally by Barrie & Rockcliff/Barrie &

Jenkins: *Chronology of the Ancient World* (BC–799 AD); *Chronology of the Medieval World* (800–1491); *Chronology of the Expanding World* (1492–1762); and *Chronology of the Modern World* (1763–1965). In these volumes the major events of each year are listed month by month, while also included are annual listings of the developments in the arts, sciences, politics, etc., together with the births and deaths of famous people. The *Pan Book of Dates* is arranged by date (1 January to 31 December) and has a good index.

Problems likely to be encountered by the writer of historical fiction and some suggestions as to how they may be solved are discussed below.

Places

Many of the places and buildings you may want to mention in your novel or play still exist today, but have changed out of all recognition in the last few hundred years, and it is not easy to find out exactly how they looked at a particular date. You should always ask at the local library or record office if they have maps of approximately the right date, and where these exist you will find it valuable to keep a photocopy of the map in front of you as you write. There is an historical series of the Ordnance Survey, which may be useful, and you can buy reprints of the first (one-inch) edition. A good historical atlas is essential. *Newnes Historical Atlas,* the *Penguin Atlas of World History* or *The Times Concise Atlas of World History* are recommended, or you may prefer to have one of the three inexpensive Penguin atlases, *Ancient History, Medieval History* or *Recent History.*

Like the writer of modern fiction, the historical novelist should try to visit every place or building that comes into his story. If this is quite impossible, the best course is to enquire at your local library or county record office for a reliable parish history and for any books about life in the district during the period in which you are interested. If your story is set in the 18th century or later, you will be able to study the local newspaper. Where buildings have to be described, Nikolaus Pevsner's *Buildings of England* series, already mentioned, will be most useful; also H.M. Colvin's *History of the King's Works.* For buildings in London, there is the very detailed *Survey of London.* Other useful sources are the guidebooks to historic castles and houses open to the public.

Dates

The problems that arise over dating have been discussed in the previous chapter. In historical fiction work the writer will most often need to find out on what day of the week a certain anniversary or religious festival fell. This can be done very easily by first looking up the date of Easter in the chronological table at the back of the *Handbook of Dates for Students of English History* and then by turning to the appropriate calendar section, in which there is a double-page spread for all the years from AD 500 to 2000 in which Easter fell (or is going to fall) on that particular day. In the same *Handbook* you will find a list of saints' days and religious festivals, but if you need more detail on festivals you should consult the *British Calendar Customs* series published by the Folklore Society. *Whitaker's Almanack* contains an 'Easy Reference' calendar from 1770.

Weather

What the weather was like on a certain day, or if a particular winter was severe, or when there was a heatwave and how long it lasted, can be vital to an historical novel. *Whitaker's Almanack* (from 1868) is a good source, and so are local and regional newspapers. *The Times* has employed a regular weather correspondent since the early 1870s, but earlier reports – from 1731 – appeared in *Gentleman's Magazine*, where you will find not only monthly tables giving temperatures and rainfall, but a calendar with brief descriptions against each day, such as 'cloudy morning, but bright later'; 'windy and wet all day'; 'heavy rain in the south, snow in the north'.

Two excellent works which are rare books and to be found nowadays only at the major libraries are T. H. Baker's *Records of the Seasons, etc. . . . observed in the British Isles* and E. J. Lowe's *Natural Phenomena and Chronology of the Seasons* (of which Part I only was ever published, containing records from AD 220 to 1753). Among other useful reference books are Ingrid Holford's *Guinness Book of Weather Facts and Feats*; D. Bowen's *Britain's Weather*, which has an appendix listing notable gales, blizzards, floods and frosts; J. H. Brazell's *London Weather*, with its useful chronology from AD 4 to 1964; and W. Andrews' *Famous Frosts and Frost Fairs in Great Britain*. For information about the weather in different regions of the globe, the best source is W. G. Kendrew's *The Climates of the Continents*.

In England, the Meteorological Office has published records since the 1860s. Its Library and Archives Department contains many earlier records, covering the entire world; researchers are allowed to use the Library, and in special cases books will be loaned by post. The Librarian will usually recommend titles or will pass a specific query on to the relevant department, who may charge a fee if extensive research has to be undertaken by staff. Enquiries should be addressed in the first instance to the National Meteorological Library, London Road, Bracknell, Berks RG12 2SZ (tel. 0344 85420242, extension 4843).

Language

Getting the idiom right in historical fiction is often a big worry to the writer. The best advice that can be given is that he should read extensively the best novels and plays of the relevant age; by so doing, he will gradually acquire the 'feel' of the spoken English of the time. The meanings of words can be checked in the big *Oxford English Dictionary*, in the *Shorter OED*, or in the *Routledge Dictionary of Historical Slang*. Eric Partridge's *Slang Today and Yesterday*, as mentioned earlier in this chapter, has useful sections on the slang spoken at different periods (16th to mid-20th century). If you are setting your story in the last war, you should look at *The Language of World War II*, which covers not only spoken expressions but also the slogans and abbreviations then current, as well as the popular songs of the time.

Cost of living, currencies and wages

How much people earned and what they paid for their food and clothing are queries that frequently crop up in historical writing. J. Burnett's *A History of the Cost of Living* will answer most needs: it has chapters dating from the Middle Ages to the present day, and also a good bibliography. Unfortunately it has been allowed to go out of print, but most libraries will have it; should you ever see it on offer secondhand, be sure to snap it up! A more recent paperback, written primarily for family and local historians, is Lionel Munby's *How Much is that Worth?* Another exceptionally informative source is the *What It Cost the Day Before Yesterday Book* by Harold Priestley, which is divided into three periods: 1851–1914, 1915–70 and (to take account of inflation) 1971–78. *Prices and Wages in England from the 12th to the 19th Century* by Lord Beveridge and others is a standard work, and Peter Wilsher's *The Pound in your Pocket 1870–1970* is a very readable and well-researched study of the pound and its purchasing power over the last hundred years. Newspapers and women's magazines are valuable sources from the early 19th century onwards – advertisements as much as text – while for a general survey A. Adburgham's *Shops and Shopping 1800–1914* is excellent. *Edwardian Shopping and*

Yesterday's Shopping, reprinted from the Army and Navy Stores' catalogues of 1898–1913 and 1907 respectively, provide a record both of changing fashion and of prices at that time.

Currency Conversion Tables: A Hundred Years of Change by R. L. Bidwell is a most useful guide to the fluctuations in rates of exchange of most countries of the world since 1870; it also has a table of London gold prices. For money values in earlier times there is Peter Spufford's *Handbook of Medieval Exchange*. A more recent title, published in the United States, is Pierre Vilar's *A History of Gold and Money 1450–1920*. If you should need other historical information or monetary rates, it is best to write or telephone to the Bank of England Reference Library, Threadneedle Street, London EC2R 8AH (tel. 071–601 4715).

Fashion, etiquette and food

The standard work on English costume is the series by C. W. and P. E. Cunnington, which consists of *Handbooks* covering the medieval period and the 16th, 17th, 18th, 19th and 20th centuries in separate volumes. For quick reference there is the *Dictionary of English Costume 900–1900* by C. W. and P. E. Cunnington and Charles Beard. Also useful is *The Evolution of Fashion: Pattern and Cut from 1066 to 1930* by M. Hamilton Hill and Peter Bucknell, while Alison Lurie's study *The Language of Clothes* is both a thoroughly researched and witty comment on dress and manners that will help both the modern and the historical novelist. The new *Fashions of a Decade* series, published by Batsford, is useful for the 20th century. Other titles are listed in the booklet *Costume: A General Bibliography*, published by the Costume Society. There is now a Costume and Fashion Research Centre at 4 Circus Road, Bath, Avon BA1 2EW (tel. 0225 461111, extension 2752), which may be able to help further. Enquiries should be addressed in writing to the Keeper of Costume in the first instance. On hairdressing there is R. Corson's *Fashions in Hair: The First 5000 Years*, R. Turner Wilcox's *Modes in Hats and Headdress* (from ancient Egyptian to the present day) and G. de Courtais' *Women's Headdress and Hairstyles in England from AD 600 to the Present Day*.

The best guides to English manners and etiquette are J. Wildeblood and P. Brinson's *The Polite World* (covering the 13th to the 19th centuries) and *A Punch History of Manners 1841–1940*, by A. Adburgham. On eating habits and diet there are Arnold Palmer's *Movable Feasts*, G. Brett's *Dinner is Served*, J. C. Drummond and A. Wilbraham's *Englishman's Food: Five*

Centuries of English Diet, J. Burnett's *Plenty and Want: A Social History of Diet in England from 1815 to the Present Day* and Reay Tannahill's *Food in History*.

Transport and travel

One of the best general studies is E. A. Pratt's *History of Inland Transport and Communications*. David & Charles of Newton Abbot, Devon, are publishers who specialise in railway and transport history, and it is worth asking for their current catalogue and stocklist. Finding out exactly how long a particular journey would have taken at a particular date is not easy, but so far as train journeys are concerned it is a good idea to look at an early Bradshaw (first published in 1839) or at the time-table nearest in date to that used in the story. Stage-coach time-tables will be found in the early London directories.

Children's Fiction

Research done by the children's writer is not much different from that carried out by the writer of stories for adults. Children of all ages being highly critical and quick to spot mistakes, it is very important that background and language are absolutely right.

The correct idiom is vital. It is a good idea, if you are embarking on a modern story, to study a selection of juvenile magazines for a time. You will also want to find out about published children's books. The Children's Book Foundation, which is part of the Book Trust (Book House, 45 East Hill, London SW18 2QZ; tel. 081–870 9055), maintains an excellent library and information service; the Trust's *Children's Books of the Year*, published annually, is free to members. You can also consult the *Children's Fiction Index*, which will be found at the children's librarian's desk in most libraries.

On sources generally, there is the recent *Children's Fiction Sourcebook*. As well as the standard work, *The Oxford Companion to Children's Literature*, you will find Arthur Mortimore's *Index to Characters in Children's Literature* very useful. If you write for young children, you may want to have works such as *The Classic Fairy Tales*, *The Fairies in Tradition and Literature* or the *Oxford Dictionary of Nursery Rhymes* on your reference bookshelf.

So far as school stories are concerned, you cannot do better than delve into Peter Opie's *The Lore and Language of Schoolchildren*. Isabel Quigly's *The Heirs of Tom Brown*, with its excellent bibliography, will help with a public school setting. Another very useful book is *Children's Games in Street and Playground*, by Iona and Peter Opie.

Various slang dictionaries have been mentioned on page 79. However, it cannot be stressed too strongly that language is changing all the time – and especially the language of the young – so that there can be no substitute for the writer mixing with, and talking and listening to, the younger generation, in order to get the idiom exactly right.

Background too must be up to date: remember single-parent families and the mixed nationalities encountered by children today in playgroup and school!

Science Fiction

The best source in this country is the Science Fiction Foundation Research Library at the Polytechnic of East London, Longbridge Road, Dagenham, Essex RM8 2AS (tel. 081–590 7222, extension 2177). The collection includes the library of the British Science Fiction Association. Intending researchers should telephone in advance for an appointment.

Finding out about Published Fiction

In addition to the specific research problems connected with his own work, the fiction writer or playwright frequently wants to know what other novels or plays or short stories have been published with similar themes or backgrounds. He may also wish to check on whether any other writer has used the title which he has in mind. (There is no copyright in titles, but for the exact legal position, see the Society of Authors' *Quick Guide* on the 'Protection of Titles'.)

Most public libraries possess copies of the *Fiction Index*, the *Play Index* and the *Short Story Index*; you should ask for them at the readers' enquiry desk. There are cumulated volumes of the *Fiction Index* for 1945–60 and 1960–69; since 1970 every five years. The *Index* is published annually in the spring following the year indexed. Titles are listed under some 3,000 subject headings.

The *Short Story Index* is also published annually, with five-year cumulations; in addition there is a single volume of *Collections Indexed 1900–1978*. There are seven volumes of the *Play Index*, covering the period 1949–87; synopses of the plots of plays are included, together with an author, title and subject listing.

Research for Writers

The researcher wishing to find out about published historical
fiction should look at the *World Historical Fiction Guide* and at
Irene Collins' *Recent Historical Novels*. J. Nield's *Guide to the Best
Historical Novels and Tales* deals with titles published before 1929;
it is out of print, but available in most reference libraries.

Literary pseudonyms may be traced in Frank Atkinson's
Dictionary of Literary Pseudonyms. There are three useful sources
for finding out about characters in published fiction: the *Dictionary
of Characters in British Novels*, the *Dictionary of Fictional
Characters* and the *Dictionary of Real People and Places in Fiction*.

*American Diaries: An Annotated Bibliography of American Diaries
written prior to Year 1861*, by William Matthews, University of
California Press, Berkeley and Los Angeles, 1945, 1959

American Diaries in Manuscript, 1580–1954, by William
Matthews, University of Georgia Press, Athens, 1974

And So To Bed: A Bibliography of Diaries published in English, by
Patricia Pate Havlice, Scarecrow, Metuchen, 1987

Autobiography of the Working Class, by John Burnett, 3 vols,
Harvester, Hemel Hempstead, 1984–89

BBC Scrapbooks, by Leslie Baily, 2 vols: 1, *1896–1914*; 2, *1918–
1939*, Allen & Unwin, London, 1966–68

Benn's Media Directory, published annually by Benn Business
Information Services Ltd, Tonbridge, 3 vols

Book of British Towns, published by Drive Publications,
Automobile Association, Basingstoke, 1979

Britain: An Official Handbook, published annually by HMSO,
London

Britain's Weather, by David Bowen, David & Charles, Newton
Abbot, 1969

*British Autobiographies: An Annotated Bibliography of British
Autobiographies published or written before 1951*, by William
Matthews, University of California Press, Berkeley and Los
Angeles, 1955

British Calendar Customs: England, 3 vols, 1936–40; *Scotland*, 3
vols, 1939–41; *Orkneys and Shetland*, 1946, published by The
Folklore Society, London

*British Diaries 1442–1942: An Annotated Bibliography of British
Diaries written between 1442 and 1942*, by William Matthews,
University of California Press, Berkeley and Los Angeles, 1950

*British Manuscript Diaries of the 19th Century: An Annotated
Listing*, by John Stuart Batts, Centaur Press, Fontwell and
London, 1976

British Trials 1660–1900, microfiche series, in progress, 1990– , Chadwyck-Healey, Cambridge

Buildings of England series, originally ed. by N. Pevsner, 46 vols, 1951 onwards, Penguin Books, Harmondsworth; revised editions in progress

Butterworth's Police Law, Butterworth, London, 2nd ed., 1988

Children's Books of the Year, published annually by Book Trust, London

Children's Fiction Index, published by Association of Assistant Librarians, London, 6th ed., 1989

Children's Fiction Sourcebook, compiled by J. Madden, M. Hobson and R. Prytherch, Gower, Aldershot, 1992

Children's Games in Street and Playground, by Iona and Peter Opie, Oxford University Press, Oxford, 1969; paperback ed., 1984

Chronology of the Ancient World, BC-799 AD, by H.E.L. Mellersh, Barrie & Jenkins, London, 1976

Chronology of the Medieval World, 800–1491, by R.L. Storey, Barrie & Rockcliff, London, 1973

Chronology of the Expanding World, 1492–1762, by N. Williams, Barrie & Rockcliff, London, 1969

Chronology of the Modern World, 1763–1965, by N. Williams, Barrie & Rockcliff, London, 1966; paperback, Penguin Books, Harmondsworth, 1975

Civilization and Capitalism 1400–1800, by F. Braudel, 3 vols, Collins, London, 1981–85

The Classic Fairy Tales, by Iona and Peter Opie, Oxford University Press, Oxford, 1974; paperback, Granada, 1980

The Climates of the Continents, by W.G. Kendrew, Clarendon Press, Oxford, 5th ed., 1961

The Common People 1746–1938, by G.D.H. Cole and R. Postgate, Methuen, London, 1938; reprinted 1965

The Common People: A History from the Norman Conquest to the Present, by J.F.C. Harrison, Fontana, London, 1984

The Concise Oxford Dictionary of English Place-Names, compiled by E. Ekwall, Oxford University Press, Oxford, 4th ed., 1960; reprinted 1974

The Concise Times Atlas of World History, ed. G. Barraclough, Times Books, London, rev. ed., 1986

Costume: A General Bibliography, by P. Anthony and J. Arnold, published by The Costume Society, London, 1974

Currency Conversion Tables: A Hundred Years of Change, by R.L. Bidwell, Rex Collings, London, 1970

Customs in Common, by E.P. Thompson, Merlin, London, 1991

Debrett's Correct Form, rev. ed., Debrett's Peerage/Futura, 1976

The Dialects of England, by Peter Trudgill, Blackwell, Oxford, 1990

Dictionary of Characters in British Novels, by John Greenfield, 2 vols, Facts on File, Oxford, 1991

Dictionary of English Costume 900–1900, by C.W. and P.E. Cunnington and Charles Beard, A & C Black, London, 1960; reprinted 1976

Dictionary of Fictional Characters, by William Freeman, Everyman Reference series, Dent, London, 3rd ed. revised, 1973

A Dictionary of First Names, by P. Hanks and F. Hodges, Oxford University Press, Oxford, 1990

The Dictionary of Historic Nicknames, compiled by Carl Sifakis, Facts on File, Oxford, 1984; paperback, 1986

Dictionary of Literary Pseudonyms, compiled by Frank Atkinson, 4th ed., Library Association, London, 1987

Dictionary of Real People and Places in Fiction, compiled by M.C. Rintoul, Routledge, London, 1991

A Dictionary of Surnames, complied by P. Hanks and F. Hodges, Oxford University Press, Oxford, 1988

Dictionary of the Underworld: British and American, compiled by Eric Partridge, Routledge, London, 3rd ed. revised, 1968

Dinner is Served, by G. Brett, Hart-Davis, London, 1968

Directory of British Associations & Associations in Ireland, published by CBD Research, Beckenham, 10th ed., 1990

Edwardian Shopping: A Selection from the Army & Navy Stores Catalogue 1898–1913, compiled by R.H. Langbridge, David & Charles, Newton Abbot, 1975

Encyclopedia of Bible Life, by Madeleine S. and J. Lane Miller, A & C Black, London, rev. ed., 1979

English Dialect Dictionary, compiled by J. Wright, 6 vols, Frowde, London, 1896–1905; new ed., Oxford University Press, Oxford, 1981

English Family Life 1576–1716: An Anthology of Diaries, ed. R. Houlbrooke, Blackwell, Oxford, 1989

English Historical Documents, ed. D.C. Douglas, 12 vols, in progress, Eyre Methuen, London

English People in the Eighteenth Century, by Dorothy Marshall, Longman, London, 1956

English Place-Name Society, volumes by county, in progress since 1923, published by the Society, c/o University of Nottingham

English Social History, by G.M. Trevelyan, Longman, London, new ed., 1978; paperback, Penguin Books, 1986

The Englishman's Food: A History of Five Centuries of English

Diet, by J.C. Drummond and A. Wilbraham, Cape, London, 1958; reprint, Pimlico, London, 1991

Evolution of Fashion: Pattern and Cut from 1066 to 1930, by M. Hamilton Hill and P. Bucknell, Batsford, London, 1967; reprinted 1987

The Fairies in Tradition and Literature, by K.M. Briggs, Routledge, London, 1977; reprinted, Bellew, London, 1989

Famous Frosts and Frost Fairs in Great Britain, by W. Andrews, Redway, London, 1887

Fashions in Hair: The First 5000 Years, by R. Corson, Peter Owen, London, 1965

Fashions of a Decade series, in progress, published by Batsford, London, 1991–

Fiction Index, published annually by the Association of Assistant Librarians, London, since 1970; cumulated vols 1945–60 and 1960–69, now every 5 years

Food in History, by Reay Tannahill, Eyre Methuen, London, 1973

Forensic Medicine, by Keith Simpson, E. Arnold, London, 9th ed., 1985

Gentleman's Magazine, 1731–1922; there are several general index volumes and a 2-volume index to biographical and obituary notices 1731–1819 (see page 58).

Georgian Delights, by J.H. Plumb, Weidenfeld & Nicolson, London, 1980

Gestures: Their Origins and Distribution, by Desmond Morris, Cape, London, 1979; paperback, Triad, 1981

Great Britain Road Atlas, Automobile Association, Basingstoke, revised regularly

Guide to the Best Historical Novels and Tales, by J. Nield, Matthews, London, 5th ed., 1929 (out of print)

Guide to Country Houses series, published by Burkes' Peerage/ Savill, London, in progress (3 vols to date)

The Guinness Book of Weather Facts and Feats, by Ingrid Holford, Guinness Superlatives, Enfield, 1977

Handbook of Dates for Students of English History, ed. C.R. Cheney, Royal Historical Society, London, 1978; reprinted 1982

Handbook of English Costume series, by C.W. and P.E. Cunnington, Faber, London, 1952–73; progressively revised

Handbook of Medieval Exchange, by Peter Spufford, Royal Historical Society, London, 1986

Handbook of Pseudonyms and Personal Nicknames, compiled by Harold S. Sharp, Scarecrow, Metuchen, N.J., 2 vols, 1972; supplements 1975, 1982

The Heirs of Tom Brown, by Isabel Quigly, Chatto & Windus,

London, 1982; paperback, Oxford University Press, Oxford, 1984

Historic Houses, Castles and Gardens in Great Britain and Ireland, published annually by British Leisure Publications, East Grinstead

A History of the Cost of Living, by John Burnett, Penguin Books, Harmondsworth, 1969

A History of Gold and Money 1450–1920, by Pierre Vilar, Verso, USA, 1991 (distributed in UK by Marston Book Services, Oxford)

History of Inland Transport and Communication, by E.A. Pratt, 1912; reprinted, David & Charles, Newton Abbot, 1970

The History of the King's Works, ed. H.M. Colvin, HMSO, London, in progress, 1963–

A History of Private Life, ed. P. Ariès and G. Duby, 5 vols, translated from French, Belknap, Harvard University Press, Cambridge, Mass. and London, 1987–91

Hollis Press & Public Relations Annual, published by Hollis Directories, Sunbury-on-Thames, Middx

How Much is that Worth?, by Leslie Munby, Phillimore, Chichester, 1989

How We Lived Then: A History of Everyday Life during the Second World War, by Norman Longmate, Hutchinson, London, 1971; paperback, Arrow, London, 1977

How We Used to Live: Victorians Early and Late, by David Evans, A & C Black, London, 1990

Human Documents series, by R.E. Pike, Allen & Unwin, London; periodically revised (some vols out of print)

Index to Characters in Children's Literature, compiled and published by Arthur D. Mortimore, Bristol, 1977

The Language of Clothes, by Alison Lurie, Heinemann, London, 1981; paperback, Hamlyn, London, 1983

The Language of World War II, compiled by A.M. Taylor, H.W. Wilson, New York, 1948

Life in the English Country House, by Mark Girouard, Yale University Press, New York and London, 1978; paperback, Penguin Books, Harmondsworth, 1980

Life in Georgian England, by E.N. Williams, Batsford, London, 1962

London Weather, by J.H. Brazell, HMSO, London, 1968

The Long Week-End: A Social History of Great Britain 1918–1939, by Robert Graves and Alan Hodge, Hutchinson, London, 1985

The Lore and Language of Schoolchildren, by Peter Opie,

Clarendon Press, Oxford, 1959; paperback, Paladin, London, 1977

The Making of the English Working Class, by E.P. Thompson, Gollancz, London, 1980

Manwatching: A Field Guide to Human Behaviour, by Desmond Morris, Cape, London, 1977; paperback, Triad/Panther, London, 1978

Mr Punch's History of Modern England, by C.L. Graves, 4 vols, Cassell, London, 1921–22

The Model Wife, by Rona Randall, Herbert Press, London, 1989

Modes in Hats and Headdress, by R. Turner Wilcox, Scribner's, New York, rev. ed., 1959

Moriarty's Police Law, Butterworth, London, 24th ed., 1981

Movable Feasts: Changes in English Eating-Habits, by Arnold Palmer, Oxford University Press, Oxford, 1984

Natural Phenomena and Chronology of the Seasons, by E.J. Lowe, Part I only, London, 1870

Newnes Historical Atlas (originally the *Hamlyn Historical Atlas*), rev. ed., Newnes, London, 1983

Newspeak: A Dictionary of Jargon, by Jonathan Green, Routledge, London, 1984; paperback, 1985

Ordnance Survey: first edition reprinted by David & Charles, Newton Abbot; modern editions, HMSO/Ordnance Survey, London and Southampton

Oxford Companion to Children's Literature, by H. Carpenter and M. Prichard, Oxford University Press, Oxford, 1984

Oxford Dictionary of Nursery Rhymes, ed. Iona and Peter Opie, Oxford University Press, Oxford, 1951

Oxford English Dictionary (*OED*), 2nd ed., 20 vols, 1989; compact edition (original edition) with supplement, 3 vols, with reading glass, 1987; also the *Shorter OED*, reset 3rd ed., 2 vols, 1973

Pan Book of Dates, compiled by Gerald Masters, Pan, London, 1990

Partridge's Dictionary of Catch Phrases, ed. P. Beale, Routledge, London, 2nd ed., 1986; paperback, 1990

Penguin Atlas of Ancient History, by C. McEvedy, Penguin Books, Harmondsworth, 1970

Penguin Atlas of Medieval History, by C. McEvedy, Penguin Books, Harmondsworth, 1979

Penguin Atlas of Recent History: Europe since 1815, Penguin Books, Harmondsworth, 1982

Penguin Atlas of World History, translated from German by H. Kinder and W. Hilgemann, Penguin Books, Harmondsworth,

1974; reprinted 1984

Penguin Dictionary of Proper Names, by G. Payton and revised by J. Paxton, Penguin Books, Harmondsworth, London, 1991

Penguin Dictionary of Surnames, by Basil Cottle, Penguin Books, Harmondsworth, 2nd ed., 1978

Penguin (formerly *Pelican*) *Social History of Britain*, Penguin Books, Harmondsworth, in progress, 1982–

Play Index, published by H.W. Wilson, New York, since 1949, 7 vols to date covering 1949–87

Plenty and Want: A Social History of Diet in England from 1815 to the Present Day, by John Burnett, 3rd ed., Routledge, 1989

The Polite World: A Guide to English Manners and Deportment from the 13th to the 19th Century, rev. ed. by J. Wildeblood and P. Brinson, Oxford University Press, Oxford, 1974

Portrait of a Decade series, published by Batsford, London, 9 vols, covering 1900 to the 1980s

The Pound in Your Pocket 1870–1970, by Peter Wilsher, Cassell, London, 1970

Prices and Wages in England from the 12th to the 19th Century, by Lord Beveridge and others, Frank Cass, London, 1965

'Protection of Titles', Society of Authors *Quick Guide*, free to members or £1.50 post free from the Publications Department of the Society, 84 Drayton Gardens, London SW10 9SD

Pseudonyms and Nicknames Dictionary, ed. Jennifer Mossman, Gale Research, Detroit, 2nd ed., 1982

A Punch History of Manners 1841–1940, by A. Adburgham, Hutchinson, London, 1961

Recent Historical Novels, ed. Irene Collins, Historical Association, London, 1990

Records of Seasons and Prices of Agricultural Produce & Phenomena observed in the British Isles, by T.H. Baker, Simpkin Marshall, London, 1883

Routledge Dictionary of Historical Slang, Routledge, London, 1973

Sea Slang of the 20th Century, by W. Granville, Winchester Publications, 1949

The Shell Book of Firsts, ed. Patrick Robertson, Michael Joseph, 2nd rev. ed., 1984

Shops and Shopping, by A. Adburgham, Allen & Unwin, London, 2nd ed., 1981

Short Story Index, published annually with 5-year cumulations by H.W. Wilson, New York; 9 permanent retrospective volumes covering 1900–88, also single-volume *Collections Indexed 1900–1978*

Slang Thesaurus, by Jonathan Green, Penguin Books, Harmondsworth, 1988

Slang Today and Yesterday, by Eric Partridge, 4th ed., Routledge, London, 1970

A Social History of England, by Asa Briggs, Weidenfeld & Nicolson, London, 1983; paperback, Penguin Books, Harmondsworth, 1987

Stately Homes, Museums, Castles and Gardens in Britain, published annually by Automobile Association, Basingstoke

Survey of English Dialects, by H. Orton and E. Dieth, introductory vol. and 4 regional vols, E.J. Arnold, Leeds, 1962–70

Survey of London, 41 vols to date, originally published by LCC, now by Athlone Press, London, 1900–

The Thesaurus of Slang, compiled by E. and A. Lewin, Facts on File, Oxford, 1988

They Saw It Happen series, published by Blackwell, Oxford; 4 vols covering 55 BC-1940 (out of print)

Titles and Forms of Address: A Guide to Correct Use, 19th ed., A & C Black, London, 1989; new ed. in preparation

Trade Associations and Professional Bodies of the United Kingdom, by P. Millard, 8th ed., Pergamon, Oxford, 1987

Useful Toil: Autobiographies of Working People from the 1820s to the 1970s, by John Burnett, Penguin Books, Harmondsworth, 1984

What It Cost the Day Before Yesterday Book, by H. Priestley, Kenneth Mason, Emsworth, 1979

Whitaker's Almanack, published annually by Whitaker, London

Willing's Press Guide, published annually by Reed Information Services Ltd, East Grinstead, 2 vols

Women's Diaries, Journals and Letters: An Annotated Bibliography, compiled by Cheryl Cline, Garland, New York and London, 1989

Women's Headdress and Hairstyles in England from AD 600 to Present Day, by G. de Courtais, Batsford, London, rev. ed., 1986

World Cruising Handbook, by Jimmy Cornell, A & C Black, London, 1991

World Historical Fiction Guide, compiled by D.D. McGarry and S. Harriman White, Scarecrow, Metuchen, NJ, 2nd ed., 1973

The World of the Forsytes, by John Fisher, Secker & Warburg, London, 1976

Yesterday's Shopping, reprinted catalogue of the Army & Navy Stores 1907, David & Charles, Newton Abbot, 1969

6

Biography

Biographical writing may consist of a short article on a celebrity, past or present, to be published perhaps in commemoration of a centenary or an eightieth birthday, or it may be a full-length study. It sometimes happens that a book grows out of the research undertaken for a newspaper or magazine article. Occasionally biographies are written of people who during their lifetime were not especially renowned or eminent, but whose papers (usually diaries or letters) make a unique contribution to the social history of their time.

There is a growing trend for biographies to be written while their subjects are still alive, or very soon after their death; this may have something to do with the fear of the modern biographer that once the biographee and his contemporaries have gone, there may be little material to work on, seeing that letter-writing is a dying art and telephoning an increasing convenience. The academic view of such work, however, is that it constitutes a 'study' or 'profile' of the person concerned rather than a true biography, and that while the study or profile as such may be of inestimable value to a future biographer, it is essential for a certain amount of time to have elapsed before any life can be properly evaluated and seen in perspective to its time.

The author who embarks on a biographical project normally has some good reason for wanting to write it – kinship to the subject, or an intimate working relationship with him or her, and/or the possession of – and access to – original papers. Or, if a number of 'lives' have already been published on the person concerned, the writer may simply have a burning desire to write from a fresh angle, to 'set the record straight' or to throw new light on some controversial aspects as a result of recent research. It is generally accepted that the famous characters of history will stand new biographies every ten years.

Whatever the motive, it is advisable to try to get the work commissioned and – especially where a full-length book is envisaged – to secure a cash advance, for there will be a considerable amount of research to be undertaken and expenses to be met. In calculating the likely total costs, you should not forget to take into account your own working time. Out-of-pocket expenditure will include travel, meals away from home, postal and telephone charges, photocopying, photographs and stationery, at the very least; there may well be 'extras' such as library search fees, fees payable to a genealogist or research assistant, the cost of professional typing and indexing, reproduction fees for illustrations, and so on.

Before a publisher signs a contract, or parts with any money to a writer who is unknown to him, he will normally ask to see a synopsis, or maybe even a chapter or two, of the proposed work. The research that has to be done for the purposes of writing this synopsis is roughly the same as what would be needed for a short biographical article: both must include the salient points of the life and mention the existence of any hitherto unpublished material and/or recent research that provide a new angle. It must be done in sufficient depth so as to convince the potential publisher that the book will be a good investment.

The writer who has reached this stage is bound to be familiar with the outline life of his subject. However, it may not be out of place to record here, as an *aide-mémoire*, the main sources open to biographers and to researchers seeking biographical information for use in other work.

The importance of researching 'in the round' has been stressed earlier in this handbook. In biographical research this is particularly important. It is essential to uncover the whole person, 'warts and all', so that at the research stage nothing should be avoided or glossed over or left unexplored. Motives for a person's actions may be discussed in the final work, and whether the biographer writes from a more or a less sympathetic angle is a matter of interpretation rather than one of research: this is a decision each individual writer must make once he has satisfied himself as to the true facts.

Private Papers

One good reason for allowing a certain amount of time to elapse before writing a biography is that there may not be access to private papers for a given number of years after a person's death; although the writer may have possession of his subject's own papers and the blessing of the family concerned to make use of them, it is very probable that some of the material required will be contained in the papers of others and that this may be subject to restrictions. Papers deposited in record offices and other archives are normally subject to the thirty-year closure rule or, exceptionally, to an even longer period; in many cases permission will be needed from the family or the estate before the documents may be seen. Although the copyright of correspondence belongs to the writer, the actual letters belong to the recipient or to his heirs or executors, from whom permission must be obtained for access; in practice, unless there is some good reason to the contrary, this is usually forthcoming – but it may be stipulated that the text of the biography must be submitted before going to press. It is important always to make due acknowledgment to the source of such material and to comply with any request for prior submission of the text.

It is true that modern biographies *are* often written without the permission of the subject's family and thus without access to the private papers, but a writer who decides to embark on such a work should be fully aware beforehand of the difficulties that can arise. Quite apart from missing out on material and close family recollections and anecdotes, it may be less easy to obtain other people's help (there is no doubt that when seeking interviews or writing for information, magic phrases such as 'the official biography', 'sanctioned by the family', and so on, *do* carry weight and often swing the balance in the biographer's favour where someone is hesitant about supplying information). More serious can be the reaction of relatives to an 'unofficial' biography, with the possibility that if they are seriously displeased they may seek an injunction through the courts.

The location of unpublished source material in general has been discussed in an earlier chapter (see pages 49–55). For the biographer needing to find out whether any private papers exist and, if so, their whereabouts, the first point of call must be the National Register of Archives, maintained by the Royal Commission on Historical Manuscripts at Quality House, Quality Court, Chancery Lane, London WC2A 1HP; enquiries should be made in person or in writing, not by telephone. By using the highly efficient catalogue and cross-referenced indexing system, now partly computerised, the researcher will be able to find out the precise location of correspondence and other papers on his subject.

The Department of Manuscripts in the British Library Reference Division and the Public Record Office are both major sources, while the National Maritime Museum at Greenwich has a comparatively recent manuscript collection of interest to the naval biographer. Many universities have important holdings. The Churchill Archives Centre at Churchill College, Cambridge is collecting papers of 20th-century politicians, scientists and both military and naval commanders. The *Guide to the Papers of British Cabinet Ministers 1900–1951*, published by the Royal Historical

Society, is a valuable reference tool for the modern biographical researcher. Use should also be made of the 'General Index to Collections' at the back of *British Archives: A Guide to Archive Resources in the United Kingdom.*

The papers of lesser-known persons are more difficult to track down. If you are not in touch with the family or cannot trace any relatives, and the local record office has no deposited papers, you may be able to trace executors or other persons likely to be in possession of a deceased person's papers through a will at Somerset House (see chapter 7, 'Family and Local History'). If you are writing a biography of someone who lived in the last fifty years, even if you do have access to family and private papers, an advertisement in the national or local press is to be recommended: many unexpected and valuable 'fish' are netted in this way, in the shape of replies from friends, teachers, colleagues, employees and others who have known or met the subject at some period of his life, and may well produce fascinating and very usable factual or anecdotal material of which you would otherwise remain unaware.

It is important to remember that the papers of even the most eminent public personages contain a certain amount of correspondence from people in lesser walks of life, and if you have reason to believe that the subject of your biography had dealings with someone whose papers have been catalogued and/or deposited, do not overlook this source. When researching for biographical information on professional people, it is always worth contacting the librarian or archivist of the relevant society or institution; some of these bodies hold collections of important private papers and most have biographical information that you may not find easily elsewhere, going back to the date of their foundation.

'Private papers' in this context are not limited to correspondence, but may consist of almost any kind of documentary material, such as account books, scrapbooks and photograph albums, visitors' books, personal diaries, and so on.

Printed and Other Sources

Biographical dictionaries

The major source of biographical information on nationals of this country is the *Dictionary of National Biography*, known to scholars, librarians and researchers as 'the *DNB*'. In the current edition there are twenty-two volumes containing entries in alphabetical sequence for the period up to 1900, and for the 20th century one volume per decade, the latest available being that for 1971–80, plus a five-year supplement spanning 1981–85. Few private individuals can afford either the shelf space or the cost of the complete set, and the two-volume micrographically reduced compact edition, marketed a few years ago, is no longer obtainable. However, there is a three-volume *Concise* edition in preparation which will combine in one alphabetical sequence entries from the earlier two-volume *Concise* edition and the new material to 1985. This new *Concise DNB* is one reference tool that should have a place on every writer's bookshelf: it contains entries for every person in the main *DNB*, with finding references to the page numbers and volume in which the main article is located. A *Chronological and Occupational Index to the DNB* was published a few years ago, and due in 1993 is a supplement containing entries for those persons 'omitted' from the main *DNB* from the beginning to 1985.

An important and ongoing modern reference tool is *The British Biographical Archive (BBA)*, which has a wide regional and occupational coverage; it is marketed on microfiche with printed index volumes. There are already equivalents to the *BBA* for America, Australia and several European countries; more are bound to follow.

Among the reliable standard works usually found in most reference libraries, and handy for quick reference, are *Chambers' Biographical Dictionary*, A. M. Hyamson's *Dictionary of Universal Biography* (now brought up to date and re-written), P. Boase's six-volume *Modern English Biography* (especially strong on people who died in the years 1851–1900), and *Webster's Biographical Dictionary*. Haydn's *Universal Index of Biography*, long out of print but often found in secondhand bookshops at a very reasonable price, is a useful source for dates of persons omitted from the modern dictionaries. Many foreign countries publish their own equivalents of the *DNB*; these are listed under 'Biography' in the *Guide to Reference Material*, vol. 2, under each country.

The *Biography Index*, published by H. W. Wilson of New York, claims to be international, but has a definite American bias. More useful is the *Biography and Genealogy Master Index*, produced by Gale Research of Detroit, USA, which, in its microfiche cumulative version, is currently available at copyright and major libraries in the United Kingdom. Information is extracted from over six hundred English language biographical dictionaries, and the 'Bio-Base' (as the microfiche is known) is regularly updated. Birth and death dates are stated, together with the source in abbreviated form, and references to sources can be verified in the accompanying booklet.

In Germany a massive international research tool, the *Index Bio-Bibliographicus Notorum Hominum*, is nearing completion, which will contain both a bibliography and an index to about two thousand bibliographical works from all countries and in all languages.

Encyclopedias are another source of brief lives; some of the articles are followed by a select bibliography which will lead the researcher on to further source-material. The *McGraw Hill Encyclopedia of World Biography* is excellent. On a national level there is the *Who's Who in British History* series, which covers the British Isles from Roman to Victorian times. Among other useful works are the three volumes *Lives of the Tudor Age, Lives of the Stuart Age* and *Lives of the Georgian Age*, each containing approximately three hundred lives of a particular period, ranging from a few hundred words to a few thousand per entry; they also include short bibliographies and an indication of the location of major portraits. Feminists may like to know of the *Europa Biographical Dictionary of British Women*, which contains one thousand entries from Boadicea to the present day; whereas the *Macmillan Dictionary of Women's Biography* and *The World Who's Who of Women* include women of outstanding achievement and influence from all parts of the world.

There are any number of biographical dictionaries relating to the various professions, and the researcher should always ask at the library desk for them. Titles include H. M. Colvin's *Biographical Dictionary of British Architects; The New Grove Dictionary of Music and Musicians*; and the two standard works of international biographical reference in the art world, the ten-volume Benézit, *Dictionnaire des peintres, sculpteurs, dessinateurs et graveurs* and the thirty-seven volume Thieme and Becker, *Allgemeines Lexikon der bildenden Künstler*. For theatrical lives, a major project is under way in the United States: a *Biographical Dictionary of Actors, Actresses, Musicians, Dancers, Managers and Other Stage Personnel in London 1660–1800*; so far, some twelve volumes (A-R) have been published. *Munk's Roll* (lives of Fellows of the Royal College of Physicians) contains biographical information on apothecaries and doctors from the 16th century to the present day.

The *Oxford Companion* series is another useful source of biographical information. Volumes include *American History, Art, Canadian Literature, Children's Literature, Classical Literature*, the *Decorative Arts, English Literature, Film, French Literature, German Literature, Law, Music, Ships and the Sea, Spanish Literature* and the *Theatre*.

The best quick reference for contemporary biography is *Who's Who*. There are also eight *Who Was Who* volumes containing entries for those who died during the years 1897–1990, and a

Cumulated Index volume (1897–1990). *Debrett's Distinguished People of Today* and *People of Today* include entries for a number of people who have not qualified for inclusion in *Who's Who*. Another useful source is the *Longman Dictionary of 20th Century Biography*. Some professions and religious groups have their own biographical volumes, for example *Crockford's Clerical Directory*, the *Jewish Year Book*, the *Medical Register*, the *Writers' Directory* and a whole series of *Who's Who* volumes in various fields (*Art, Journalism, Music*, the *Theatre, Government, Finance and Industry, Yachting* and many more), some of which are annual and others published at irregular intervals. There are also *Who's Who* volumes for many foreign countries.

Among the more international reference works of contemporary biography are the *International Who's Who* and the *Dictionary of International Biography*, both of which include entries on a world-wide basis. Other useful sources are the *International Authors' and Writers' Who's Who*, the *International Year Book and Statesman's Who's Who* and *Who's Who in International Affairs*. Foreign biographical sources are listed under selected individual countries (see pages 145–57).

Bibliographies

The best way to find out what has already been published about a person is to consult the British Library *Bibliography of Biography* and the Bowker *International Bibliography of Biography*, both from 1970. You should also look in the general catalogue of one of the major libraries, using whatever 'Recent Acquisitions' or computer-updated listing is available, and also – remembering that new books take some time to reach the library shelf and catalogue – checking recent issues of the *BNB*. In the case of a prominent figure of history or literature, there may already be a published bibliography, and this can be traced in the *World Bibliography of Bibliographies*, usually to be found on the reference shelves of major libraries, and comprehensive up to 1974. Again, this should be supplemented by a search in the general catalogue and/or *BNB* for works published since that date.

Up-to-date bibliographies will be found in the most recently published studies of the subject, and it is a good investment to buy rather than borrow such a book, so that you can keep it at your elbow and make notes and underlinings in it of special sources; alternatively, make a photocopy of the bibliography section. Such bibliographies make an excellent starting point for research; with luck, they will include references to newspaper and periodical articles. Where this is not so, a search should be made in the *British Humanities Index* and the earlier subject indexes to periodicals (see pages 45–6).

Obituaries

Obituaries are an excellent source and often the starting point for biographical research, since the more recent notices usually provide both an outline of a person's life and an evaluation of his career.

To find notices of people who died earlier than the mid-19th century, the six-volume *Musgrave's Obituary* is the first place to look; you should also use the *Indexes to the Biographical and Obituary Notices* in the *Gentleman's Magazine* (the two volumes cover the years 1731–1819) and, if you know the approximate year of death, the *Annual Register*. For obituaries of prominent persons who have died since the early 1800s, *The Times* is the best source; in recent years as many as six hundred obituary notices have been printed annually in that paper. Provided you have an approximate date of death, a search in the *Times Index* should not take long, while for recent obituary notices there are now three published volumes, *Obituaries from The Times*, for the years 1951–60, 1961–70 and 1971–75. A more recent compilation, *Annual Obituary*, covers the years from 1980, one volume per year.

Not everyone you may expect to find in *The Times* has achieved an obituary there (much depends on how many other eminent people died the same day), and so the *Daily Telegraph*, the *Guardian* and the relevant local newspapers should be checked. The local paper of the area in which a person was resident often prints a notice that did not 'make' the nationals or one that goes into greater detail. Professional and trade journals, where appropriate, are especially useful for the evaluation of a person's career.

International notices, but with an American bias, are best checked in the *New York Times Obituaries Index*, from 1858, or in the *New York Times Personal Name Index*, from 1851. For notices relating to persons of other countries, look also at the relevant national paper.

Diaries, letters and memoirs

A great deal of information will be obtained about a person from the published diaries, letters or memoirs of his friends and contemporaries. As research progresses, therefore, it is an excellent plan to keep an ongoing list of all names that crop up and systematically to check these out at the library. Use the indexes to these books to locate the relevant passages. If you think there may be unpublished journals or correspondence, consult the National Register of Archives, as explained earlier in this chapter under the heading 'Private Papers'.

School and university records

School and university records provide excellent source-material, not only for details of a person's scholastic and academic achievement, but also for information concerning his extra-curricular activities (sports, drama, public-speaking, etc.) and – especially important – the names of his contemporaries and friends, schoolmasters and tutors. Should any of these people still be alive, they may have useful contributions to make and can usually be traced through the school or university, or – if they themselves have achieved eminence – in the current *Who's Who*.

The Institute of Historical Research pamphlet *Registers of the Universities, Colleges and Schools of Great Britain and Ireland* lists the printed registers that existed at the date of publication (1966); others may be looked up in library catalogues. Where no register exists, the school secretary or secretary of the relevant 'Old Boys' or 'Old Girls' association will often be of great assistance. Research of this kind may involve you in a visit to the educational establishment concerned. Addresses, with names of current headmasters and headmistresses, will be found in the *Independent Schools Yearbook* (one volume for boys' schools, co-educational schools and preparatory schools, and one for girls' schools), or may be obtained from the local education authority. Universities and colleges are listed in the *World of Learning*. The registers of Oxford and Cambridge, *Alumni Oxonienses* and *Alumni Cantabrigienses*, and A. B. Emden's *Biographical Registers* of both these universities to 1500 are of special value to the historian, while the *Historical Registers* series for Oxford and Cambridge brings the records up to the present day.

Service records

You should encounter no great problem in obtaining details of a person's Service career. All records more than one hundred years old are at the Public Record Office, where there are also complete runs of the *Army, Navy* and *Air Force Lists*; current volumes of these are usually available in all reference libraries.

Regimental histories are another good source and may be traced in the Society for Army Historical Research's *Bibliography of*

Regimental Histories. J.M. Brereton's *Guide to the Regiments and Corps of the British Army* includes, along with other information, addresses of regimental headquarters to whom to write for further details; the same author's more recent publication, *The British Soldier: A Social History*, is essential reading for writers needing to know about Army life from the mid-17th century onwards. Another highly recommended book is G. Hamilton-Edwards' *In Search of Army Ancestry*. The Public Record Office leaflet no. 9, 'British Military Records as Sources for Biography and Genealogy', is obtainable on request from the PRO, Ruskin Avenue, Kew, Richmond, Surrey TW9 4DU.

So far as naval records are concerned, ask at the Public Record Office for handbook no. H22, 'Naval Records for Genealogists'. The National Maritime Museum has published a useful list, *The Commissioned Sea Officers of the Royal Navy 1660–1815*; another informative source-book is the *Dictionary of British Ships and Seamen*.

The first port of call for research into Air Force records should be the Royal Air Force Museum (Department of Aviation Records, Grahame Park Way, Hendon, London NW9 5LL; tel. 081–205 2266, extension 210/211/250).

The whereabouts of the records of all three Services can be ascertained from R. Higham's admirable *Guide to the Sources of British Military History*.

Business records

Details of a person's business career can often be obtained from the organization or company by whom he was employed. Naturally there are sometimes restrictions on the amount of information that will be divulged to an outsider, but in special circumstances the researcher may be allowed access to the relevant files.

There may be a company history, either published or printed for private circulation, which will provide extremely useful background material. You can check this in the *International Directory of Company Histories*. Annual returns and other statutory documents, including lists of all directors and company secretaries, of public, private limited and guarantee companies may be inspected (on microfiche) at Companies House (Department of Trade and Industry), 55 City Road, London EC1Y 1BB (tel. 071–253 9393) or at the Companies Registration Office, Crown Way, Maindy, Cardiff CF4 3UZ (tel. 0222 388588); a modest search fee is payable per file, and there are full photocopying facilities. The Business Archives Council, Denmark House, 185 Tower Bridge Road,

London SE1 2UF (tel. 071–407 6110) maintains a library and will advise researchers about records available; its Scottish counterpart, the Business Archives Council of Scotland, is at Glasgow University Archives and Business Records Centre, 13 Thurso Street, Glasgow G11 6PE (tel. 041–339 8855, extension 6494). Researchers should also make use of the British Library Business Information Service, which is currently at 25 Southampton Buildings, London WC2A 1AW (tel. 071–323 7457), but will move to St Pancras in 1993 (see pages 67–8).

Members of Parliament and government officials

Dod's Parliamentary Companion, first published in 1832, is the indispensable British biographical source-book for the modern period. Earlier information will be found in the Institute of Historical Research series (nine volumes published to date), *Office Holders in Modern Britain*. There is one volume per ministry, some of the lists beginning in 1660 and covering the entire period up to 1870; the latest volume in the series lists officials of Royal Commissions of Inquiry 1815–70. Another good source is the four-volume *Members of Parliament*, in which you will find the names of all MPs in England from 1213 and in Scotland and Ireland from 1357 and 1559 respectively; the lists continue up to 1874, for the United Kingdom, and there is an index volume. For further information, or if you fail to find what you are seeking in printed sources, write to the Clerk of the Records at the House of Lords Record Office, House of Lords, London SW1A 0PW. For the location of private papers of Members of Parliament and selected public servants, consult *Sources in British Political History 1900–1951*.

Bidwell's Guide to Government Ministers 1900–1972 is international in coverage.

Public speeches and broadcasts

Speeches of any significance are usually reported in the national press and may be traced in the *Times Index* either under the speaker's name or under the name of the society or conference addressed. The texts of Members' speeches in Parliament are printed in *Hansard: Parliamentary Debates* (separate series for the House of Commons and the House of Lords). Lectures or papers read before learned or professional bodies will normally be found in the transactions or proceedings of such institutions at a later date.

To check on broadcast or televised speeches and interviews, your best plan is first to contact the National Sound Archive, 29

Exhibition Road, London SW7 2AS (tel. 071–589 6603); an appointment will be made for you to listen to or view the relevant transmission, provided it is in their collections. (Note that the NSA includes a collection of Parliamentary sound recordings.) Once you have ascertained the date, it may be possible to obtain a transcript from the BBC Written Archives Centre at Caversham Park, Reading RG4 8TZ (tel. 0734 472742) or the independent radio or television company. (The availability of transcripts is subject to certain copyright restrictions.)

Travel

Obtaining information about a person's travel may be unexpectedly complicated, where no diary or travelogue was kept. Hotel registers and shipping company records are not always retained for more than a few years, although it is always worth asking. (For example, the P. & O. Group's archives were deposited at the National Maritime Museum in Greenwich in the autumn of 1977.)

British Transport historical records are now at the Public Record Office in Kew, and so are the records of the former Board of Trade (now the Department of Trade and Industry) from *c.* 1890; the latter contain lists of all arrivals in, and departures from, the United Kingdom, but only a sample (roughly one-tenth) of passengers' lists and ships' logs, so that it is very much a matter of luck whether the information you seek will be obtainable. For more recent information you should write to the Registrar-General of Shipping and Seamen, Llantrisant Road, Llandaff, Cardiff CF5 2YS. Factual details such as dates of departure, ports of call, tonnage, and which company owns a particular vessel may be quite easily verified in *Lloyd's Shipping Index* or *Lloyd's Voyage Record*.

Further Research

Having cast your net, and hauled in your initial catch of material, your next task as biographer will be to sort the documentation into periods, or other natural chapters, of the life and, as you proceed, to make a note of any supplementary research to be undertaken. For a short biographical feature or the synopsis of a book, you can fairly safely rely on the standard or most recent work, plus your own special knowledge; but if you are embarking on a full-length biography you must go through and evaluate for yourself all the published material. It is a good idea to make index cards or slips for each book or article read, and to keep these in alphabetical sequence; this will take only a few minutes at the time and will be of immense value both for quick reference as you write and at the end of the day, when it comes to compiling the bibliography (see chapter 10, 'Preparation for the Press', pages 159–60).

Some professional help may be required for your chapter on family ancestry (see chapter 8, 'Specialist Research', pages 136–40) and if so, this should be arranged at the earliest possible moment, as good genealogists are frequently booked up for several months ahead. At the same time the question of employing outside researchers should also be carefully considered: where the source material is located at some distance from your home, or if it is essential to go through several years of a particular paper that is available only at the British Newspaper Library at Colindale, for instance, it may pay you to off-load part of the routine research and leave yourself free to tackle the more complicated aspects of the work.

Inevitably some travelling will be involved, and it makes sense to plan this so that several sources and/or interviews can be combined on each trip. A visit to the family home, if it still exists, is essential, and on such a visit time must be allowed for conversations with local inhabitants and – particularly important – with anyone close to the family who is still alive, such as a gardener, nanny or cook, where appropriate, or perhaps the vicar or local schoolmaster or publican. It goes without saying that this applies only when you are researching for biographies of people who are either still alive or recently deceased; in the case of subjects who were born earlier than the turn of the century, you have no choice but to rely on documentary sources such as the local newspaper or church magazine, or the records of any local societies with which the family is known to have been connected. The local librarian or secretary of the local historical society will usually be helpful in this respect, and you could strike lucky in that the descendants of an old family retainer may have cherished stories handed down verbally from one generation to the next, along with old photographs or other mementoes, so that any opportunity of visiting such people should always be taken up.

Corroboration of family births, marriages and deaths since 1837 can be obtained at the General Register Office, and of divorces (since 1852) and wills (since 1858) from the Principal Registry of the Family Division at Somerset House (for details and how to trace earlier records, see chapter 7, 'Family and Local History', pages 117–35). To verify the date of an engagement you may need to search the appropriate pages of *The Times, Daily Telegraph* or local paper; these papers will also carry reports of christenings, weddings, funerals and memorial services in the case of prominent members of society.

If the subject of your biography was involved in any major legal proceedings, you will be able to check this in the *All England Law Reports*, which begin in 1558 and are indexed; or use the *Times Index* and look up the law report in that paper (these have been published since January 1788). Once you have the date of the court proceedings you can, if you require a more popular account or a 'sensational' headline to quote, then look up other newspapers of the same date.

Special Problems

Names

In private correspondence and diaries people are often mentioned by nickname or given name only, and their identity may not be clear to you at the outset of research. It is an excellent idea to keep an alphabetical list or card index of everyone who crops up in the course of your work on a biography; apart from its value to you personally as a private 'who's who' of identification, it will come in very useful should any editorial note be required and also later on for the index. Among pitfalls to avoid are the danger of confusing titles (always check on which duke or earl you are referring to at any one time) and the various names by which a woman may be known during her life, due to a series of marriages and/or divorces and the possibility that she may have reverted to her maiden name for professional or other reasons. To add to the confusion, titled persons are sometimes referred to by title and sometimes by surname, which may not be the same.

Dating letters

Letters all too frequently present the biographer with unforeseen problems. Far too many people had (and still have) the habit of dating their correspondence 'Thursday', 'Sunday, 12th' or 'Amsterdam, Monday', or – which is worse from the researcher's point of view – of not dating them at all. You should also be aware that some individuals are prone to stuff free hotel or club stationery into their briefcases and to use it weeks or even months later, so that although such correspondence may be dated, you cannot be absolutely certain that the writer was actually resident at the hotel or club at the time: if there is any doubt at all in your mind on this score, try to verify the date and/or place in another source.

Some expert detective work will sometimes be needed before you can establish the correct chronological sequence of a bundle of correspondence. The most obvious clues are: the address from which the letter is, or is alleged to be, written; the person to whom it is written; the subject-matter. Look also at the handwriting; the ink; the paper: should there be a watermark, this will not give you the precise date of the letter, but it will provide firm evidence that the document cannot have been written earlier than the date of the watermark.

If, on first reading, a letter does not appear to offer any clue of this kind, do not despair. Re-examine it closely for mention of any family, national or world event – perhaps the death of a well-known person, an exhibition or play seen, a new novel read, and so on, the dates of which can then be checked out in the national press, *Whitaker's Almanack* and other sources. Letters that you cannot even guess at dating should be kept apart from the rest; sooner or later, as work progresses, you are more than likely to stumble on some information (nearly always when you are not looking for it) that will enable you to slot such letters into their right sequence. The use of the *Handbook of Dates for Students of English History* for checking the day of the week of given dates has been explained on page 71.

Handwriting is a great revealer of character, and biographers are sometimes tempted to send a few letters for professional analysis. If you decide to do this, write to the British Institute of Graphologists, Bell Court House (4th floor), 11 Blomfield Road, London EC2M 7AY, for a recommendation, and be sure to send the graphologist correspondence of varying dates. Diane Simpson's *The Analysis of Handwriting* contains much practical information, as well as an entertaining short chapter on the analysis of 'doodles'. Other titles to look at are Barry Branston's *Graphology Explained* and Claude Santoy's *ABC of Handwriting Analysis*.

Verbal information

It is beyond the scope of this chapter to examine in detail all the possibilities open to the biographical researcher, but if the basic principle is followed of taking each natural phase of the life in turn, verifying dates and events in printed and other records and supplementing the documentary material with the recollections of contemporaries wherever obtainable, you will not go far wrong. A word of warning about the use of verbal information, however: human nature being what it is, people do frequently tend to try to enhance their own status (either in the researcher's eyes or their own or with a view to their name appearing in print) by exaggerating their intimacy or acquaintance with a well-known person, and memories in general are, sadly, far from infallible. Always, therefore, make a point of double-checking, so far as you can, any story that is told to you. If you cannot verify it from a reliable printed source, try to get corroboration from a second person. Confidences must, of course, be respected at all times, and care must be taken to avoid giving offence to relatives or other persons who are still alive.

Where private individuals have been especially helpful or informative, it is good manners to let them see the draft text before going to press, and to acknowledge their assistance in the book.

The ABC of Handwriting Analysis, by Claude Santoy, Hale, London, 1991

Air Force List, published annually since 1949 by HMSO, London

All England Law Reports: reprint 1558–1935, 36 vols + index, Butterworth, London, 1966–68; since 1936 weekly, with annual cumulative index, Butterworth, London

Allgemeines Lexikon der bildenden Künstler, by U. Thieme and F. Becker, 37 vols; photographic reprint of original 1907 edition published by Seeman Verlag, Leipzig, 1978

Alumni Cantabrigienses: A Biographical List of all known Students, Graduates and Holders of Office to 1900, by J. & J. A. Venn, 10 vols, Cambridge University Press, 1940–54; Kraus reprint, 1974

Alumni Oxonienses: The Members of the University of Oxford 1500–1886, 8 vols, by J. Foster, Parker, Oxford, 1888–92; Kraus reprint, 1968

The Analysis of Handwriting, by Diane Simpson, A & C Black, London, 1985

Annual Obituary, published since 1981 by St James Press, London

Annual Register, published since 1758 by Longman, London

Army List, now published bi-annually by HMSO, London (first published 1814; but an earlier series exists from 1754 and may be seen at the PRO, Kew)

Bibliography of Biography, microfiche cumulation 1970–84 and two bound vols, 1988 and 1989, published by British Library, Boston Spa; irregular

Bibliography of Regimental Histories, compiled by A. S. White, Society for Army Historical Research with The Army Museums Ogilby Trust London, 1965 (now out of print, but the library of the National Army Museum, Royal Hospital Road, London SW3 4HT (tel. 071–730 0717) maintains a fully up-dated interleaved version)

Bidwell's Guide to Government Ministers 1900–1972, 3 vols, Frank Cass, London, 1973–74

Biographical Dictionary of Actors, Actresses, Musicians, Dancers, Managers and Other Stage Personnel in London 1660–1800, published by Southern Illinois Press, USA, and in progress since 1973 (12 vols to date)

Biographical Dictionary of British Architects 1660–1840, rev. ed., by H. M. Colvin, Murray, London, 1978

Biographical Register of the University of Cambridge to 1500, by A. B. Emden, Cambridge University Press, Cambridge, 1963

Biographical Register of the University of Oxford to 1500, 3 vols, by A. B. Emden, Clarendon Press, Oxford, 1957–59; supplement (1501–1540), 1974

Biography and Genealogy Master Index, 8 vols, Gale Research, Detroit, 1980, updated regularly on microfiche

Biography Index, published by H.W. Wilson, New York, since 1946; now quarterly, with annual and 2-year cumulative volumes; available on-line and CD-ROM from July 1984

British Archives: A Guide to Archive Resources in the United Kingdom, by Janet Foster and Julia Sheppard, Macmillan, London, 2nd ed., 1989

The British Biographical Archive (BBA), ongoing microfiche series published by Saur, Munich; printed index, 4 vols to date

British Humanities Index, published quarterly since 1963, with annual cumulations, by the Library Association, London

'British Military Records as Sources for Biography and Genealogy', Public Record Office leaflet no. 9, PRO, London

British National Bibliography (BNB), weekly since 1950, with cumulative monthly, annual and some 5-yearly volumes; now published by British Library, London; also available on microfiche, CD-ROM and on-line via BLAISE-LINE

The British Soldier: A Social History, by J. M. Brereton, Bodley Head, London, 1986

Chambers' Biographical Dictionary, ed. M. Magnusson, Chambers, Edinburgh, 1990; paperback rev. ed., 1991

Commissioned Sea Officers of the Royal Navy 1660–1815, National Maritime Musuem, London, 1954

Crockford's Clerical Directory, first issued in 1858; latest ed., 1991–92, by Church House Publishing, London, 1991

Debrett's Distinguished People of Today, published by Debrett's Peerage, London, 1988

Debrett's People of Today, published by Debrett's Peerage, London, annually from 1990

Dictionary of British Ships and Seamen, by G. Uden and R.

Cooper, Allen Lane, Harmondsworth, 1980

Dictionary of International Biography, published annually since 1963, now by International Biographical Centre, Cambridge

Dictionary of National Biography (DNB), to 1900, 22 vols, Oxford University Press, London, 1885–1900; 8 later vols, each covering 10 years, for the period 1901–1980, the most recent (1971–80) published 1981; compact edition, 2 vols, 1975 (now out of print); *The Concise DNB, Part 1, Beginnings to 1900*, 2nd ed., 1906; *Part 2, 1901–1970*, 1982 (new 3-vol ed. in preparation); *A Chronological and Occupational Index to the DNB*, 1985

Dictionary of Universal Biography, by A. M. Hyamson, first published by Routledge, London, 1916; re-written, 1976; reprinted Routledge, London and Gale Research, Detroit, 1981

Dictionnaire des peintres, sculpteurs, dessinateurs et graveurs, ed. E. Benézit, new ed., 10 vols, Gründ, Paris, 1976

Dod's Parliamentary Companion, published annually since 1832 by Dod's Parliamentary Companion Ltd, Herstmonceux, E. Sussex

Europa Biographical Dictionary of British Women, Europa, London, 1983; paperback ed., 1985

Gentleman's Magazine: Index to the Biographical and Obituary Notices, 2 vols, *1731–1780*, British Record Society, London, 1891; *1781–1819*, by B. Nangle, Garland Publishing, New York and London, 1980

Graphology Explained: A Workbook, by Barry Branston, Piatkus, London, 1989

Guide to Reference Material, vol 2, 5th ed., ed. A. J. Walford, Library Association, London, 1990

Guide to the Papers of British Cabinet Ministers 1900–1951, compiled by C. Hazelhurst and C. Woodland, Royal Historical Society, London, 1974

Guide to the Regiments and Corps of the British Army, by J. M. Brereton, Bodley Head, London, 1985

Guide to the Sources of British Military History, ed. R. Higham, Routledge, London, 1972; supplement, ed. G. Jordan, Garland, New York and London, 1988

Handbook of Dates for Students of English History, ed. C. R. Cheney, Royal Historical Society, London, 1978, latest reprint, 1982

Hansard: Parliamentary Debates, 1803 onwards; now published daily during sessions by HMSO, London. Chadwyck-Healey, Cambridge, publishes various series of Parliamentary Papers from 1715, on microfilm and microfiche.

Haydn's Universal Index of Biography, ed. J. Bertrand Payne, Moxon, London, 1870

Historical Register series (Universities of Cambridge and Oxford):

Cambridge, to year 1910, with supplementary vols, Cambridge University Press; latest vol. (1971–75), 1977

Oxford, 1220–1900, with supplementary vols to 1965, Oxford University Press, 1900, 1970

In Search of Army Ancestry, by G. Hamilton-Edwards, Phillimore, Chichester, 1977

Independent Schools Yearbook: Boys' Schools, Co-educational Schools & Preparatory Schools (formerly entitled *Public & Preparatory Schools Yearbook*), published annually by A & C Black, London

Independent Schools Yearbook: Girls' Schools (formerly entitled *Girls' Schools Yearbook*), published annually by A & C Black, London

Index Bio-Bibliographicus Notorum Hominum, Biblio Verlag, Osnabrück, in progress, 1972–

International Authors' and Writers' Who's Who, 12th ed., International Biographical Centre, Cambridge, 1991

International Bibliography of Biography 1970–1987, 12 vols, published by Bowker, New Providence, N.J., 1988

The International Directory of Company Histories, published by St James Press, London; in progress, 1988–

International Who's Who, published annually by Europa Publications, London

International Year Book and Statesman's Who's Who, previously published by Burke's Peerage, London, now by Reed Information Services, East Grinstead, W. Sussex

Jewish Year Book, published annually by Jewish Chronicle Publications, London

Lives of the Georgian Age, Lives of the Stuart Age, Lives of the Tudor Age, 3 vols, Osprey, London, 1976–78

Lloyd's Shipping Index, first published 1880, now daily by Lloyd's of London Press Ltd, Colchester, Essex

Lloyd's Voyage Record, published weekly since 1946 by Lloyd's of London Press Ltd, Colchester, Essex

Longman Dictionary of 20th Century Biography Longman, Harlow, 1985

McGraw Hill Encyclopedia of World Biography, 12 vols, McGraw Hill, New York and London, 1973

Macmillan Dictionary of Women's Biography, ed. J. S. Uglow, Macmillan, London, 2nd ed., 1989

Medical Register, published annually by the General Medical Council, London

Members of Parliament, 4 vols, HMSO, London, 1878–91 (vols I–II, England 1213–1702; III, Great Britain 1705–1796, United Kingdom 1801–1874, Scotland 1357–1707, Ireland 1559–1800;

IV, Index)

Modern English Biography, compiled and privately printed by P. Boase, Truro, 6 vols, 1892–1921; reprinted, F. Cass, London, 1965

Munk's Roll (Lives of the Fellows of the Royal College of Physicians), 8 vols published to date, covering 16th century to 1988, IRL Press, Oxford, continuing

Musgrave's Obituary prior to 1800, 6 vols, ed. Sir G. J. Armytage, Harleian Society, London, 1899–1901

'Naval Records for Genealogists', Public Record Office Handbook H22, PRO, London, 1988

Navy List, published annually since 1814 by HMSO, London (earlier listings at PRO, Kew)

The New Grove Dictionary of Music and Musicians, ed. Stanley Sadie, 20 vols, Macmillan, London, 1981

New York Times Obituaries Index, from 1858; cumulative volumes 1858–1968 and 1969–79, Glen Rock, N.J., now annually by Mecklen Corporation, N.Y.

New York Times Personal Name Index 1851–1974, supplement *1975–1984*, compiled by B.A. and V.R. Falk, Roxbury Data, Succasunna, N.J.

Obituaries from The Times, 3 vols covering the period 1951–75, Research Publications, Reading, 1975–79

Office Holders in Modern Britain, 9 vols, Institute of Historical Research, London, 1972–84

Oxford Companion series, Oxford University Press, regularly revised; some paperback editions

Registers of the Universities, Colleges and Schools of Great Britain and Ireland, by P. M. Jacobs, Institute of Historical Research, London, 1964 (reprinted from the Institute's *Bulletin*, 37 (November 1964))

Sources in British Political History, 1900–1951, edited by Chris Cook, 6 vols, Macmillan, London, 1985: 1, *A Guide to the Archives of Selected Organisations and Societies*; 2, *A Guide to the Papers of Selected Public Servants*; 3, *A Guide to the Private Papers of Members of Parliament, A-K*; 4, *A Guide to the Private Papers of Members of Parliament, L-Z*; 5, *A Guide to the Private Papers of Selected Writers, Intellectual Publicists*; 6, *First Consolidated Supplement*

The Statesman's Year Book, published annually since 1864 by Macmillan, London

The Times Index, first published 1790; now monthly, with annual cumulations, Research Publications, Reading

Webster's Biographical Dictionary, Merriam, Springfield, Mass., latest edition, 1980

Whitaker's Almanack, published annually by Whitaker, London

Who Was Who, published by A & C Black, London; 8 vols to date, covering the period 1897–1990; *Cumulated Index 1897–1990*, 1991

Who's Who, published annually by A & C Black, London

Who's Who in British History, ed. G. Treasure, 7 vols to date, Shepheard Walwyn, London; vol. 8 due 1993

Who's Who in International Affairs, published by Europa, London, 1st ed., 1990

World Bibliography of Bibliographies, 4th ed. by T. Besterman, Lausanne, 4 vols and index, 1965–66; *Supplement 1964–1974*, ed. A.F. Toomey, 2 vols, Rowman & Littlefield, Totowa, N.J., 1977

The World of Learning, now published annually by Europa, London

The World Who's Who of Women, published since 1973 by the International Biographical Centre, Cambridge; updated approximately every 2 years (latest ed., 11th, 1991)

The Writers Directory, St James Press, London/St Martin's Press, New York, latest ed. (9th), *1990–92*, published 1990

Note: Space does not permit a complete listing of *Who's Who* volumes for the various professions and foreign countries, of which there are now more than seventy titles published by a number of different firms; however, the researcher should have no difficulty in tracing these in the major library catalogues.

7

Family and Local History

In recent years people have become increasingly interested in tracing their own family ancestry, and, largely as a result of teaching in schools and evening classes, many students embark on a local or family history project which they later wish to develop into a full-length study. Biographers and authors of historical novels also need to do some research in this field, and some of the problems they are likely to encounter have been outlined in the sections of this handbook on 'Factual and Historical Research' and 'Biography'.

The first thing to be said is that research for family or local history can be exceedingly complex. For those who look on it as a hobby and for whom time is no object, it will be a lengthy and often frustrating, but always in the end rewarding, task. Writers with publishers' press deadlines to meet, and who need only certain facts to fill out their work – for example, ancestral research for the first chapter of a biography, or the tracing of a particular will, or the detail of some event in a certain parish needed for an historical novel – would be well advised to use the services of a professional genealogist or record agent (see 'Specialist Research', pages 136–40). Those who wish to undertake their own research in this field should be prepared to do a considerable amount of preliminary study so as to familiarise themselves with the classes of records available and the kind of information to be derived from them.

Space does not permit to do more here than suggest the major sources of information, as well as some of the standard textbooks on genealogy and local archives. Most adult education centres run courses on local history and genealogy, but very few on palaeography (the study of old handwriting). For details of a comprehensive course, leading to a diploma, that may be followed on a full- or part-time basis, or as a correspondence course, write to the Secretary, the Institute of Heraldic and Genealogical Studies, 79–82 Northgate, Canterbury, Kent CT1 1BA (tel. 0227 68664).

The Society of Genealogists, 14 Charterhouse Buildings, Goswell Road, London EC1M 7BA (tel. 071–251 8799) periodically organizes day conferences and lectures for beginners (members only). Members of the Society have free use of the library, with its unique collection of printed, manuscript, microfiche and microfilmed material, free attendance at lectures and the benefit of a reduced rate for research carried out by members of the staff; they also receive a quarterly journal, *Genealogists' Magazine*. The society's other quarterly periodical, *Computers in Genealogy*, is offered to members at a reduced subscription. A leaflet, 'Using the Library of the Society of Genealogists', is available. The writer who intends to do any extensive genealogical research, and who lives in or with good access to London, will find membership very worthwhile. Non-members may use the library on payment of a small fee, currently £2.50 for one hour, £6.00 for 3½ hours, £8.00 for a whole day, and may subscribe to both publications.

There are family history societies and local history groups in most counties of the United Kingdom, and writers researching in this field should consider joining their local group. Subscriptions are usually quite modest, and in return members benefit from advice on their researches as well as the exchange of information with fellow genealogists and historians. An up-to-date list of these societies, giving the secretaries' names and addresses, is available on receipt of first-class stamped addressed envelope or two international reply coupons from the Administrator, Federation of Family History Societies (FFHS), c/o Benson Room, Birmingham & Midland Institute, Margaret Street, Birmingham B3 3BS.

A subscription to the Guild of One-Name Studies, which is closely associated with the Society of Genealogists and the FFHS, would be worthwhile in the long term, but probably not if you are engaged on a 'one-off' search for the ancestry chapter of one book. Members receive a quarterly journal, *One-Name Studies*, and also a Register listing the names that are currently being researched worldwide, with the name and address of a 'registered member' to contact for information on each name. A select bibliography is in preparation. Members may register a name for a small fee, provided it has not already been registered; but when you do this, you give an undertaking to deal with all reply-paid enquiries about that name – so consider carefully before you commit yourself (it could be a drain on your writing time!). The Hon. Secretary of the Guild may be contacted at Box 6, 14 Charterhouse Buildings, Goswell Road, London EC1M 7BA.

The leading publishers of family and local history in this country are Phillimore & Co. Ltd, Shopwyke Hall, Chichester, Sussex PO20 6BQ (tel. 0243 787636). The Phillimore bookshop, at the same address, also stocks titles from other publishers and will supply books by post. Ask to be put on the catalogue mailing list. Both the Society of Genealogists and the FFHS publish handbooks and leaflets to assist the amateur family and local historian (the FFHS list includes the popular 'Gibson' and 'McLaughlin' guides).

Among a number of journals of interest are *Family History News and Digest*, published twice a year (spring and autumn) by the FFHS; *Family Tree Magazine*; and *The Local Historian* (formerly *The Amateur Historian*). Finally, a subscription to the annual *Genealogical Research Directory* (currently £12.50 plus postage in the UK) entitles you to register up to fifteen names in which you are interested; the book is circulated throughout the world and may eventually bring you the bonus of an exchange of information with other subscribers. *The National Genealogical Directory* is an annual publication listing genealogists in Britain and their current research interests.

Using County Record Offices, Archaeological Societies and Other Collections

The writer embarking on a family or local history should first of all visit his local record office, where the archivist or an assistant archivist will usually be glad to discuss the project and to explain what records are available. Some county record offices publish useful pamphlets for students on how to trace the history of a parish or of a family, and most have a printed or microfiche guide to their collections, as well as regularly updated lists of parish registers and other documents that have been deposited.

A short list of record offices will be found in Appendix I, but more detailed information is given in the HMSO pamphlet *Record Repositories in Great Britain*, which is revised every few years. An excellent guide is Jeremy Gibson's *Record Offices: How to Find Them*.

The principal public libraries have local history collections, and those of local archaeological societies are usually open to *bona fide* researchers (non-members may be asked to pay a modest search fee). Where information is needed from outside your own district, it is always worth sending a preliminary letter (with self-addressed stamped envelope) to the local archivist or chief reference librarian. Most county archivists are happy to answer simple enquiries, such as the verification of not more than one or two entries in a parish register (a baptism, marriage or burial), but especially nowadays, owing to the severe cutback in local government expenditure, staff are not available to undertake extensive searches. However, advice will always be given on the records to consult, as well as practical help over any problems encountered in the search room; and most county record offices will, on request, also supply the names and addresses of local record agents. Occasionally a record office or public library will offer to do research for you, on a fee-paying basis; however, it has to be said that you will almost certainly obtain results faster by employing a freelance record agent direct. You should nevertheless always enquire on your first visit whether there is any member of staff who happens to have a special knowledge of, or interest in, your subject. Photocopies and photographs of most documents are usually obtainable.

A list of local archaeological societies, with names and addresses of secretaries, will be found in *Whitaker's Almanack*.

Family History

A family history may have as its starting point a rough tree drawn up by a relative or ancestor, or – if you are lucky – a more professional pedigree and possibly also a collection of papers handed down from one generation to another or recently discovered in an attic of the ancestral home. The first thing to do is to make reasonably sure that a history has not already been written or a tree drawn up. This can be checked in one of several ways: in the catalogue or subject index of one of the copyright libraries; at the library of the Society of Genealogists; at the College of Arms; at the local record office nearest to the family home. Remember that many family histories are privately printed or may be deposited at the record office, or donated to the local library, in typescript.

If the family is likely to have been recorded in any of Burke's publications, the place to look is *Burke's Family Index*. This useful volume has references to some twenty thousand different family histories.

The next step is to verify, one by one, the dates of all births, marriages and deaths, and – other people's memories being what they are – also to check the names, allowing for variations in spelling. The usual procedure is to work methodically backwards in time, either from yourself or from the person you are writing about, first to the parents, then the grandparents, and so on, generation by generation. If you are fortunate enough to own a personal computer, you could invest in some specially designed software to help you store and sort the fruits of your research. Alternatively, set up a card index system, with a separate card for each individual, on which you enter each piece of information as it is verified; or there are specially printed genealogical record cards or 'research workbooks' on the market (available from the Society of Genealogists, among others).

You can draw up your own draft family tree as you proceed; but if the tree is to be published, it is best to have it professionally drawn.

Terrick Fitzhugh's *How to Write a Family History* is highly recommended reading.

Verifying births, marriages and deaths

Since 1 July 1837 all births, marriages and deaths in England and Wales, together with some overseas (consular) and service returns, births and deaths at sea, etc. have been centrally recorded at the General Register Office in London. Formerly at Somerset House, these records are now permanently at St Catherine's House, 10 Kingsway, London WC2B 6JP. In Scotland registration began in 1855, the records being housed at the office of the Registrar General, New Register House, Edinburgh EH1 3YT. In Ireland, the records from 1864 to 1921 are at the office of the Registrar General, Joyce House, 8–11 Lombard Street East, Dublin 2, for the whole of the country and for the Republic since 1922; Northern Ireland records dating from partition are in the care of the Registrar General, Oxford House, 49–55 Chichester Street, Belfast BT1 4HL.

Searches may be made in person at St Catherine's House but access is only to the indexes, not to the actual registers. The index volumes are arranged according to the quarter of the year in which the event (birth, marriage or death) was registered, and alphabetically under surnames. Unless you have an approximate date to go on, you must be prepared for a long haul – and an exhausting one, as pulling out one heavy volume after another is exceedingly tiring. The information printed in the indexes is minimal, so that sometimes you may not be certain that you have found the correct entry; but if you request a copy of the relevant certificate and the parentage and/or spouse does not match with the information you have to give on the application form, a refund will be made. As full certificates now cost £5.50 apiece, this is an important consideration. (There is a shorter form of certificate – available for births only – but this is not normally sufficient for genealogical research purposes as it contains only the name, sex, date and place, but *not* the parentage.)

It is always worth getting copies of birth, marriage and death certificates, as the detail given on them, such as the occupation of a child's father, the witnesses to a marriage, the cause of death and the address at which it occurred, will be invaluable and may lead you on to other channels of enquiry. For those who live a long way from London (or Edinburgh, Dublin or Belfast), copies of certificates may be obtained by post, in which case a higher fee is charged (currently £12 if you supply references or £15 without references; this includes a five-year search carried out by staff). Certificates ordered in person are available for collection after four working days; those requested by post will take three to six weeks. There may be slight variations between the different registries. It all sounds very involved to the uninitiated, but Eve McLaughlin's booklet *St Catherine's House* will give you confidence.

More than eighty million birth and baptismal entries, and some marriage entries, may be seen on the International Genealogical Index (IGI), formerly known as the Computer File Index, of the Genealogical Society of the Church of Jesus Christ of Latter-Day Saints, Salt Lake City, Utah, USA (known more familiarly as the Mormon Church), which is available on microfiche in the UK. The complete world listing of the IGI may be seen in London at the Mormon Branch Library (its official title is the London Regional Genealogical Library), 64–68 Exhibition Road, South Kensington, London SW7 2PA (tel. 071–589 8561) and at the Society of Genealogists; most county record offices and some public libraries hold smaller sections relevant to their own areas. An updated, revised version of the IGI will be available in the UK from 1992. The index is a useful starting point for family history research, as within each county the entries are arranged in alphabetical order of surname. You can obtain on-the-spot print-outs for study at home; in addition, microfilms with fuller information will be sent from Salt Lake City (you pay only for postage). Time-saving as this great research tool is, users of the IGI should, however, be aware that it is neither comprehensive nor, sadly, 100% accurate: coverage and the degree of accuracy vary from county to county (a computer index is, after all, only as accurate as the information fed into it by the human computer operator), so that researchers should always double-check entries in the original sources. Also at this library are the Parish and Vital Records Listings (a guide to parishes, towns and other centres worldwide whose records have been transcribed and/or indexed); an index to the Genealogical Library Catalogue (microfilms obtainable from Salt Lake City); and the Family Registry List (names and addresses of people doing genealogical research and the names which they are researching).

Nonconformist registers were required by law to be surrendered to the Registrar General in 1840, and these are now at the Public Record Office. (Some registers were exempt – where they were kept in the same books as other records, such as members' lists, minutes of meetings, etc. – and you may be lucky enough to find them at local record offices.) The Religious Society of Friends, before surrendering their records, prepared 'Digest Registers' which, together with other valuable Quaker material, may be seen at Friends' House, Euston Road, London NW1 2BJ (tel. 071–387 3601). Records of Huguenots in England since the mid-16th century have been published by the Huguenot Society, University College, Gower Street, London WC1E 6BT. For further information on the existence and whereabouts of Nonconformist registers, see *Sources for Nonconformist Genealogy and Family History* (volume 2 of the *National Index of Parish Registers*).

Researchers seeking material on Roman Catholic or Jewish families should look at volume 3 of the same series, *Sources for Roman Catholic and Jewish Genealogy and Family History*.

Parish registers

Ministers in England were first ordered to keep records of all baptisms, marriages and burials in 1538; some registers therefore start in that year, but others were not commenced until a few years later or the earliest volumes have not survived. Not all parish registers have been deposited at the relevant local record office, but recent legislation provides that clergy who do not have adequate facilities for preservation and storage must deposit them within a reasonable time.

The best way to find out whether or not a particular parish register has been deposited is to telephone to the local record office; with new registers being deposited all the time, the situation is constantly changing. If the record office does not have what you require – and often they will not have registers of recent date – they will give you the name and telephone number of the incumbent in whose possession the relevant registers are, or you can look this up in the current *Crockford's Clerical Directory*. To obtain access to these registers, you must write or telephone to make an appointment, as either the minister or his parish clerk must be present. A fee is payable to the incumbent for this service: based either on the time spent or on the number of years searched, this is no longer standard, but you can expect to be asked for up to £3 per hour. If you are making a long search, you will normally be able to negotiate a special rate. To avoid any difficulty, it is wise to establish the fee before you make the appointment. (N.B. If you cannot get to the vestry yourself and the incumbent agrees to do the search for you, he is entitled to charge a higher fee.)

It is as well to remember that directories such as *Crockford's* go to press months ahead of publication and cannot therefore be totally up to date. (The same, alas, applies to this book.) To avoid your letter of enquiry being forwarded on to another parish, should the incumbent listed have moved (which at best will cause delay and may mean that you never receive a reply), it is wise to address it impersonally, i.e. to 'The Incumbent', 'The Rector' or 'Vicar'.

It is important for the novice researcher to remember that parish registers do not give the exact dates of birth or death, but only those of baptism and burial. (Some of the more diligent parish priests also noted the dates of births and deaths, but not often.) In some parishes there are separate registers for baptisms, marriages and burials; in others, the baptisms and burials may be recorded in the same book, starting at different ends, and where the incumbent ran out of space the entries are sometimes continued a few pages later or, worse, may be merged – be careful not to overlook these.

Many registers have been transcribed and/or printed, and the Society of Genealogists issues a very useful booklet: *Parish Register Copies, Part One, Society of Genealogists Collection*. (*Part Two, Other than the Society of Genealogists Collection* has been discontinued.) The *National Index of Parish Registers*, a vast project started over twenty years ago, is now periodically revising or reprinting some of its earlier volumes. The first three volumes of the *Index* constitute a guide to the pre-1837 registers of all denominations in England, Scotland and Wales; the final two volumes deal with sources for Scottish genealogy and family history and the parish registers of Wales respectively. Six regional volumes have been published so far; others are in progress. *The Phillimore Atlas and Index of Parish Registers* is the best quick reference tool.

Other useful sources, especially when it is difficult to gain access to the registers, are Bishop's Transcripts (copies of parish registers made by each minister and sent annually to the Bishop of his diocese). Unfortunately these are not altogether reliable and indeed are sometimes different, as entries were often copied wrongly, or even omitted. It is essential to make a double-check in the original registers.

Marriage indexes

Boyd's Marriage Index, compiled by Mr Percival Boyd from parish registers, Bishop's Transcripts and the marriage licences of England, covers most of the English counties in the period 1538–1837. It contains more than $3\frac{1}{2}$ million names and is housed at the Society of Genealogists in London; a booklet is available from the society listing the parishes and dates included. This is an important source for the researcher who already knows the place or county of the marriage he wishes to trace. However, it is neither complete nor infallible (Mr Boyd died in 1955), and entries should always be verified in the relevant parish register. This is a golden rule in genealogical research when using any printed or transcribed registers or indexes.

Another important marriage index is *Pallot's*, containing some 4½ million marriages between 1780 and 1837; this is held at the Institute of Heraldic and Genealogical Studies in Canterbury. Enquiries may be sent by post, and searches will be made on a fee-paying basis, currently £10 for one entry, £15 for up to twenty entries.

There are also a number of local marriage indexes compiled both by family history groups and by individuals, and more are in progress. Ask at your local record office, or consult the FFHS booklet, *Marriage, Census and Other Indexes for Family Historians*.

Marriage registers generally are separate from those of baptisms and burials; some are more informative than others. Supplementary information may be obtained from records of the intention to marry, such as banns, licences, marriage bonds and allegations. Advice on the availability of these will be given by staff on duty in the record office.

Divorce records

The Divorce Registry at Somerset House, Strand, London WC2R 1LP, holds records of all divorces since 1852 and will supply photocopies of decrees. These are useful to the researcher, as they give the date and place of the marriage.

Wills and administrations

Probate records constitute one of the most useful sources of genealogical information. Since 11 January 1858 copies of all wills and administrations in England and Wales have been centralised at the Principal Registry of the Family Division at Somerset House (address as above); they are calendared alphabetically under surnames in the year in which probate was granted (which may be the same as the year of death, but is sometimes later). The calendar volumes are on open shelves, and once you have traced the will or administration you need, the volume containing it will be produced on demand. Brief notes may be made (in pencil), or alternatively a photocopy ordered.

Prior to 1858 wills and administrations were proved by the courts which had general jurisdiction, of which the most important were the Prerogative Court of Canterbury (PCC) and the Prerogative Court of York (PCY). The PCC wills are at the Public Record Office in Chancery Lane, London (*not* at Kew), and those of the PCY at the Borthwick Institute, York. Ask at your local record office for details of other courts.

The British Record Society's *Index Library* lists the wills held at the PRO and at many local record offices, but as a general guide the researcher should first consult J.S.W. Gibson's *Wills and Where to Find Them*, which discusses the availability of probate records in each English county and also explains the jurisdiction of the different courts, as well as the systems operating in Scotland, Ireland, the Channel Islands and the Isle of Man. *An Index to the Wills proved in the Prerogative County of Canterbury 1750–1800* is in progress under the supervision of Anthony J. Camp, Director of Research of the Society of Genealogists. The latter's *Wills and Their Whereabouts* is a standard guide and Eve McLaughlin's *Wills before 1858* is a useful introduction.

Census returns

The 19th-century census returns are a valuable source for the family historian and may be seen on microfilm in the Census Room of the Public Record Office, now in the basement of the Chancery Lane building. Returns exist from 1801, but individual names were not recorded until 1841. The most recent return available for public inspection is that of 1891. A PRO reader's ticket is not required for access to the census.

The great value of the census to the genealogist is that he will usually find the whole family (or at least those living under the same roof at the appropriate date) recorded together. The returns of 1851 onwards are the most informative, since they give exact ages and places of birth, and also each person's marital status and relationship to the household, whereas the 1841 census return states only their occupations, in what area of the country they were born and, for those over fifteen, ages to the lowest term of five.

It is of course essential to know, if not the exact address at which the family is believed to have been living at the date of the census, at least the parish. The relevant dates are:

> 6 June 1841
> 30 March 1851
> 7 April 1861
> 2 April 1871
> 3 April 1881
> 5 April 1891

Index books are on open shelves in the Census Room, in which you can look up the number of the book and the enumerator's district; this helps you to locate the precise place on the spool. Most towns are now street-indexed. There are pitfalls in that streets may appear half in one enumerator's district and half in another, and not all enumerators, especially in the earlier returns, were scrupulously accurate. It is a little complicated at first, but the PRO staff will assist anyone in difficulties over tracing the right entry or in deciphering the handwriting, which is often far from clear. As delving into census returns nearly always takes longer than one imagines it will, the wise researcher allows plenty of time for it. An excellent and reasonably up-to-date (1989) handbook is E. Higgs' *Making Sense of the Census*. The FFHS 'Gibson' and 'McLaughlin' guides on the subject seem certain to be revised to take in the availability of the 1891 census returns. (Editions in print at the time of writing are *Census Returns on Microfilm: 1841–81* by Jeremy Gibson and *Censuses 1841–1881: Use and Interpretation* by Eve McLaughlin.)

Other records

The above-mentioned are but a few of the sources open to the genealogist/family historian. Searching these will enable you to draw up at least a skeleton family tree as a basis from which to work. The next stage will be to explore the various other classes of records likely to yield further information. Elucidation of the mysteries of Court rolls, Quarter Sessions records, poll books, service records, and so on, is best left to the expert. The classic study by Sir Anthony Wagner, *English Genealogy*, has recently been reprinted. Recommended textbooks include *Genealogy for Beginners* by A.J. Willis and M. Tatchell; *In Search of Ancestry* and *In Search of Scottish Ancestry*, both by G. Hamilton-Edwards; *A Genealogist's Bibliography* by C.R. Humphery-Smith; *The Family History Book* and *Family Roots*, both by Stella Colwell; *Tracing Your Ancestors in the Public Record Office* by Amanda Bevan and Andrea Duncan; and *Tracing Your Scottish Ancestors* by Cecil Sinclair. The *Family History Annual* contains articles by experts on a wide range of genealogical studies and research methods, while *The Family Historian's Enquire Within* by Pauline Saul and F.C. Markwell should ideally be kept at the researcher's elbow. Terrick FitzHugh's recently published *Dictionary of Genealogy* will be invaluable both to the professional and to the amateur researcher: it has over a thousand entries, and includes descriptions and locations of records by county, as well as explanations of obsolete terms and translations of those Latin phrases most likely to be encountered in ancestry research.

Use should also be made of the indexes to proceedings of local archaeological societies and to publications of local family history societies (see page 118). Most public libraries and county record offices possess complete sets of those relating to their districts. The standard works and guides mentioned above contain details of the records of special groups such as the Baptists, Huguenots, Methodists and Quakers.

The major printed biographical sources have been discussed under 'Biography' (pages 96–116), but special mention should be made here of the publications issued by Burke's Peerage Ltd. Publication of the long-awaited new (106th) edition of *Burke's Peerage and Baronetage* is still pending. *Burke's Family Index* has already been mentioned. Other titles include *Burke's Dormant and Extinct Peerages*, *Burke's Guide to the Royal Family*, *Burke's Irish Family Records*, *Burke's Landed Gentry* and, international in scope, *Ruvigny's Titled Nobility of Europe* (originally published in 1914, reprinted recently by Burke), *Burke's Presidential Families of the United States of America*, and *Burke's Royal Families of the World*.

Debrett's Peerage and Baronetage is up to date (1990), while the older, but more comprehensive, *Cockayne's Complete Peerage*, covering extant, extinct and dormant titles to 1938, and out of print for many years, has been reprinted, as has *Cockayne's Complete Baronetage*. *Boutell's Heraldry* and A.C. Fox-Davies' *A Complete Guide to Heraldry* are standard works, while for the amateur there is a useful booklet entitled *How to Read a Coat of Arms*. Debrett's *Guide to Heraldry and Regalia* is a new work. The best place to look up a coat of arms when you come across one and do not know to which family it belongs is Papworth's *Ordinary of British Armorials*. F.L. Leeson's *Directory of British Peerages*, which covers earliest times to the present day in one continuous alphabetical listing of titles and surnames, is an invaluable finding aid.

Local History

Local history writing may range from a short article in the local newspaper or county magazine to a full-length academic study. In all cases painstaking research and a good deal of detective work will be necessary; care must be taken to transcribe original documents accurately and to keep a note of all sources. References should normally be quoted in all but the shortest and most 'popular' articles.

There is a vast store of printed and manuscript material open to the local historian, much of it as yet untapped. Some of these sources have been discussed already under chapter 3, 'Basic Sources of Information and their Location' (pages 32–64). As with family history, before embarking on a project it is wise to check with the local record office whether the same ground has been covered by someone else; even if nothing has yet been published or deposited, archivists notoriously have their 'ears to the ground' and will usually be aware of any other writers, researchers or students working on parallel lines. A preliminary study of a work of similar nature, even if it deals with a totally different district, can be of considerable help to a writer wondering how to tackle the particular subject he has in mind.

Difficulty may be encountered in reading early documents, and unless you have some knowledge of palaeography and Latin, you may need to use the services of an expert. E.E. Thoyt's *How to Read Old Documents* is a modern guide, while both F.G. Emmison's popular booklet *How to Read Local Archives 1500–1700* and Eve McLaughlin's *Reading Old Handwriting* will greatly assist the beginner; but if you are seriously interested in learning more about handwriting, you should read L. C. Hector's *The Handwriting of English Documents* and Hilda Grieve's *Examples of English Handwriting 1150–1750*. Lionel Munby's *Secretary Hand: A Beginner's Introduction* is another useful aid.

The Latin of local records differs considerably from school Latin, and Eileen A. Gooder's *Latin for Local History* is an excellent textbook. C. T. Martin's *The Record Interpreter*, with its invaluable list of Latin abbreviations and glossary of Latin words used in English historical manuscripts and records, first published in 1892 and out of print for many years, became available again in a facsimile edition a few years ago; and another useful reference work is Baxter and Johnson's *Medieval Latin Word List*.

C. R. Cheney's *Handbook of Dates for Students of English History* and Fryde's *Handbook of British Chronology* are indispensable aids to dating: they contain not only lists of rulers (with regnal years), popes, archbishops and other officers of state, but also include saints' days and tables that enable you to work out the day of the week of any date from AD 500 to the year 2000.

All the above-mentioned standard works should be found on the open shelves in county record offices and good reference libraries.

As general introductions to the subject, the researcher should read David Dymond's *Writing Local History* and also two titles by

F. G. Emmison: *Archives and Local History* and *Introduction to Archives*. Books recommended for further reading include W. G. Hoskin's *Local History in England* and *Fieldwork in Local History*, and W. E. Tate's classic, *The Parish Chest*. Titles in the Historical Association's 'Helps for Students of History' series are always worth studying; especially worthwhile is *British and National Archives and the Local Historian*. In preparation is *Oral History and the Local Historian*. The *Victoria County Histories* (a varying number of volumes per county and still in progress) are standard works. John Richardson's *The Local Historian's Encyclopedia*, handy for reference purposes, and the more recent *Batsford Companion to Local History*, are very comprehensive.

Depositing Papers

Every writer of family or local history, whether or not his work achieves publication, should consider depositing a copy of it, together with any original papers that may have come into his possession, and possibly also his research notes, at the appropriate local record office or, in the case of a family history, at the Society of Genealogists in London. By so doing he will be making a valuable contribution to the store of material on English social history and genealogy for the use of future generations of students and researchers.

Archives and Local History, by F.G. Emmison, Phillimore, Chichester, 2nd ed., 1978

The Batsford Companion to Local History, by Stephen Friar, Batsford, London, 1991

Boutell's Heraldry, rev. ed. by J.P. Brooke-Little, Warne, London, 1983

British and National Archives and the Local Historian, by A. Morton and G. Donaldson, 'Helps for Students of History' series, Historical Association, London, 1980

Burke's Dormant and Extinct Peerages, Burke's Peerage, London, reprinted 1985

Burke's Family Index, Burke's Peerage, London, 1976

Burke's Guide to the Royal Family, Burke's Peerage, London, 1973

Burke's Irish Family Records, Burke's Peerage, London, 1976

Burke's Landed Gentry, Burke's Peerage, London, 3 vols, 1965–72

Burke's Peerage and Baronetage, 105th ed., Burke's Peerage, London, 1970; rev. ed. pending

Burke's Presidential Families of the United States of America, Burke's Peerage, London, 1981

Burke's Royal Families of the World, Burke's Peerage, London, 2 vols, 1977, 1980

[*Burke's*] *Ruvigny's Titled Nobility of Europe*, originally published 1914; reprinted by Burke's Peerage, London, 1980

Census Returns on Microfilm: A Directory to Local Holdings, compiled by Jeremy Gibson, FFHS, Birmingham, 5th ed., reprinted 1990

Censuses 1841–1881: Use and Interpretation, by Eve McLaughlin, FFHS, Birmingham, 4th ed., 1990

[*Cockayne's*] *Complete Baronetage*, reprinted in 6 vols, Alan Sutton, Gloucester, 1982

[*Cockayne's*] *Complete Peerage of England, Scotland, Ireland, Great Britain and the United Kingdom, Extant, Extinct or Dormant*, 13 vols, London, 1910–59; reprinted in 6 vols, Alan Sutton, Gloucester, 1982

A Complete Guide to Heraldry, by A.C. Fox-Davies, rev. by J.P. Brooke-Little, Orbis, London, 1985

Computers in Genealogy, quarterly periodical published by the Society of Genealogists, London, 1982–

Crockford's Clerical Directory, first issued in 1858; latest edition (1991–92), by Church House Publishing, London, 1991

Debrett's Guide to Heraldry and Regalia, by David Williamson, Webb & Bower, Exeter, 1992

Debrett's Peerage and Baronetage, published by Debrett's Peerage Ltd and Macmillan, London; latest ed., 1990

Dictionary of Genealogy, by Terrick Fitzhugh, 3rd ed., A & C Black, 1991

A Directory of British Peerages, by F.L. Leeson, Society of Genealogists, London, 1985

English Genealogy, by Anthony Wagner, Phillimore, Chichester, 3rd ed., reprinted 1990

Examples of English Handwriting 1150–1750, by Hilda Grieve, Essex Record Office, Chelmsford, reprinted 1981

The Family Historian's Enquire Within, eds. P. Saul and F.C. Markwell, FFHS, Birmingham, 4th ed., 1991

Family History Annual, ed. and published by M.J. Burchall, Brighton, 1985–

The Family History Book, by Stella Colwell, Phaidon, Oxford, 1980; reprinted 1984

Family History News and Digest, published twice a year (spring and autumn) by the Federation of Family History Societies (FFHS), Birmingham

Family Roots: Discovering the Past in the Public Record Office, by Stella Colwell, Weidenfeld and Nicolson, London, 1991

Family Tree Magazine, published monthly by J.M. and M. Armstrong, 141 Great Whyte, Ramsey, Huntingdon, Cambs PE17 1HP

Fieldwork in Local History, by W.G. Hoskins, 2nd ed., Faber, London, 1982

Genealogical Research Directory, published annually since 1982: UK agent, Mrs E. Simpson, 2 Stella Grove, Tollerton, Notts NG12 4EY

A Genealogist's Bibliography, by C.R. Humphery-Smith, Phillimore, Chichester, 1985

Genealogist's Magazine, published quarterly by the Society of Genealogists, London

Genealogy for Beginners, by A. Willis and M. Tatchell, Phillimore, Chichester, 1984

Handbook of British Chronology, ed. E.B. Fryde *et al*, 3rd ed., Royal Historical Society, London, 1985

Handbook of Dates for Students of English History, by C.R. Cheney, Royal Historical Society, London, 1978; reprinted 1982

The Handwriting of English Documents, by L.C. Hector, originally published by E. Arnold, London, 1958; now in facsimile reprint by Kohler & Coombes, Dorking, 1980

How to Read a Coat of Arms, by Peter Summers, rev. ed., Alphabooks, Sherborne 1986

How to Read Local Archives 1550–1700, by F.G. Emmison, Historical Association, London, 1967; latest reprint, 1988

How to Read Old Documents, by E.E. Thoyt, Phillimore, Chichester, 1980

How to Write a Family History, by Terrick Fitzhugh, Alphabooks, Sherborne, 1988

Index Library, published for the British Record Society by Phillimore, Chichester, continuing

An Index to the Wills proved in the Prerogative Court of Canterbury 1750–1800, ed. A.J. Camp, Society of Genealogists, London, in progress, 5 vols to date, 1976–

In Search of Ancestry, by G. Hamilton-Edwards, Phillimore, Chichester, 1983

In Search of Scottish Ancestry, by G. Hamilton-Edwards, Phillimore, Chichester, 1983

Introduction to Archives, by F.G. Emmison, Phillimore, Chichester, 1977

Latin for Local History, by Eileen A. Gooder, Longman, Harlow, 1978; reprinted (7th impression of 2nd ed.), 1990

List of Parishes in Boyd's Marriage Index, Phillimore, Chichester, for the Society of Genealogists, London, 6th ed., 1987

The Local Historian (formerly *The Amateur Historian*), published quarterly by Phillimore, Chichester, for the British Association for Local History (BALH)

The Local Historian's Encyclopedia, by John Richardson, 2nd ed., Phillimore, Chichester, 1986

Local History in England, by W.G. Hoskins, Longman, Harlow, 3rd ed., 1984

Making Sense of the Census, The Manuscript Returns for England and Wales 1801–1901, by E. Higgs, PRO Handbook no. 23, HMSO, London, 1989

Marriage, Census and Other Indexes for Family Historians, by Jeremy Gibson, FFHS, Birmingham, 4th ed. due 1992

Medieval Latin Word List, by J.H. Baxter and C. Johnson, rev. ed. by R.E. Latham, Oxford University Press, Oxford, 1965

National Genealogical Directory, published annually by M.J. Burchall and J. Warren, Brighton

National Index of Parish Registers, series ed. Cliff Webb, published by Phillimore, Chichester, for the Society of Genealogists, in progress (some vols revised/reprinted, some out of print, others in preparation): I, *Sources for Births, Marriages and Deaths before 1837*, 1968, reprinted 1976; II, *Sources for Nonconformist Genealogy and Family History*, 1973, reprinted 1981; III, *Sources for Roman Catholic and Jewish Genealogy and Family History*, 1974, reprinted 1986; IV, *South East England*, 1980: Part 1, *Surrey*, reprinted 1990; V, *South Midlands and Welsh Border*, 1966, 3rd ed. revised, 1976; VI, *North Midlands*: Part 1, *Staffordshire*, 1982, rev. ed. due 1991/2; Part 2, *Nottinghamshire*, 1988; VII, *East Anglia*, 1983; VIII, Part 1, *Berkshire*, 1989; IX, Part 1, *Bedfordshire and Huntingdonshire*, 1991, Part 2, *Northamptonshire*, 1991; X, in preparation; XI, *North-East England*: Part 1, *Durham and Northumberland*, 2nd ed. 1984, rev. ed. due 1992; XII, *Sources for Scottish Genealogy and Family History*, 1970, reprinted 1980; XIII, *The Parish Registers of Wales*, 1986

One-Name Studies, quarterly journal of the Guild of One-Name Studies, London

Oral History and the Local Historian, by Robert Perks, 'Helps for Students of History' series, Historical Association, London; in preparation

Ordinary of British Armorials, by A.W.W. Papworth, 1874; facsimile ed., Tabard Publications, London, 1961

The Parish Chest, by W.E. Tate, Phillimore, Chichester, 3rd rev. ed., 1983; reprinted 1985

Parish Register Copies, booklets in two parts published by

Phillimore, Chichester, for the Society of Genealogists, London, and updated at intervals: 1, *Society of Genealogists' Collection*, 8th ed., 1987; 2, *Other Collections*, 1978 (discontinued)

Phillimore Atlas and Index of Parish Registers, ed. C. Humphery-Smith, Phillimore, Chichester, 1984

Reading Old Handwriting, by Eve McLaughlin, FFHS, Birmingham, 1987

The Record Interpreter, by Charles Trice Martin, originally published 1892; facsimile of 2nd ed. (1910), Kohler & Coombes, Dorking, 1976; reprinted 1982

Record Offices: How to Find Them, by Jeremy Gibson, FFHS, Birmingham, 5th ed., 1991

Record Repositories in Great Britain: A Geographical Directory, published by HMSO, London, for the Royal Commission on Historical Manuscripts and updated every few years; latest ed., 1991

St Catherine's House, by Eve McLaughlin, FFHS, Birmingham, 7th ed., 1988

Secretary Hand: A Beginner's Introduction, by Lionel Munby, British Association for Local History (BALH), 1984 (now c/o Phillimore & Co. Ltd, Shopwyke Hall, Chichester, Sussex PO20 6BQ)

Tracing Your Ancestors in the Public Record Office, 4th ed. by Amanda Bevan and Andrea Duncan (formerly by Jane Cox and Timothy Padfield), PRO Handbook no. 19, HMSO, London, 1991

Tracing Your Scottish Ancestors: A Guide to Ancestry Research in the Scottish Record Office, by Cecil Sinclair, HMSO, Edinburgh, 1990

'Using the Library of the Society of Genealogists', leaflet available from the Society of Genealogists, London; updated at intervals

Victoria History of the Counties of England (*VCH*): first vol. published 1901 by Oxford University Press for the Institute of Historical Research, London; continuing

Whitaker's Almanack, published annually by Whitaker, London

Wills and Their Whereabouts, by A.J. Camp, Phillimore, Chichester, 1974

Wills and Where to Find Them, by Jeremy Gibson, Phillimore, Chichester, 1974

Wills Before 1858, by Eve McLaughlin, FFHS, Birmingham, 1985

Writing Local History, by David Dymond, Phillimore, Chichester, for the British Association for Local History (BALH), 1988

Note: Publications of the Federation of Family History Societies are distributed from Birmingham. Orders should be sent to FFHS, c/o Benson Room, Birmingham & Midland Institute, Margaret Street, Birmingham B3 3BS; mark envelope 'PUBLICATIONS'. *The National Genealogical Directory* is available from the Society of Genealogists, 14 Charterhouse Buildings, Goswell Road, London EC1M 7BA.

8

Specialist Research

While the writer will always find it more rewarding to undertake his own research, and should do so whenever feasible, there are times when it pays to employ the expert. Books or records to be consulted may be accessible only at some distance from the writer's home; specialist knowledge of a subject may be required, or knowledge of local records which it would take the inexperienced researcher, or one from another district, months, if not years, to acquire – in such events the employment of an expert will usually save the client time and money in the long term. If he has press deadlines looming, or other commitments, it may even pay him to off-load some of the more routine research as well.

Writers wishing to get in touch with a freelance researcher will find some names listed in the *Writers' and Artists' Yearbook*, under 'Editorial, Literary and Production Services', and in the Cassell and Publishers Association *Directory of Publishing*, under 'Trade and Allied Services: publishing consultancies and research services in Great Britain'. The British Library Reference Division, the Public Record Office and some other libraries and local record offices maintain lists of researchers/record agents and will pass on names and addresses to enquirers (send a stamped addressed envelope); naturally, they do not accept any responsibility for the work undertaken by these people. Experts willing to do research may also sometimes be contacted through the secretaries or librarians of professional or trade societies or institutions; alternatively, an advertisement in a professional or trade journal may yield a suitable result. Some freelancers advertise their service in *The Times*, the *Times Literary Supplement, The Author, Books and Bookman* and similar papers. Schoolmasters and university students often seek research assignments during the long vacation. For details of how to obtain the services of a qualified indexer, see page 164.

Contacting a suitable researcher abroad is rather more difficult. You can write to the national library of the country concerned, or to the library or archives centre where you want the research to be done (always enclose a sufficient number of International Reply Coupons for airmail if writing overseas – one is not enough); or you can approach the cultural attaché of the relevant embassy, legation or high commission in London.

The most obvious occasions when a writer may need this kind of help are in the fields of genealogy, when a complicated ancestral search may be necessary for the first chapter of a biography; in local or family history, for which not only a knowledge of the classes of records available is required, but also some skill in reading Latin and palaeography (transcribing old handwriting); in picture research; and in translation.

Genealogy

Experience in palaeography and genealogy is acquired only after considerable study, and there are many traps into which the unwary novice can fall. A working knowledge of Latin is essential for the study of medieval or earlier texts, while later source material demands the ability to read and transcribe both the 'secretary hand' (the script in use in England from the mid-16th to the mid-17th centuries) and the later 'court hand', each with distinctive forms of capital letters and contractions. Unless you are embarking on your family or local history as a hobby, therefore, and can afford the time to qualify yourself in these subjects, some professional assistance will be desirable.

It is wise to employ someone who lives in the area in which the relevant search is to be made, for he will be familiar both with the local records and with local family names, and thus can save the client time and money. Most local record offices maintain lists of recommended searchers; alternatively, names and addresses of professional genealogists and record agents who are members of the Association of Genealogists and Record Agents (AGRA) may be obtained from the Joint Hon. Secretaries, Mr & Mrs D. R. Young, 29 Badgers Close, Horsham, W. Sussex RH12 5RU (enclose £1.50 to cover cost and postage). All AGRA members have satisfied their Council as to integrity, qualifications and experience, and they adhere to a strict professional code of practice.

The College of Arms (Queen Victoria Street, London EC4V 4BT) is open to enquiries of a genealogical and heraldic nature from members of the public (arms and pedigrees of English, Northern Irish and Commonwealth families). For personal visitors only a brief search will be made free of charge to ascertain whether or not a family tree has been drawn up; further research will be conducted on a fee-paying basis. Debrett Ancestry Research Ltd, P.O. Box 7, New Alresford, Hants. SO24 9EN (tel. 0962 732676), which formerly catered only for royalty and the aristocracy, now offers a worldwide genealogical research service to the commoner. So does Burke's Ancestry Research Department, 12 Rickett Street, London SW6 1RU (tel. 071–385 4206); this firm will give advice on a genealogical search for approximately £15–£20 or a feasibility assessment for £20–£35, the cost of which will be deducted if they are commissioned to do further research. Other firms and individuals offering genealogical research services in various parts of the United Kingdom and abroad advertise in the *Genealogists' Magazine*, the quarterly journal of the Society of Genealogists. The Society itself will carry out research, on a fee-paying basis, for members and non-members. Enquiries, accompanied by a stamped addressed envelope, should be addressed to the Director of Research, The Society of Genealogists, 14 Charterhouse Buildings, London EC1M 7BA.

Picture Research

Picture research is an immensely complicated field and therefore beyond the scope of this handbook. Sometimes a writer will be expected to provide all the illustrative material for his book or article; in other cases the publisher will employ a professional picture researcher, who may be a member of his staff or a freelance, to locate and select pictures, commission photographers, and clear the copyright and reproduction fees on a particular project. Whether the author or the publisher foots the bill for the picture researcher is a matter for negotiation. But a wise author makes sure that it is stipulated in his contract that it will be the publisher who bears responsibility for print and reproduction fees, since these can be very costly.

Writers wishing to obtain the services of a qualified picture researcher are recommended to contact the freelance register of the Society of Picture Researchers and Editors (SPREd): telephone Ruth Smith on 0727 833676. For other information about the Society, write or telephone to SPREd, BM Box 259, London WC1N 3XX (tel. 071–404 5011).

For those who are tempted to do their own picture research and need a good introduction to the subject, the *Writers' & Artists' Yearbook*, published annually by A & C Black, contains an excellent article by Judith Harries. Among a variety of useful manuals and source-books are the following:

The Art of Picture Research, by Hilary and Mary Evans, David & Charles, Newton Abbot, 1979

BAPLA Directory, published annually by the British Association of
  Picture Libraries and Agencies, PO Box 4, Andoversford,
  Cheltenham, Glos.
Directory of British Photographic Collections, ed. J. Wall,
  Heinemann, London, on behalf of the Royal Photographic
  Society, 1977
The Picture Researcher's Handbook by Hilary and Mary Evans,
  4th ed., Van Nostrand Reinhold, London, 1989
Picture Source Book for Social History, 6 vols, Allen & Unwin,
  London, 1961
*Picture Sources UK: A Guide to more than 1200 Public and Private
  Picture Collections*, Macdonald, London, 1985 (to be updated
  regularly)
Sources of Illustration 1500–1900, Adams & Dart, London, 1971

Translation

Translation is another field in which professional help may be
required from time to time. For basic research purposes a rough
translation or précis may be adequate to work on, but any passage
to be quoted in print should be prepared by a qualified translator.
The best way to find one is to contact the Institute of Translation
and Interpreting (ITI), 318A Finchley Road, London NW3 5HT
(tel. 071–794 9931). The languages and skills of qualified members
of the Institute, together with those of members of the Translators
Association of the Society of Authors, will be found in the *ITI
Index*. Alternatively, translation agencies are listed in the yellow
pages of most telephone directories, but these normally handle
commercial rather than literary texts.

The Translator's Handbook by Catriona Picken (2nd ed., Aslib,
London, 1989) is an excellent introduction and source-book for all
members of the profession; it will also be of use to writers who need
to commission a translator.

Research Fees

Fees for professional freelance assistance are negotiable and depend
on the nature and complexity of the task. Genealogists, record
agents and researchers usually work on an hourly basis plus out-of-
pocket expenses (travelling, search fees, photocopying, postages,
telephone, etc.); short pieces of translation are charged per thousand words. Most freelance workers have a sliding scale of fees; the
professional bodies to which the majority of them belong recom-

mend standard rates for the job, and if you are asked to pay 'above the odds' it will be either because the assignment is very specialised or complicated, or is needed in a great rush (necessitating week-end and evening work), or because the person engaged has special qualifications.

It is normal practice for the client commissioning the work to pay a lump sum on account (up to 50% of the total cost estimated) and the balance on completion, but in the case of long-term commissions accounts may be rendered monthly. Estimates will be given on request; but do not expect your researcher to give one with any accuracy – neither he nor you will know at the outset precisely how much time he will spend on the job.

Fees paid to researchers, genealogists, translators and other workers may be set against a writer's tax.

9

Information from and about Foreign Countries

The British writer who needs to use foreign sources – published or unpublished documentary material – or to obtain background information on other countries should first of all explore what is available in the United Kingdom. All the copyright libraries and major reference libraries here have substantial foreign language holdings, and there should be little difficulty encountered in obtaining most standard works.

National encyclopedias, bibliographies and current works of reference are usually to be found on the open shelves. If these do not provide what you are looking for, you should next consult the library's subject index, first under the relevant country and then under the desired subject sub-heading.

The principal foreign newspapers and weeklies going back many years are held at the British Library Newspaper Library in Colindale, although there are some gaps during the two world wars; nowadays most are purchased on microfilm. The whereabouts of foreign periodicals in British libraries can be traced in *Serials in the British Library*. Current publications worldwide are listed in *Benn's Media Directory*, *Ulrich's International Periodicals Directory* and *Willing's Press Guide*.

Subscriptions to foreign newspapers and periodicals can be arranged, with payment in sterling, through J.E.M. Subscriptions Services, 23 Waveney Close, Bicester, Oxon. OX6 8GP (tel. 0993 840346), or the London booksellers Grant & Cutler, 55–57 Great Marlborough Street, London W1V 2AY (tel. 071–734 2012). The latter firm holds a large stock of foreign language titles and will order on any subject. Bay Foreign Language Books, 19 Dymchurch Road, St Mary's Bay, Romney Marsh, Kent TN29 0ET (tel. 0679 64417) also import books and offer, in addition, an out-of-print search for foreign titles.

The use of bibliographies and how to trace books has been dealt with earlier in this handbook (see pages 33–41). In Walford's *Guide to Reference Material* and its US equivalent, Sheehy's *Guide to Reference Books* (details in chapter 3), encyclopedias, national bibliographies and major works are listed, subject by subject, under the relevant sub-heading of each country. For quick factual reference the following single-volume mini-encyclopedias are recommended additions to the writer's own bookshelf: *Le Petit Larousse* (French); *Der Brockhaus in einem Band* (German); *Pequeño Larousse Illustrado* (Spanish). It is always worthwhile keeping an eye open for these as they appear (they are updated regularly), and you can often pick them up secondhand: some of the information they contain is not always included in English language encyclopedias. It goes without saying that if you are using foreign sources you will need at least a working (reading) knowledge of the language or languages concerned; otherwise you must be prepared to go to the considerable expense of translation. A series of good foreign-language/English dictionaries is essential, along with the basic grammars.

Tourist information offices (listed in the London telephone directory) will provide up-to-date travel and basic background material on foreign countries, while the press offices of the relevant embassies and high commissions, or the cultural attachés (names and addresses in the current *London Diplomatic List*, published twice yearly by HMSO and available at most library enquiry desks) are usually extremely helpful, either with specific problems or in suggesting where you should address your enquiries in the country concerned. Another good source is the new *World Directory of Diplomatic Representation*, published by Europa (first edition 1992). Public relations officers of the major international companies may also provide useful source material; names and addresses will be found in the current *Hollis Press & Public Relations Annual*.

There are biographical dictionaries for most countries, and up-to-date biographical information will be found in the *Who's Who* of the country concerned; where no publications exist for the country in which you are interested, it is best to ask the relevant embassy or high commission in London.

Details of foreign libraries in the United Kingdom will be found in the *Aslib Directory*. The researcher who lives in or near London will be able to make use of the following:

Bibliothèque de l'Institut Français, 15 Queensberry Place, London SW7 2DT (tel. 071–589 6211). Use of reference facilities is free; books may be borrowed on subscription. Open Mon. 11–8; Tues, Wed., Fri., 11–6.

British Library Oriental and India Office Collections (formerly the India Office Library), Orbit House, 197 Blackfriars Road, London SE1 8NG (tel. 071–412 7873). Mon.–Fri., 9.30–5.45, Sat., 9.30–1. N.B. These collections will be moving to the new British Library at St Pancras in 1996.

German Institute Library, 50–51 Princes Gate, Exhibition Road, London SW7 2PG (tel. 071–581 3344). Open to the public, free of charge, for reference and study, Mon.–Thurs., 10–8; Sat., 10–1.

Institute of Commonwealth Studies Library, 27–28 Russell Square, London WC1B 5DS (tel. 071–580 5876). Open (during term) Mon.–Wed., 10–7, Thurs, Fri., 10–6; (during vacations), Mon.–Fri., 10–5.30.

Italian Institute Library, 39 Belgrave Square, London SW1X 8NX (tel. 071–235 1461). Mon.–Fri., 9.30–5, for reference only.

Polish Library, 238–246 King Street, London W6 0RF (tel. 081–741 0474). Mon., Wed., 10–8, Tues., Fri., 10–5, Thurs., Sat., 10–1, for reference (loans to scholars).

Royal Commonwealth Society Library, 18 Northumberland Avenue, London WC2N 5BJ (tel. 071–930 6733). Open to members and to *bona fide* researchers, Mon.–Fri., 10–5.30.

School of Oriental and African Studies Library, Thornhaugh Street, Russell Square, London WC1H 0XG (tel. 071–323 6112). Mon.–Thurs., 9–8.45, Fri., 9–7, Sat., 9.30–5; summer vacation, Mon.–Fri., 9–5, Sat., 9.30–5. Reader's ticket required (letter of introduction).

Spanish Institute Library, 102 Eaton Square, London SW1W 9AN (tel. 071–235 1484/5). Mon.–Thurs., 9.30–1, 2.30–5, Fri., 9.30–2, for reference only.

United States of America Information Service Reference Center, American Embassy, 55/56 Upper Brook Street, London W1A 2CH (tel. 071–499 9000, ext. 2925). Open Mon.–Fri., 10–12.

When material cannot be located in this country and it is necessary to make enquiries at libraries or research institutions abroad, it is not only good manners but will also avoid possible confusion or delay at the other end if you have your initial letter professionally translated. (For details of how to find translation services, see page 139.) If any extensive research is involved, the foreign librarian or archivist will usually be able to put you in touch with a local freelance researcher.

The leading libraries abroad are listed in *The World of Learning*, published by Europa, London, and in two excellent guides by Helga Lengenfelder: *World Guide to Libraries* and *World Guide to*

Special Libraries, both published by Saur, Munich, 1990–91 (distributed in the UK by Bowker-Saur, see page 63). The two Bowker annuals, *Literary Market Place* and *International Literary Market Place*, covering the United States and the rest of the world respectively, are good sources of information on libraries and the book trade generally, with reference books, periodicals, literary associations and prizes detailed under individual countries.

The best place to look initially for information on foreign countries is in the *World Bibliographical Series* published by Clio Press of Oxford. There is also an excellent series on *International Historical Statistics* (separate volumes for Europe; Africa and Asia; The Americas and Australasia) published by Macmillan, London. A good historical source is the multi-volume *Guide to the Sources for the History of the Nations* series, published by Saur, Munich, for the International Council on Archives (ICA). *Archivum, The International Review on Archives*, published by the ICA, is also of interest: volume XXXIII (1988) is an International Directory of Archives, listed by country, and volume XXXVI (1990) an International Bibliography of Directories and Guides to Archival Repositories, also listed by country, with subject guides.

Space does not permit the examination in any detail of specific foreign sources or guides to sources, of which there are many. Bearing in mind that readers of this book are most likely to want access to foreign material in the UK, in this edition I have expanded the lists of printed sources and dropped the lists of libraries in the United States and France. (Details of these and other libraries will, as mentioned above, be found in the current editions of *The World of Learning* and the two *World Guides* by Helga Lengenfelder.)

A bewildering and ever-increasing quantity of foreign-language and overseas reference material is becoming accessible to researchers in this country. The convenience factor (irrespective of the time- and money-saving aspect) of being able to search the catalogues of some of the great national library collections of Europe without needing to trek, say, to Paris or Madrid, is of inestimable value. Publishers everywhere seem to be jumping on the bandwagon of the new technology to produce bigger and better research tools, yearbooks and directories. There can be no excuse nowadays for failing to obtain the information you need on foreign countries. A few suggestions, offered purely as a starting point, are listed below, alphabetically under area or country.

Useful international sources include the microfiche *Biographical Archive* project, which now covers several countries, the US *Public Affairs Information Service Index* (*PAIS*) with its worldwide coverage, Europa's *Regional Surveys of the World* series, and old favourites already mentioned such as the *Europa World Year Book*, the *International Who's Who* and the *Yearbook of International Organizations*.

Short List of Foreign Source-material (arranged alphabetically under area or country)
Africa

Sources of information in the UK:

African Studies Centre Library, University of Cambridge, Free School Lane, Cambridge CB2 3RQ (tel. 0223 334398)

The School of Oriental and African Studies, University of London, Thornhaugh Street, Russell Square, London WC1H 0XG (tel. 071–637 2388)

Recommended books:

Africa: A Guide to Reference Material, Zell, Munich, 1992
Africa South of the Sahara 1992, Europa, London, 1991
The African Book World and Press: A Directory, Zell, Munich, 4th ed., 1989
African Books in Print, 3rd ed., 2 vols, Mansell, London, 1984
African Political Facts since 1945, Macmillan, London, 2nd ed., 1990
African Studies Companion, Zell, Munich, 1989
Bibliographies for African Studies 1970–1986, Zell, Munich, 1988
International African Bibliography, quarterly since 1971, Mansell, London, with regular cumulative volumes
Statistics Africa, CBD Research, Beckenham, updated regularly

Note: The publishers Hans Zell, of Munich, specialise in African studies. Titles are distributed in the UK by Bowker-Saur Ltd., Borough Green, Sevenoaks, Kent TN15 8PH (tel. 0732 884567).

Arab States and the Middle East

Sources of information in the UK:

British Library Oriental and India Office Collections, Orbit House, 197 Blackfriars Road, London SE1 8NG (tel. 071–412 7873). Moving to the new British Library at St Pancras in 1996.

Centre for Arab Gulf Studies, Documentation Unit, University of Exeter Old Library, Prince of Wales Road, Exeter, Devon EX4 4JZ (tel. 0392 264041)

Middle East Centre, St Anthony's College, Woodstock Road, Oxford OX2 6JF (tel. 0865 259651, ext. 64) (collections of papers of individuals involved in the Middle East from 1800 to the present day)

Recommended books:

Book World Directory of the Arab Countries, Turkey and Iran, Mansell, London, 1981

Index Islamicus 1906–1955, with 5-yearly supplements to 1985, Mansell, London, 1958–91; published quarterly since 1977

Who's Who in the Arab World, published by Publitec, Beirut, Lebanon

The Middle East and North Africa 1992, Europa, London, 1991

Saudi Arabia: A Bibliography on Society, Politics and Economics from the 18th Century to the Present, Saur, Munich, 1984

Theses on Islam, the Middle East and NW Africa 1880–1978, Mansell, London, 1983

Union Catalogue of Arabic Serials and Newspapers in British Libraries, Mansell, London, 1977 (indexed in English and Arabic)

Asia and the Far East

Sources of information in the UK:

Asian Studies Centre, St Anthony's College, Woodstock Road, Oxford OX2 6JF (tel. 0865 59651, ext. 260)

British Library Oriental and India Office Collections, Orbit House, 197 Blackfriars Road, London SE1 8NG (tel. 071–412 7873). Moving to the new British Library at St Pancras in 1996.

Centre of South Asian Studies, University of Cambridge, Laundress Lane, Cambridge CB2 1SD (tel. 0223 338094).

School of Oriental and African Studies, University of London, Thornhaugh Street, Russell Square, London WC1H 0XG (tel. 071–637 2388)

Recommended books:

Asia: A Selected and Annotated Guide to Reference Works, Mansell, London, 1980

Cumulative Bibliography of Asian Studies 1941–1965, Association for Asian Studies Inc., Boston, Mass.; annually with cumulative volumes

The Far East and Australasia 1992, Europa, London, 1991

Statistics Asia and Australasia, CBD Research, Beckenham, updated regularly

Who's Who in Australasia and the Far East, Melrose, Cambridge, 2nd ed., 1991

Who's Who in the People's Republic of China, Bowker, New Providence, N.J., 3rd ed., 1991

The Commonwealth

Sources of information in the UK:

Commonwealth Institute Library, Kensington High Street, London W8 6NQ (tel. 071–603 4535)

Commonwealth Secretariat Library, 10 Carlton House Terrace, Pall Mall, London SW1Y 5AH (tel. 071–839 3411, ext. 5013)

Foreign & Commonwealth Office Library (tel. 071–271 3000). Moving to main FCO building, Whitehall, during 1992.

Institute of Commonwealth Studies, University of London, 27–28 Russell Square, London WC1B 5DS (tel. 071–580 5876)

Rhodes House Library, South Parks Road, Oxford OX1 3RG (tel. 0865 270909)

Royal Commonwealth Society Library, 18 Northumberland Avenue, London WC2N 5BJ (tel. 071–930 6733)

Researchers should also contact the various high commissions in London, i.e. Australia House, Canada House, India House, New Zealand House, etc. (addresses and telephone numbers in *Whitaker's Almanack* under 'The Commonwealth' or in *Hollis Press & Public Relations Annual* under 'International and Overseas Information Sources in the UK', and the London telephone directory).

Recommended books:

General

Commonwealth Political Facts, ed. Chris Cook, Macmillan, London, 1979

The Commonwealth Yearbook, HMSO, London, annually

Who's Who in the Commonwealth, International Biographical Centre, Cambridge, updated regularly

Note: The library of the Institute of Commonwealth Studies in London (see page 147) publishes a quarterly *Accessions List* and an annual list of *Theses in Progress in Commonwealth Studies*; it also maintains a card catalogue of completed theses.

Australia

Australian Books in Print, D. W. Thorpe, Melbourne

Australian Dictionary of Biography, Melbourne University Press, 12 vols to date plus index vol

Australian National Bibliography, National Library of Australia, Canberra (previously known as *Annual Catalogue of Australian Publications*, published 1936–60): since 1972 published weekly, with monthly and 4-monthly cumulations and annual volumes

Official Year Book of the Commonwealth of Australia, published annually by the Government Printing Office, Canberra

Resources for Australian and New Zealand Studies: A Guide to Library Holdings in the United Kingdom, British Library, London and Australian Studies Centre, University of London, 1986

Who's Who in Australia, published triennially since 1906, now by Information Australia, Melbourne

Canada

Canadian Almanac and Directory 1991, available from Europa, London

Canadian Reference Sources: A Selective Guide, rev. ed., ed. D. E. Ryder, Canadian Library Association, Ottawa, 1981

Canadiana, national bibliography published monthly since 1951, with annual cumulations, National Library of Canada, Ottawa

Dictionary of Canadian Biography, University of Toronto Press, 1966– (in progress)

Encyclopedia Canadiana (standard national encyclopedia). A new *Canadian Encyclopedia* was published by Hurtig in 3 volumes in September 1985.

Historical Statistics of Canada, Statistics Canada, Ottawa, 2nd ed., 1983

How to Find Out about Canada, by H. C. Campbell, Pergamon, Oxford, 1967 (out of print, but contains useful information)

Statistics Canada, published annually by the Information Department of Canada, Ottawa

Who's Who in Canada, published annually since 1907, now by Global Press, Toronto

India

Index India, published quarterly by Rajasthan University, Jaipur, since 1967

India: A Reference Manual, published annually since 1953 by the Ministry of Information and Broadcasting, New Delhi

India Who's Who, published annually since 1969 by INFA Publications, New Delhi

Indian National Bibliography, published monthly, with annual cumulations, since 1957 by the Central Reference Library, Calcutta

New Zealand

Bibliography of New Zealand Bibliographies, New Zealand Library Association, Wellington, 1967

Books and Pamphlets relating to Culture and the Arts in New Zealand, compiled by B. Smyth and H. Howorth, Christchurch, 1978

Encyclopedia of New Zealand, ed. A. H. McLintock, 3 vols, Owen, Wellington, 1966

New Zealand National Bibliography, monthly since 1967, National Library of New Zealand, Wellington

New Zealand Official Year Book, published annually by the Department of Statistics, Wellington

Resources for Australian and New Zealand Studies, see page 148 under 'Australia'.

Regrettably, space does not permit the listing of other Commonwealth countries in this section.

Europe

Given the vast amount of material published each year, readers will understand that it is impossible to do more in the space of this chapter than to list some of the countries of Europe, with the location of their national libraries/archives and a selection of reference works (by title only). There are, however, a number of general guides which should first be mentioned. These include:

Directory of European Industrial & Trade Associations and *Directory of European Professional & Learned Societies*, both CBD Research, Beckenham; updated regularly

The Documentation of the European Communities, by Ian Thomson, Mansell, London, 1989

European Biographical Dictionary, Database, Brussels, 8th ed., 1989

The European Communities Encyclopedia and Directory 1992, a new publication from Europa, London, 1991

European Historical Facts and *European Political Facts* series, Macmillan, London

Hollis Europe, annually by Hollis Directories, Sunbury-on-Thames

Official Publications of Western Europe, ed. E. Johansson, Mansell, London, 2 vols, 1984, 1988

Statistics Europe, CBD Research, Beckenham, updated regularly

Who's Who in Europe, Servi-Tech, Brussels, updated at intervals and available in English and French

The Press and Information Office of the Commission of the European Communities is at 8 Storey's Gate, London SW1 3AT (tel. 071–222 8122).

Note: For purposes of this chapter, 'Europe' refers to Western Europe. The countries of Eastern Europe are included under the heading 'Russia, the Commonwealth of Independent States and Eastern Europe'.

Austria

The Österreichische Nationalbibliothek in Vienna is the national library, and there is also the Staatsarchiv (national archives) in the same city.

Austria, Facts and Figures
Dokumentation und Information in Österreich
Österreichische Bibliographie
Österreichisches Biographisches Lexikon 1815–1950
Österreich Lexikon
Who's Who in Austria

Belgium

The Bibliothèque royale Albert Ier/Koninklijke Bibliotheek Albert I and the Archives générales du Royaume, both in Brussels, are the major library and archive sources.

Bibligraphie de Belge/Belgische bibliografie
Documentation sur la Belgique: bibliographie sélective et analytique

Inventaire des centres belges de recherche
Who's Who in Belgium and the Grand Duchy of Luxembourg

Denmark – see under 'Scandinavia'.

France

The national library is the Bibliothèque Nationale (BN), 58 rue Richelieu, 75084 Paris (tel. 47 03 81 26). A project to move the collection to a new building in 1995 has (at the time of writing) temporarily been shelved. Intending users of the BN will obviously have a reading knowledge of French and will appreciate two booklet guides, the *Guide du lecteur* (reader's guide), 4th edition, 1985 and the *Guide pratique* (practical guide), 1987. The general catalogue is in three parts: printed books, manuscripts and periodicals; it is now on microfiche and available at the British Library and other major UK libraries, and may also be searched on-line. An annex to the BN was opened in 1981 at Provins, east of Paris, to house the newspaper and periodicals collection.

Another excellent reference library in Paris is the Bibliothèque du Centre National d'Art et de Culture Georges Pompidou, at the Centre Beaubourg: 19 rue Beaubourg, 75191 Paris (tel. 42 77 12 33).

The Archives Nationales are at 60 rue des Francs-Bourgeois, 75141 Paris (tel. 40 27 60 00).

Recommended books:

Annuaire Statistique de la France, published annually by the I.N.S.E.E., Paris
Archives Biographiques Françaises, covering the 18th to 20th centuries, on microfiche with printed index vols, Saur, Munich, 1988–90
Le Bottin Administratif (yearbook of government departments and public offices), Bottin, Paris, annually
Dictionnaire de biographie française, Letouzey, Paris, in progress, 1929–
Grand Larousse Encyclopédique, Larousse, Paris, 10 vols, 1960–64; supplements, 1968, 1975
Livres Hebdo: Bibliographie de la France, published weekly, with monthly and quarterly supplements, since 1979, now by Editions Cercle de la Librairie, Paris. (*Hebdo* has superseded the earlier *Bibliographie de la France*, published since 1811, and *Biblio*, since 1933.)

Qui est Qui en France/Who's Who in France, published biennially
since 1953 by Éditions Jacques Lafitte, Paris

The Press Division of the French Embassy in London issues a
compact and informative publication, regularly updated (latest
edition 1990) entitled *France: A Journalist's Guide*, which is available free on request. Anyone who has to do research in or about
France will find it invaluable.

Germany

The three major libraries are the Deutsche Bibliothek in Frankfurt,
the Staatsbibliothek Prüssischer Kulturbesitz and the Deutsche
Staatsbibliothek (formerly the Prüssische Staatsbibliothek), both in
Berlin.

Allgemeine Deutsche Biographie
Der Grosse Brockhaus (encyclopedia)
Deutsche Bibliographie (former Federal Republic of Germany)
Deutsche Nationalbibliographie (former German Democratic
Republic)
Neue Deutsche Biographie
Wer ist Wer? (includes some Austrian and Swiss entries)
Who's Who in Germany

As a result of the unification of the two German republics some of
these titles may change in the near future.

Greece

The National Library is in Athens.

Greek Bibliography
Guide to Greek Libraries and Cultural Organizations
Hellenika Vivla (bibliography)
Modern Greece: A Bibliography
Mega Hellenikon Biographikon Lexikon (biographical dictionary),
in progress

Italy

The major libraries are the Biblioteca Nazionale Centrale Vittorio
Emanuele II in Rome and the Biblioteca Nazionale Centrale in
Florence; there are also national libraries in Milan, Naples,
Palermo, Turin and Venice.

Bibliografia Nazionale Italiana
Dizionario Biografico degli Italiani
Enciclopedia Italiana di Scienze, Lettre ed Arti
Guida delle Bibliothece Italiane
How to Find Out about Italy
Italian Books in Print
Lui, Chi, E?
Who's Who in Italy

The Netherlands

The major collection is at the Koninklijke Bibliotheek (Royal Library) in The Hague.

Brinkman's Cumulatieve Catalogus van Boeken (bibliography)
Digest of the Kingdom of the Netherlands (Government Information Service publication)
Grote Nederlandse Larousse Encyclopedie
Grote Winkler Prins Encyclopedie
Nieuw Nederlandsch Biografisch Woordenboek
Who's Who in the Netherlands
Wie is Dat?

Norway – see under 'Scandinavia'.

Scandinavia

Two biographical dictionaries covering the region are the *Dictionary of Scandinavian Biography* and *Who's Who in Scandinavia*; the latter publication (1st ed., Bowker, New York, 1981) includes an appendix listing societies, associations and institutions.

Denmark

The Kongelige Bibliotek (Royal Library) in Copenhagen is the national library; the archive collection is at the Kobenhavns Stadsarkiv.

Bibliography of Books on Denmark 1900–1965
Dansk Biografisk Leksikon
Dansk Bogfortegnelse (national bibliography)
Denmark: An Official Handbook
Denmark: A Select Bibliography
Who's Who in Denmark

Norway

The national library is the Universitetsbiblioteket i Oslo (Royal University Library), and the national archives are at the Riksarkivet, also in Oslo.

Facts about Norway
Guide to Norwegian Statistics
Hvem or Hvem? (Norwegian who's who)
Norsk Biografisk Leksikon
Norsk Bokfortegnelse (national bibliography)
Norway Year Book

Sweden

The Kungliga Biblioteket (Royal Library), the Riksarkivet (National Record Office) and the Statistika Centralbyráns Biblioteket (Library of Statistics) are all in Stockholm.

Facts about Sweden
Svenskt Biografiskt Lexikon
Svensk Bokforteckning (national bibliography)
Vem är Det? (Swedish who's who)

Spain

The Biblioteca Nacional is in Madrid, as are the Archivo General de la Administracion Civil del Estado (the General Archives of the Civil Administration of the State) and the Archivo Historico Nacional (the National Historical Archives). There is also the Real Biblioteca (Royal Library) at El Escorial, near Madrid. The Archivo de la Corona de Aragon (the Royal Archives of Aragon) are in Barcelona, where there is also the Biblioteca de Catalunya (the Library of Catalonia).

Bibliografia Española
Enciclopedia Universal Ilustrada Europeo-Americana
Gran Enciclopedia Rialp
Indice Cultural Español (Spanish cultural index)
Quién es quién (Spanish who's who)
Who's Who in Spain

Switzerland

The national library is the Schweizerische Landesbibliothek/ Bibliothèque Nationale Suisse in Berne; the Archives Fédérales (national archives) are in the same city. In Geneva there are the United Nations Library and the International Labour Office Library.

Das Schweizer Buch/Le Livre Suisse (national bibliography)
Who's Who in Switzerland

For the next two areas of the world – Latin America and the Caribbean, and Russia, the former USSR and Eastern Europe – space does not permit the listing of even major libraries in the different countries and states. The general works and bibliographies included should be useful to the researcher.

Latin America and the Caribbean

Bibliografía Latinoamericana, CERLAL, Bogotá, 1974–
Cambridge Encyclopedia of Latin America and the Caribbean, ed. H. Blakemore, S. Collier and T. Skidmore, Cambridge University Press, 1985
Caribbeana, 1900–1965: A Topical Bibliography, by L. Comitas, University of Washington Press, Seattle and London, 1968
CARICOM Bibliography, Caricom Secretariat, Georgetown, Guyana, 1977–
South America, Central America and the Caribbean 1991, Europa Publications, London, 1990

Russia, the Commonwealth of Independent States and Eastern Europe

Archives and Manuscript Repositories in the USSR, Estonia, Latvia, Lithuania and Byelorussia, by Patricia Kennedy Grimsted, Bibliotheca Slavica, Princeton University Press, N.J., 3 vols, 1972–81
Biographical Dictionary of the Soviet Union 1917–88, Bowker, New Providence, N.J., 1989
Eastern Europe and the USSR 1992, Europa, London, 1991
Encyclopedia of the USSR 1905–1990, Mansell, London, 1990
The Great Soviet Encyclopedia (translation of *Bol'shaya Sovetskaya Entsiklopediya*, 3rd ed.), 31 vols + 3 index vols, Macmillan, New York/Macmillan, London, 1973–83
Guide to Documents and Manuscripts in the United Kingdom relating to Russia and the Soviet Union, compiled by J.M. Hartley, Mansell, London, 1987
Guide to Russian Reference Books, in progress at Stanford University, California, 1962–

Official Publications of the Soviet Union and Eastern Europe 1945–1980: A Select Bibliography, ed. G. Walker, Mansell, London, 1982

Who's Who in the Soviet Union Today, Saur, Munich, 1991

Inevitably, following recent events in the former USSR, much of the information given above will need up-dating.

United States of America

The Library of Congress, Washington, DC 20540 (tel. (202) 707 5000) is the national library, but it is not the exact equivalent of the British Library in that it does not automatically acquire a copy of every book published in the United States; it does, however, collect and catalogue books published in other countries. The *National Union Catalog*, which has replaced the old *Library of Congress Catalog*, will be found on open access at the British Library and in major libraries of the UK. The *Pre-1956 Imprints*, an impressive run of 755 volumes, are clear and easy to use; their great value to the researcher is that they provide in one alphabetical sequence, under authors, the holdings of the Library of Congress together with those of the principal libraries of North America. Another bonus is that the *NUC* gives dates of authors (otherwise sometimes difficult to obtain). The *NUC* from 1968 may be accessed through BLAISE-LINE (LC MARC).

The National Archives and Records Administration is at the National Archives Building, 8th Street at Pennsylvania Avenue NW, Washington DC 20408 (tel. (202) 501 5400).

Recommended books:

American Biographical Archive (ABA), microfiche + printed index vols, Saur, Munich, 1986–90

Books in Print, published annually by Bowker, New Providence, N.J.; also *Subject Guide to Books in Print*

Dictionary of American Biography (period up to 1960), 21 vols + 6 supplements, Scribner, New York, 1928–80

Directory of Special Libraries and Information Centers, 2 vols, Gale Research, Detroit, 13th ed., 1990

Encyclopedia of Associations, published annually in 5 vols by Gale Research, Detroit

Guide to Manuscripts relating to America in the United Kingdom, ed. J.W. Raimo, Mansell, London, 1979

Guide to Reference Books, by E.P. Sheehy, American Library

Association, Chicago, 9th ed., 1992

Information Please Almanac, published annually since 1947, now by Houghton Mifflin, Boston, Mass.

National Inventory of Documentary Sources in the United States, on microfiche in three parts: 1, *Federal Records*; 2, *Manuscript Division, Library of Congress*; 3, *State Archives, State Libraries, Historical Societies, Academic Libraries and Other Repositories*; 5 units per year, with cumulating index, Chadwyck-Healey, Cambridge

Oxford Companion to American History, Oxford University Press, Oxford, 1966

Statistical Abstract of the United States, published annually since 1879 by the Government Printing Office, Washington DC

Who was Who in America 1897–1981, 7 vols, 1942–81; *Historical* volume (1607–1896), 1963; *Index* volume (1607–1981), 1981, Marquis, Chicago

Who's Who in America, published biennially in 2 vols by Marquis, Chicago

At the British Library Newspaper Library in Colindale, North London, there are on open access indexes to the *New York Times* (from 1851), *Washington Post* (from 1955), *Chicago Tribune* (from 1972), and a few other US newspapers. Check with the librarian as to availability on microfiche and CD-ROM.

10

Preparation for the Press

The research is done, the final draft completed, the length approximately right. (Some word processor owners will have a built-in word-count facility, but those less fortunate must do it the hard way, taking an average number of words per page and multiplying by the number of pages – remembering to allow for any short pages and inserts – and rounding up the total to the nearest hundred words.)

If the great work is a novel or a play, all that remains is for the author either to print it out on his daisy-wheel, letter-quality or laser printer, or to type the fair copy himself electronically or manually, or – if he simply cannot face this task – to go to the expense of having it professionally typed. Those lucky enough to own word processors or computers with word processing programs will have made their final check on screen before printing out; everyone else should go through the typescript carefully once more before despatching it to literary agent or publisher.

The non-fiction book requires a little extra attention. The prelims must be written, the notes and references section and the bibliography (if any) compiled, some thought given to the provision of an index, although this will not actually be prepared until later. None of these chores, strictly speaking, comes within the province of 'research', but their importance as a whole in putting a professional finish on the typescript is such that they merit a brief mention here.

For the writer who needs to refresh his memory, the current *Writers' & Artists' Yearbook* carries short articles on the 'Preparation of Typescripts' and 'Correcting Proofs'. Judith Butcher's booklet *Typescripts, Proofs and Indexes*, sadly one of only two titles still available in the *Cambridge Authors' and Printers' Guides* series, is an excellent quick reference aid; while for the word processing author there is Michael Barnard's *Making Electronic Manuscripts*. Another excellent little handbook for the writer to keep at his elbow during this stage of his work is *The Typist's* A-Z by Edith Mackay. This useful publication deals with everything from punctuation, abbreviations and layout to the intricacies of square brackets; it also contains sections on the correction signs for typescripts, titles and forms of address, and the meaning of foreign words and phrases, among others. G. V. Carey's *Mind the Stop* is the layman's bible on punctuation.

Judith Butcher's *Copy-Editing*, on the other hand, is highly professional and directed more towards publishers' editors than to the layman; it too merits a place on the writer's bookshelf, however, since it gives many valuable hints for the final preparation of typescripts for the printer. The *MHRA Style Book* is a standard work. Finally, the relevant British Standards are listed at the end of this chapter.

Prelims

These are the preliminary pages at the beginning of a book, known in the printing and publishing trade as 'prelims'. Normally they will consist of a title page, dedication, list of contents, list of illustrations, acknowledgments, abbreviations, preface or foreword. Not all of these will be required for every kind of book, and the publisher will have some say in the matter. It is up to the author to indicate, at this stage, what he intends to provide – i.e. if he wishes to include an 'Author's Note' or not. It will not matter if he cannot write the text of these as yet – it is quite sufficient to put a blank sheet in the typescript at the appropriate place or places, stating, for example, 'Acknowledgments' and below this, 'copy to follow'. The important thing is for the production manager and book designer to know that they are coming, so that they can allow for them in their calculations.

Notes and References

Consistency is the keyword here. If the book has been commissioned, the publisher may have sent the author a copy of the 'house style', or at least have stated a preference for the numbering and style of notes and references, such as whether they should appear at the foot of each page, after each chapter, or in a separate section at the end of the book. Failing such instruction, or if you do not yet have a publisher, it is advisable to study some published titles in a similar category of book and follow the same system.

Bibliography

Depending on whether the work is aimed at the popular or academic market, the bibliography may be selective or as comprehensive as you can make it. If the latter, it is usual to divide the entries into 'primary' and 'secondary' (or 'printed' and 'manuscript') sources, and to include not only books, but articles in periodicals and learned journals, as well as references to private papers consulted. Provided careful notes have been kept of all material used in the course of research, as suggested earlier in this handbook, the compilation of a bibliography should be quite straightforward. The normal arrangement of books and articles is in an alphabetical sequence, under the surname of the author. Care should be taken to list the particular editions used and to indicate any subsequent revised editions or reprints of each work, where possible.

The British Standard *BS 1629, Recommendations for references to published materials*, details an internationally accepted set of rules for the guidance of those compiling bibliographies in books.

Preparation of the Typescript

The cardinal rules for typing material for publication stipulate that the text should be typed on one side of the paper only, in double spacing, with good margins (at least 1½ inches (4 cm) on the left-hand side). Nowadays A4 size paper is preferable to the old quarto or foolscap, and it is helpful to the publisher if approximately the same number of lines are typed per page. Headings should be consistent throughout, and quoted matter of more than a few lines should be indented, without the use of quotation marks. Indent five spaces at the beginning of each paragraph, unless the publisher's house style asks for anything different. Start each chapter on a new page.

You do not need to be over-meticulous about the appearance of the typescript. There are bound to be a few additions, deletions or corrections when you come to re-read the text, and so long as these are absolutely legible and their place of insertion or deletion clear to the printer, it is unnecessary to go to the trouble of re-typing each amended page. Be very careful, however, about numbering pages: an insertion between pages 14 and 15, for example, would be numbered 14a, 14b and so on; but if page 15 is to be deleted altogether, the previous page should be numbered 14/15. Where an insertion does not take up the full page, always rule a line obliquely from left to right through the remaining part of the page to indicate that the text is continuous. It is far better to use white correcting fluid and to type the correction in than to risk an erasure and handwritten alteration that may be ambiguous to the typesetter. (A few publishers producing small runs of specialized books require what is known as 'camera-ready' copy, typed on electronic machines with carbon ribbon, variable spacing and justified lines, which is then photographed and reproduced lithographically; here, each page must of course be perfect, although pure spelling mistakes and punctuation may be corrected – very carefully – with the aid of correction fluid.)

It is wise to make three copies of the final text, a top copy and two carbons; the publisher may ask for two, and the author should always retain one copy. If additional copies should be required later on, i.e. for an American or paperback publisher, photocopies can be made.

There are on the market special packs of carbonless typing paper that produce one top and one copy without the need for a carbon; the quality of the copy is consistent and good (essential for photocopying purposes), but the cost so high at present that they are to be recommended only for short typescripts such as poems, articles or short stories. On the other hand, good film carbon is expensive too, and the sheets should be renewed every ten or fifteen pages when typing a full-length book so as to achieve some uniformity. (The discarded carbons can be used again for less important copies, such as correspondence.)

Writers who are in the habit of leaving the final typing to the very last moment before their delivery deadline may find it useful to prepare in advance sets of paper (bond + bank paper interleaved with carbons to the number required); this can be done at any odd moment, while listening to the radio, for instance, or when suffering from 'writer's block'. The saving of time is remarkable.

Never staple pages together. Short stories or features may be fastened with paper clips, and so may individual chapters of a book; but a full-length typescript is best put into a ring binder or packed loose into a box. (Use the boxes in which reams of bond typing paper are sold.)

Proof-correction

One of the last pre-publication chores facing the book author will be the correction of proofs, sometimes in both galley and page but, depending upon the type of book, often only in page. This will give him the opportunity to amend dates or statistics, to correct wrong spellings and any grave errors, but he must bear in mind that corrections exceeding a certain percentage (usually 10%) of the original cost of setting are payable by the author; even the insertion of a few commas can be quite costly. Printer's errors are not charged.

Sometimes, where a work of topical interest is involved and some major event has taken place between the date of completion of the manuscript and delivery of proofs, the publisher will find the space to include a brief note to the effect that 'Since this book went to press [such and such] has occurred', but it cannot always be counted on.

A list of signs used in proof correction will be found in the *Writers' & Artists' Yearbook* and in the British Standard *BS 5261, Part II, Specification for typographical requirements, marks for copy preparation and proof correction, proofing procedure*. Other valuable guides for spelling, punctuation, division of words, and the use of capital and lower case, are *Hart's Rules for Compositors and Readers* and the *Oxford Writers' Dictionary*.

The Index

Every non-fiction book merits a good index, and reviewers these days are not only paying more attention than ever before to the quality of indexing but are commenting unfavourably, where appropriate, on the lack of indexes.

Most authors' contracts stipulate that the author shall provide the index. It is however sometimes possible – and when, if ever, most publishers have accepted the proposed Minimum Terms Agreement negotiated by the Society of Authors and the Writers' Guild it may hopefully become the norm – to get the publisher to agree to contribute 50% of the cost, especially if a professional indexer is to be employed. Some publishers have their own team of freelance indexers on whom they can call; others seek recommendations from the Society of Indexers, which was founded in 1957 to safeguard and improve indexing standards and which maintains a register of indexers suitably qualified in different subjects and types of indexing. To assist those seeking an indexer for their work, the Society now issues annually a booklet entitled *Indexers Available*, which is distributed throughout the book trade; it lists practising members' names, addresses, telephone numbers and their specialist subjects. At the time of writing (1991) the Society's recommended minimum rate for indexing is £9 per hour for basic skills; specialist work commands more. Rates are normally increased annually.

There has long been controversy as to whether writers should or should not index their own books. Some people feel that an author is the ideal person, but others hold very strongly to the view that he may be too close to his own work to be able to produce a truly objective index. Certainly, as a general rule, it will almost always take him far longer than the expert. It is not generally realised that there is a great deal more to indexing than extracting the names of people and places and stringing them together in alphabetical order, so that when an author does decide to attempt it, he would be well advised to take the time and trouble to learn the basic rules.

Firstly, he must choose – and stick to – the form of alphabetical arrangement most suited to his book: either 'letter-by-letter' or 'word-by-word'. Then – and this is governed largely by space – he should give some thought to the layout and balance of the index and whether the sub-headings and sub-sub-headings (if any) will be indented or run on; both in layout and wording the sub-headings throughout must be consistent. There must be adequate cross-referencing of names and concepts, but not so much as to make the index unnecessarily long; care must be taken to avoid what is known as a 'wild goose chase', i.e. cross-references that never lead to the location of the subject-matter in the text, as in, for example, 'Indexers, Society of, *see* Society of Indexers' and 'Society of Indexers, *see* Indexers, Society of'. The main function of an index is to direct the user quickly to the place or places in the text where he will find precisely the information he seeks.

Indexing is normally undertaken at page proof stage and, for this reason, it nearly always has to be done at speed in order to meet the printers' deadline. Here the computer has really come into its own, and now that there is sophisticated software available that has been specially designed to meet the professional indexer's needs, two of the most time-consuming stages of the job – the sorting of entries into the required order, and the printing out of the edited index copy – can be accomplished very quickly. Although a growing number of indexers now use computers, much manual indexing still goes on, the usual method being to mark on the page proofs (either with highlighter pen or by underlining) each name or concept to be indexed, and to write these on separate cards or slips which are filed alphabetically in a box as work proceeds; a certain amount of tightening up and editing of entries has to take place when all entries are assembled. In the course of his work the indexer may come across inconsistencies or inaccuracies that both the author and the publisher's editor have missed; these should be telephoned through to the editorial office immediately. A few printers will accept index copy on cards or slips, but it is preferable to type the index (double-spaced, allowing thirty-two characters per line) and to keep a carbon copy. The publisher will usually say that his tight production deadline does not permit him to send the indexer a proof for correction, but this should be insisted on wherever possible. Even the best printer can make a nonsense out of an index by failing to indent a sub-heading or by omitting or misprinting the occasional page reference – something that may not be spotted if the index is checked in the editorial office – and an index that is inaccurate is worse than no index at all.

These are but a few of the problems that confront the indexer. Authors interested in acquiring some basic training in indexing may take the Training in Indexing correspondence course tutored by the Society of Indexers, which leads to accreditation as a 'registered indexer'; the various units of this course may be purchased separately. Probably the most comprehensive and up-to-date manual, recently published in the United States but distributed in the UK, is Hans Wellisch's *Indexing A to Z*. Among older works, M. D. Anderson's booklet *Book Indexing* is still an excellent short introduction, and other recommended titles are R. L. Collison's *Indexes and Indexing* and Norman Knight's *Indexing, The Art of*. The two *British Standards*, *BS 1749* and *BS 3700* (details at the end of this chapter) are the authoritative guides to current practice.

Names of suitably qualified indexers (general or specialist) may be obtained from the Registrar of the Society of Indexers, Mrs E. Wallis, 25 Leyborne Park, Kew Gardens, Surrey TW9 3HB (tel. 081–940 4771). For details of the correspondence course, a copy of *Indexers Available*, or other information about the Society, write to the Hon. Secretary, Mrs H. C. Troughton, 16 Green Road, Birchington, Kent CT7 9JZ, or telephone (answerphone) 071–916 7809.

A Last Word of Advice

Once the proofs have been corrected and returned to the publisher, the author may safely return all borrowed books and documents to their respective libraries and/or owners. He may also wish to parcel up and store his original notes and early drafts. *It is important not to throw these away*. When eventually his book is published, there is always the possibility that it may arouse unexpected interest and may even lead to other related commissions; almost certainly he will receive a number of readers' letters either asking him to justify certain statements or to give further information. Some of these enquiries may come from researchers working in the same field. Bearing in mind the enormous help he himself has derived from the work of others, would it not be churlish and ungenerous to refuse or not to be in a position to pass on the fruits of his own research – especially any information gathered but not used – to other *bona fide* writers?

It should not be forgotten that all writers feed to a lesser or greater extent on the work of other writers. As the Californian playwright Wilson Mizner put it, 'When you steal from one author, it's plagiarism; if you steal from many, it's research'.

Book Indexing, by M. D. Anderson, *Cambridge Authors' & Printers' Guides* series, Cambridge University Press, Cambridge, 1971; rev. ed., 1985

British Standards (available from the British Standards Institution, Sales Department, Linford Wood, Milton Keynes MK14 6LE):

BS 1629: 1989	*Recommendations for references to published materials*
BS 3700: 1988	*Recommendations for preparing indexes to books, periodicals and other documents*
BS 5261 Part I: 1975	*Recommendations for preparation of typescript copy for printing*
BS 5261 Part II: 1976	*Specifications for typographical requirements, marks for copy preparation and proof correction, proofing procedure*
BS 5261 C: 1976	*Marks for copy preparation and proof correction* (extract from *BS 5261 Part II*)

Copy-Editing, by Judith Butcher, 3rd ed., Cambridge University Press, Cambridge, 1992

Hart's Rules for Compositors and Readers at the University Press Oxford, 39th ed., Oxford University Press, Oxford, 1983

Indexers Available, annual list of freelance registered indexers, Society of Indexers (order from Hon. Secretary, Mrs H. C. Troughton, 16 Green Road, Birchington, Kent CT7 9JZ.)

Indexes and Indexing, by R. L. Collison, 4th rev. ed., Benn, London, 1972

Indexing, The Art of, by G. Norman Knight, Allen & Unwin, London, 1979; out of print, new ed. in preparation

Indexing A to Z, by Hans Wellisch, H. W. Wilson, New York, 1991 (distributed in UK by Thompson Henry Ltd., London Road, Sunningdale, Berks SL5 OEP)

Making Electronic Manuscripts: A Word Processing Guide for Writers, by Michael Barnard, Blueprint Publishing, Chapman & Hall, London, 1989

MHRA Style Book, ed. A.S. Maney and R.L. Smallwood, Modern Humanities Research Association, London, 1981

Mind the Stop: A Brief Guide to Punctuation, by G.V. Carey, Penguin, Harmondsworth, 1971

Oxford Writers' Dictionary, Oxford University Press, Oxford, 1990

Typescripts, Proofs and Indexes, by Judith Butcher, *Cambridge Authors' & Printers' Guides* series, Cambridge University Press, Cambridge, 1980

The Typist's A to Z, by Edith Mackay, Pitman, London, 1988

APPENDIX I

Selective List of Major Sources in the United Kingdom

This list is limited by space and should be used as a guideline only, in conjunction with the *Aslib Directory*, the HMSO booklet *Record Repositories in Great Britain* and other reference source guides mentioned in various sections of this handbook. Unless otherwise stated, the libraries and record offices are open to the public without formality. Addresses, telephone numbers and hours of opening are subject to change with alarming frequency (all London numbers will acquire an additional digit by 1994), and while every effort has been made to bring information up to date at the time of going to press, intending visitors are advised to check in advance before travelling any distance.

The Copyright Libraries

British Library, Reference Division, Department of Printed Books, Great Russell Street, London WC1B 3DG (tel: Reader Admissions Office, 071–323 7677/8; Main Reading Room, 071–323 7676; North Library, 071–323 7665; North Library Gallery, 071–323 7767). Admission by reader's ticket (special pass required for access to Department of Manuscripts Students' Room). Mon., Fri., Sat., 9–5; Tues., Wed., Thurs., 9–9. Most services are closed for one week at the end of October/beginning of November.

Note: The British Library is in the process of moving to its new building at St Pancras, North London. During the transition period, up to 1996, intending users should telephone for information in advance of their visit. The main switchboard number, for general enquiries concerning the British Library as a whole, is 071–636 1544. There are two special 'St Pancras Helpline' numbers: for the humanities, 071–323 7766; for the sciences, 071–323 7915. The address of the new British Library is 96 Euston Road, St Pancras, London NW1 2DB.

Bodleian Library, University of Oxford, Broad Street, Oxford OX1 3BG (tel. 0865 277000). Admission by reader's ticket (fee payable). Mon.–Fri., 9–10 (term), 9–7 (vacation); Sat., 9–1; closed last week in August.

Cambridge University Library, West Road, Cambridge CB3 9DR (tel. 0223 333000). Admission by reader's ticket. Mon.–Fri., 9–7; Sat., 9–1; closed for one week in September.

National Library of Scotland, George IV Bridge, Edinburgh EH1 1EW (tel. 031 226 4531). Admission by reader's ticket. Mon.–Fri., 9.30–8.30; Sat., 9.30–1.

National Library of Wales, Aberystwyth, Dyfed SY23 3BU (tel. 0970 623816). Admission by reader's ticket. Mon.–Fri., 9.30–6; Sat., 9.30–5.

N.B. Trinity College Library, College Street, Dublin 2, in the Republic of Ireland (tel. 0001 772941) is also a copyright library.

Public Record Offices

Public Record Office, Ruskin Avenue, Kew, Richmond, Surrey TW9 4DU (tel. 081–876 3444) and Chancery Lane, London WC2A 1LR (same tel. no.). Admission by reader's ticket. Mon.–Fri., 9.30–5; closed for two weeks in October.

Scottish Record Office, H.M. General Register House, Edinburgh EH1 3YY (tel. 031 556 6585). Admission by reader's ticket. Mon.–Fri., 9–4.45.

Public Record Office of Northern Ireland, 66 Balmoral Avenue, Belfast BT9 6NY (tel. 0232 661621/663286). Admission by reader's ticket. Mon.–Fri., 9.15–4.45; closed first two weeks in December.

General Register Offices

General Register Office (The Office of Population Censuses and Surveys): indexes to registers of births, marriages and deaths at St Catherine's House, 10 Kingsway, London WC2B 6JP (tel. 071–242 0262). Mon.–Fri., 8.30–4.30.

N.B. Census returns open for public inspection are in the basement of the Public Record Office, Chancery Lane, London WC2A 1LR. Admission without ticket.

Principal Registry of the Family Division, Somerset House, Strand, London WC2R 1LP (tel. 071–936 6960). Mon.–Fri., 10–4.30.

General Register Office for Scotland, New Register House, Edinburgh EH1 3YT (tel. 031 334 0380). Mon.–Thurs., 9.30–4.30; Fri., 9.30–4.

General Register Office for Northern Ireland, Oxford House, 49–55 Chichester Street, Belfast BT1 4HL (tel. 0232 235211). Mon.–Fri., 9.30–3.30.

N.B. The records for the whole of Ireland from 1864 to 1921 are at the office of the Registrar General, Joyce House, 8–11 Lombard Street East, Dublin 2, which houses the records of the Republic only since 1922.

Manuscript Collections/Registers of Archives

British Library Reference Division, Department of Manuscripts, Great Russell Street, London WC1B 3DG (tel. 071–323 7513) Admission to Students' Room by reader's ticket (applications at least 2 days in advance).* Mon.–Sat., 10–4.45; closed first week in November.

British Library Oriental and India Office Collections (formerly the India Office Library), Orbit House, 197 Blackfriars Road, London SE1 8NG (tel. 071–412 7873). Admission by reader's ticket. Mon.–Fri., 9.30–5.45, Sat., 9.30–1.

N.B. The above-mentioned collections will move to the new British Library at St Pancras by 1996. During the transition period readers should telephone either the main British Library switchboard, 071–636 1544, or the St Pancras 'Helpline' number for the humanities, 071–323 7766, in advance of their visit, for up-to-date information.

Royal Commission on Historical Manuscripts/National Register of Archives, Quality House, Quality Court, Chancery Lane, London WC2A 1HP (tel. 071–242 1198). Mon.–Fri., 9.30–5.

National Register of Archives (Scotland), West Register House, Charlotte Square, Edinburgh EH2 4DF (tel. 031 556 6585). Mon.–Fri., 9–4.45.

Large collections of manuscripts are also housed at the Public Record Offices (see page 168) and at the various County Record Offices and University Libraries (see pages 170–79).

* The normal reader's ticket for the British Library does not admit to the Department of Manuscripts Students' Room. A higher level pass will also be required for access to the manuscript collections at St Pancras.

County Record Offices/Regional Archives Centres

In this list opening times are not given for the individual offices: some are open all day throughout the working week, others close for lunch (or do not produce material during the lunch period), some are open late one evening in the week (but material must be ordered beforehand), others are shut either on Mondays or Saturdays. It is advisable to check prior to making a visit, as these opening hours are subject to change, and to reserve a seat.

Avon

Bath City Record Office, Guildhall, Bath BA1 5AW (tel. 0225 461111, ext. 2420/1)

Bristol Record Office, The Council House, College Green, Bristol BS1 5TR (tel. 0272 222377).

Bedfordshire

Bedfordshire Record Office, County Hall, Bedford MK42 9AP (tel. 0234 228833)

Berkshire

Berkshire Record Office, Shire Hall, Shinfield Park, Reading RG2 9XD (tel. 0734 233182)

Buckinghamshire

Buckinghamshire Record Office, County Hall, Aylesbury HP20 1UA (tel. 0296 382587)

Cambridgeshire

Cambridge County Record Office, Shire Hall, Castle Hill, Cambridge CB3 0AP (tel. 0223 317281); also at Grammar School Walk, Huntingdon PE18 6LF (tel. 0480 425842)

Cheshire

Cheshire Record Office, Duke Street, Chester CH1 1RL (tel. 0244 602559)

Chester City Record Office, Town Hall, Chester CH1 2HJ (tel. 0244 324324, ext. 2108)

Cleveland

Cleveland County Archives Department, Exchange House, 6 Marton Road, Middlesbrough TS1 1DB (tel. 0642 248321)

Cornwall

Cornwall County Record Office, County Hall, Truro TR1 3AY (tel. 0872 73698)
Royal Institution of Cornwall, County Museum, River Street, Truro TR1 2SJ (tel. 0872 72205)

Cumbria

Cumbria County Record Office, The Castle, Carlisle CA3 8UR (tel. 0228 23456, ext. 2416); also at County Offices, Kendal LA9 4RQ (tel. 0539 721000, ext. 4329) and at Duke Street, Barrow-in-Furness LA14 1XW (tel. 0229 831269)

Derbyshire

Derbyshire Record Office, New Street, Matlock DE4 3AG (tel. 0629 580000, ext. 7347)

Devon

Devon Record Office, Castle Street, Exeter EX4 3PQ (tel. 0392 384753)
West Devon Record Office, Clare Place, Coxside, Plymouth PL4 0JW (tel. 0752 385940)

Dorset

Dorset Record Office, Bridport Road, Dorchester DT1 1RP (tel. 0305 250550)

Durham

Durham County Record Office, County Hall, Durham DH1 5UL (tel. 091–386 4411, ext. 2575)

Essex

Essex Record Office, P.O. Box 11, County Hall, Chelmsford CM1 1LX (tel. 0245 492211); and Central Library, Victoria Avenue,

Southend-on-Sea SS2 6EX (tel. 0702 612621); Colchester and NE Essex Branch, Stanwell House, Stanwell Street, Colchester CO2 7DL (tel. 0206 572099)

Gloucestershire

Gloucestershire Record Office, Clarence Row, Alvin Street, Gloucester GL1 3DW (tel. 0452 425295)

Hampshire

Hampshire Record Office, 20 Southgate Street, Winchester SO23 9EF (tel. 0962 846142)

Portsmouth City Records Office, 3 Museum Road, Portsmouth PO1 2LE (tel. 0705 829765)

Southampton City Records Office, Civic Centre, Southampton SO9 4XL (tel. 0703 832251)

Hereford and Worcester

Hereford and Worcester Record Office, County Hall, Spetchley Road, Worcester WR5 2NP (tel. 0905 763763, ext. 6350)

Hereford Record Office, The Old Barracks, Harold Street, Hereford HR1 2QX (tel. 0432 265441)

St Helen's Record Office, Fish Street, Worcester WR1 2HN (tel. 0905 763763, ext. 5922)

Hertfordshire

Hertfordshire Record Office, County Hall, Hertford SG13 8DE (tel. 0992 555105)

Humberside

Humberside County Record Office, County Hall, Beverley, North Humberside HU17 9BA (tel. 0482 885005)

South Humberside Area Record Office, Central Library, Town Hall Square, Grimsby DN31 1HX (tel. 0472 353481)

Kingston upon Hull City Record Office, 79 Lowgate, Kingston upon Hull HU1 2AA (tel. 0482 222015/6)

Kent

Centre for Kentish Studies, County Hall, Maidstone ME14 1XQ (tel. 0622 694363) and at (SE Kent branch) Folkestone

Central Library, Grace Hill, Folkestone CT20 1HD (tel. 0303 850123)

Lancashire

Lancashire Record Office, Bow Lane, Preston PR1 2RE (tel. 0772 54868, ext. 3039)

Leicestershire

Leicestershire Record Office, 57 New Walk, Leicester LE1 7JB (tel. 0533 544566)

Lincolnshire

Lincolnshire Archives Office, The Castle, Lincoln LN1 3AB (tel. 0522 525158)

London

Greater London Record Office, 40 Northampton Road, London EC1R 0HB (tel. 071–606 3030, ext. 3820). Tues.–Fri., 9.30–4.45, late night Tues. to 7.30. Closed third and fourth weeks of October.

Manchester

Greater Manchester Record Office, 56 Marshall Street, New Cross, Ancoats, Manchester M4 5FU (tel. 061–832 5284)

Merseyside

Merseyside Record Office, Cunard Building (4th floor), Pier Head, Liverpool L3 1EG (tel. 051–236 8038)
Liverpool Record Office, City Libraries, William Brown Street, Liverpool L3 8EW (tel. 051–225 5417)
Wirral Archives Service, Birkenhead Reference Library, Borough Road, Birkenhead L41 2XB (tel. 051–652 5106/7/8)

Midlands

Birmingham Reference Library, Central Library, Chamberlain Square, Birmingham B3 3HQ (tel. 021–235 4217)
Coventry City Record Office, Mandela House, Bayley Lane, Coventry CV1 5RG (tel. 0203 832418)

Warwick University Modern Records Centre, The University Library, Coventry CV4 7AL (tel. 0203 24011, ext. 2014)

Norfolk

Norfolk Record Office, Central Library, Norwich NR2 1NJ (tel. 0603 761349)

Northamptonshire

Northamptonshire Record Office, Wootton Hall Park, Northampton NN4 9BQ (tel. 0604 762129)

Northumberland

Northumberland Record Office, Melton Park, North Gosforth, Newcastle-upon-Tyne NE3 5QX (tel. 091–236 2680)

Nottinghamshire

Nottinghamshire Archives Office, County House, High Pavement, Nottingham NG1 1HR (tel. 0602 504524)

Oxfordshire

Oxfordshire Archives, County Hall, New Road, Oxford OX1 1ND (tel. 0865 815203)

Shropshire

Shropshire Records and Research Unit, The Shirehall, Abbey Foregate, Shrewsbury SY2 6ND (tel. 0743 252852)

Somerset

Somerset Record Office, Obridge Road, Taunton TA2 7PU (tel. 0823 278805)

Staffordshire

Staffordshire Record Office, County Buildings, Eastgate Street, Stafford ST16 2LZ (tel. 0785 223121, ext. 8380)
Lichfield Joint Record Office, Lichfield Library, The Friary, Lichfield WS13 6QG (tel. 05432 256787)

Suffolk

Suffolk Record Office, Gateacre Road, Ipswich IP1 2LQ (tel. 0243 264541)

Suffolk Record Office, Bury St Edmunds Branch, Raingate Street, Bury St Edmunds IP33 1RX (tel. 0284 722522)

Surrey

Surrey Record Office, County Hall, Penrhyn Road, Kingston-upon-Thames, KT1 2DN (tel. 081–541 9065); Guildford Muniment Room, Castle Arch, Guildford GU1 3SX (tel. 0483 573942)

East Sussex

East Sussex Record Office, The Maltings, Castle Precincts, Lewes BN7 1YT (tel. 0273 482349)

West Sussex

West Sussex Record Office, Sherburne House, 3 Orchard Street, Chichester PO19 1RN (tel. 0243 533911)

Tyne and Wear

Tyne and Wear Archives Department, Blandford House, West Blandford Street, Newcastle-upon-Tyne NE1 4JA (tel. 091–232 6789); Local Studies Collection, Gateshead Central Library, Prince Consort Road, Gateshead NE8 4LN (tel. 091–447 3478)

Warwickshire

Warwick County Record Office, Priory Park, Cape Road, Warwick CV34 4JS (tel. 0926 412735)

Isle of Wight

Isle of Wight County Record Office, 26 Hillside, Newport PO30 2EB (tel. 0983 823821, ext. 3820/1)

Wiltshire

Wiltshire Record Office, County Hall, Trowbridge BA14 8JG (tel. 0225 753641)

North Yorkshire

North Yorkshire County Record Office, Malpas Road, Northallerton DL7 8TB (tel. 0609 777585)

York City Archives, Art Gallery Building, Exhibition Square, York
    YO1 2EW (tel. 0904 651533)

South Yorkshire

Barnsley Archive Service, Central Library, Shambles Street,
    Barnsley S70 2JF (tel. 0226 733241)
Doncaster Archives Department, King Edward Road, Balby,
    Doncaster DN4 0NA (tel. 0302 859811)
Sheffield Archives, 52 Shoreham Street, Sheffield S1 4SP (tel. 0742
    734756)

West Yorkshire

West Yorkshire Archive Service, Wakefield Headquarters, Registry
    of Deeds, Newstead Road, Wakefield WF1 2DE (tel. 0924
    295982)

Scotland

Argyll and Bute District Archives, Kilmory, Lochgilphead, Argyll
    PA31 8RT (tel. 0546 2127, ext. 4120)
Central Regional Council Archives Department, Unit 6, Burghmuir
    Industrial Estate, Stirling FK7 7PY (tel. 0786 50745)
Dumfries and Galloway Regional Council Library Service, Ewart
    Public Library, Catherine Street, Dumfries DG1 1JB (tel. 0387
    53820)
Dundee District Archive and Record Centre, 14 City Square,
    Dundee DD1 3BY (tel. 0382 23141, ext. 4494)
City of Edinburgh District Archives, City Chambers, High Street,
    Edinburgh EH1 1YJ (tel. 031–225 2424, ext. 5196)
Grampian Regional Archives, Old Aberdeen House, Dunbar Street,
    Aberdeen AB2 1UE (tel. 0224 481775)
Orkney Archives, Orkney Library, Laing Street, Kirkwall KW15
    1NW (tel. 0856 3166, ext. 5)
Shetland Archives, 44 King Harald Street, Lerwick ZE1 0EQ (tel.
    0595 3535, ext. 269)
Strathclyde Regional Archives, Mitchell Library, North Street,
    Glasgow G3 7DN (tel. 041–227 2405)

Wales

Clwyd Record Office, The Old Rectory, Hawarden, Deeside CH5
    3NR (tel. 0244 532364) and 46 Clwyd Street, Ruthin LL15 1HP
    (tel. 08242 3077)

Dyfed Archives Service, Carmarthenshire Area Record Office, County Hall, Carmarthen SA3 1JP (tel. 0267 233333, ext. 4182)

Glamorgan Record Office, County Hall, Cathays Park, Cardiff CF1 3NE (tel. 0222 780282)

Gwent County Record Office, County Hall, Cwmbran NP44 2XH (tel. 06333 832266)

Gwynedd Archives Service: Caernarfon Area Record Office, Victoria Dock, Caernarfon (tel. 0286 679095); Dolgellau Area Record Office, Cae Penarlag, Dolgellau LL40 2YB (tel. 0341 422341, ext. 261); Llangefni Area Record Office, Shire Hall, Llangefni LL77 7TW (tel. 0248 750262, ext. 269)

University Libraries (other than Oxford and Cambridge) with Important Manuscript Collections

Students, undergraduates and graduates of other universities are normally admitted without formality; temporary tickets will be issued to other *bona fide* researchers at the Librarian's discretion. At some libraries there are slightly amended opening hours during vacations. Please note that opening times and telephone extensions, where stated, are for the departments of manuscripts and archives. In all cases you should write in advance of your visit.

The main libraries of the University of Cambridge and the University of Oxford are listed under 'Copyright Libraries' (pages 167–68).

England

Birmingham University Library, Edgbaston, Birmingham B15 2TT (tel. 021–414 5838). Mon.–Fri., 9–5. Closed Christmas and Easter vacations.

Durham University Library, Palace Green, Durham DH1 3RN (tel. 091–374 3001). Mon.–Fri., 9–6; Sat., 9–12.30. Vacations, Mon.–Fri., 9–5

Durham University Department of Palaeography and Diplomatic, 5, The College and The Prior's Kitchen, The College, Durham DH1 3EQ (tel. 091–374 3610). Mon.–Fri., 10–1, 2–5; 5–8 during term by arrangement.

Exeter University Library, Stocker Road, Exeter EX4 4PT (tel. 0392 263870). Mon.–Fri., 9–5.30.

Hull University, Brynmor Jones Library, Cottingham Road, Hull HU6 7RX (tel. 0482 465265). Mon.–Fri., 9–1, 2–5.

Keele University Library, Keele ST5 5BG (tel. 0782 621111, ext. 3741. Mon.–Fri., 9.30–5.

Leeds University, Brotherton Library, Leeds LS2 9JT (tel. 0532 335518). Mon.–Fri., 9–1, 2.15–5.

Liverpool University, Sydney Jones Library, P.O. Box 123, Liverpool L69 3DA (tel. 051–794 2696). Mon.–Fri., 9–5.

University of London Library, Senate House, Malet Street, London WC1E 7HU (tel. 071–636 4514, ext. 5030). Mon.–Fri., 10–5. Also the Institute of Historical Research (tel. 071–636 0272).

John Rylands University Library of Manchester, Deansgate, Manchester M3 3EH (tel. 061–834 5343). Mon.–Fri., 10–5.30; Sat., 9.30–1.

Newcastle-upon-Tyne University, Robinson Library, Newcastle-upon-Tyne NE2 4HQ (tel. 091–222 7671). Mon.–Fri., 9.15–5.

Nottingham University Library, University Park, Nottingham NG7 2RD (tel. 0602 484848). Mon.–Fri., 9–5.

Reading University Library, Whiteknights, Reading RG6 2AE (tel. 0734 318776). Mon.–Fri., 9–1, 2–5.

Sheffield University Library, Western Bank, Sheffield S10 2TN (tel. 0742 768555, ext. 4334). Mon.–Thurs., 9–9.30, Fri., 9–5 (term); Mon.–Fri., 9–5 (vacation); Sat., 9–12.30.

Southampton University Library, Highfield, Southampton SO9 5NH (tel. 0703 593724). Mon.–Fri., 9–1, 2–5.

Sussex University Library, Falmer, Brighton BN1 9QL (tel. 0273 678157). Mon.–Thurs., 9–1, 2–5.

Warwick University Modern Records Centre, University Library, Coventry CV4 7AL (tel. 0203 524219). Mon.–Thurs., 9–1, 1.30–5; Fri., 9–1, 1.30–4.

York University, Borthwick Institute of Historical Research, St Anthony's Hall, Peasholme Green, York YO1 2PW (tel. 0904 642315). Mon.–Fri., 9.30–12.50, 2–4.50.

Scotland

Aberdeen University Library, Department of Special Collections and Archives, King's College, Aberdeen AB9 2UB (tel. 0224 272598). Mon.–Fri., 9.30–4.30.

Dundee University Library, Dundee, Tayside DD1 4HN (tel. 0382 23181, ext. 4095). Mon.–Wed., 9–5; Thurs. 9–1.30; Sat. a.m. by appointment (term only).

Edinburgh University Library, 30 George Square, Edinburgh EH8 9LJ (tel. 031–667 1011, ext. 6628). Mon.–Fri., 9–5.

Glasgow University Library, Department of Special Collections, Hillhead Street, Glasgow G12 8QE (tel. 041–339 8855, ext.

6767). Mon.–Fri., 9–9.30, Sat., 9–12.30 (term); Mon.–Fri., 9–5, Sat., 9–12.30 (vacation).
St Andrews University Library, North Street, St Andrews KY16 9TR (tel. 0334 76161, ext. 514). Mon.–Fri., 9–12, 2–5; Sat. 9–12 (term only).

Wales

University College of North Wales Library, Department of Manuscripts, Bangor LL57 2DG (tel. 0248 351151, ext. 2966). Mon.–Fri., 9–1, 2–5; Wed. to 9 (term only).

Cathedral Archives and Libraries

Canterbury City and Cathedral Archives, The Precincts, Canterbury, Kent CT1 2EH (tel. 0227 463510). By appointment, Mon.–Thurs., 9–4.30. Letter required to Archivist or Keeper of the Printed Books.
Durham Dean and Chapter Library, The College, Durham DH1 3EH (tel. 091–386 2489). Mon.–Fri., 9–1, 2.15–5. Closed in August.
Exeter Cathedral Library and Archives, Bishop's Palace, Exeter EH1 1HX (tel. 0392 72894). Mon.–Fri., 2–5.
Salisbury Cathedral Chapter Archives, 6 The Close, Salisbury SP1 2EF (tel. 0722 22519), by appointment (written application required)
York Minster Library, Dean's Park, York YO1 2JD (tel. 0904 625308), by appointment
Westminster Abbey Library and Muniment Room, Westminster Abbey, London SW1P 3PA (tel. 071–222 5152, ext. 228). Written application to Librarian or Keeper of the Muniments required.
Westminster Diocesan Archives (Roman Catholic), 16a Abingdon Road, London W8 6AF (tel. 071–938 3580), by appointment
Winchester Cathedral Library, The Close, Winchester SO23 9LS (tel. 0962 68580). Written application required, opening times vary.

Other Major Reference Libraries

Belfast: Irish and Local Studies Department, Central Library, Royal Avenue, Belfast BT1 1EA (tel. 0232 243233)

Birmingham Reference Library, Central Library, Chamberlain
Square, Birmingham B3 3HQ (tel. 021–235 4511)
Cardiff Arts and Social Studies Library, University College, Corbett
Road, P.O. Box 430, Cardiff CF1 3XT (tel. 0222 874000)
Edinburgh City Libraries, George IV Bridge, Edinburgh EH1 1EG
(tel. 031–225 5584)
Glasgow: Mitchell Library, North Street, Glasgow G3 7DN (tel.
041–221 7030)
Liverpool City Libraries, William Brown Street, Liverpool L3 8EW
(tel. 051–225 5429/30/31)
London: City of Westminster Central Reference Library, 35 St
Martin's Street, London WC2H 7HP (tel. 071–798 2034/2036)
Manchester: Central Library, St Peter's Square, Manchester M2
5PD (tel. 061–236 9422, ext. 204)

Private Subscription Libraries

Highgate Literary and Scientific Institution Library, 11 South
Grove, Highgate Village, London N6 6BS (tel. 081–340 3343).
Mon., Sat., 10–1; other weekdays 10–5. £26 per year (£40
family subscription).
London Library, 14 St James's Square, London SW1Y 4LG (tel.
071–930 7705). Mon.–Sat., 9.30–5.30; Thurs. to 7.30. £80 per
year.

Space does not permit the listing of the few other surviving private
subscription libraries in the provinces, but these will be well known
to readers living locally; or consult the yellow pages of the local
telephone directories. A descriptive leaflet is available from the
Secretary of the Association of Independent Libraries: Mrs Janet
Allan, Portico Library, 57 Mosley Street, Manchester M2 3HY.

Short List of Subjects and Sources

Advertising

Advertising Association Library, Abford House, 15 Wilton Road,
London SW1V 1NJ (tel. 071–828 2771). Mon.–Fri., 10–1, 2–5.
Open to public for reference, but only members may borrow
books.

Agriculture

Institute of Agricultural History and Museum of English Rural Life,
University of Reading, Whiteknights, Reading RG6 2AG (tel.

0734 875123, ext. 475). Mon.–Fri., 9.30–1, 2–5, by appointment.

Air Force

Royal Air Force Museum, Department of Aviation Records, Aerodrome Road, Hendon, London NW9 5LL (tel. 081–205 2266). Mon.-Fri., 10–4.30, by appointment only.
See also Ministry of Defence Library under '*Military*', and under '*World Wars I and II*'.

Architecture

British Architectural Library, Royal Institute of British Architects, 66 Portland Place, London W1N 4AD (tel. 071–580 5533). Mon., 10–5; Tues.–Thurs., 10–8; Fri., 10–7; Sat., 10–1.30. Closed in August.

Art

Art and Design Library (incorporating the Preston Blake Library) City of Westminster Central Reference Library, 2nd floor, 35 St Martin's Street, London WC2H 7HP (tel. 071–798 2038). Mon.–Fri., 10–7; Sat., 10–5.
British Museum, Department of Prints and Drawings, Great Russell Street, London WC1B 3DG (tel. 071–636 1544). Admission by ticket (apply in advance). Mon.–Fri., 10–1, 2.15–4; Sat., 10–12.30.
Courtauld Institute of Art Library, Somerset House, London WC2R 2LS (tel. 071–872 0220). Mon.–Fri., 10–7 (term); 10–6 (vacation). Closed in August.
National Portrait Gallery Archive and Library, The Mill, 72 Molesworth Street, Lewisham, London SE13 7EW (tel. 081–318 2888). Open to the public by appointment.
Victoria & Albert Museum Library, Cromwell Road, London SW7 2RL (tel. 071–589 6371). Mon.–Thurs., 10–1, 2–5; Sat., 10–1; closed on Fridays. N.B. A specially endorsed reader's ticket is required for access to certain MSS and reserved material in the National Art Library.

Banking and Commerce

Bank of England Reference Library, Threadneedle Street, London EC2R 8AH (tel. 071–601 4715). Telephone or written enquiries only. The Bank of England and other major banks will grant access to historical records only when applications are supported by a university or other centre of research.

City of Westminster Central Reference Library, 35 St Martin's Street, London WC2H 7HP (tel. 071–798 2034/3036). Computer search and information for business services available.

Births, Marriages and Deaths

See under 'General Register Offices' (pages 168–69) and '*Genealogy*'.

Broadcasting and Television

BBC Enterprises Data Enquiry Service, Room 7, 1 Portland Place, London W1A 1AA (tel. 071–927 5998). Written or telephone enquiries only. Fees on request.

BBC Written Archives Centre, Caversham Park, Reading RG4 8TZ (tel. 0734 472742, ext. 281/282). Tues.–Fri. 9.45–1, 2–5.15, by appointment only. Postal research queries undertaken by staff; fees on request.

National Sound Archive, 29 Exhibition Road, Kensington, London SW7 2AS (tel. 071–589 6603). Mon.–Fri., 10–5; Thurs. to 9. Listening service by appointment 3–4 days in advance. Northern listening service at British Library Document Supply Centre, Boston Spa, W. Yorks (tel. 0937 843434). Charged listening service at North Devon Library Services HQ, Barnstaple, Devon.

Visnews Television News Library, Cumberland Avenue, London NW10 7EH (tel. 081–965 7733). By appointment.

Recommended title: *Broadcasting in the U.K.: A Guide to Information Sources*, by Barrie MacDonald, Mansell, London, 1988

Business

British Library Business Information Service, Science Reference Library, 25 Southampton Buildings, Chancery Lane, London WC2A 1AW. (tel. for basic enquiries, 071–323 7454, for priced research service, 071–323 7457). Mon.–Fri., 10–5. Will be moving to the new British Library at St Pancras in 1993.

Business Archives Council, 185 Tower Bridge Road, London SE1 2UF (tel. 071–407 6110). Will assist in tracing records of commercial and industrial undertakings.

City Business Library, 106 Fenchurch Street, London EC3M 5JB (tel. 071–638 8215). Mon.–Fri., 9.30–5.30.

Companies House (Department of Trade and Industry), 55–71 City Road, London EC1Y 1BB (tel. 071–253 9393) and Companies Registration Office, Crown Way, Maindy, Cardiff CF4 3UZ (tel. 0222 388588). Mon.–Fri., 9.30–3.45. Microfilm copies of company records in London, files in Cardiff.

Census Returns

Public Record Office, basement, Chancery Lane, London WC2A 1LR (tel. 081–876 3444). Mon.–Fri., 9.30–5. Open to public without ticket.

Children's Books

Book Trust, Book House, 45 East Hill, London SW18 2QZ (tel. 081–870 9055). Children's Book Foundation Reference Library and information service, membership by subscription.

Costume

Costume and Fashion Research Centre, 4 Circus Road, Bath, Avon BA1 2EW (tel. 0225 461111, ext. 2752). Enquiries to Keeper of Costume.

European Economic Communities

European Commission Information Unit and Library, Jean Monnet House, 8 Storey's Gate, London SW1P 3AT (tel. 071–973 1992). Mon.–Fri., 10–1, 2–5.

Films and Cinema History

British Film Institute Library, 21 Stephen Street, London W1P 1PL (tel. 071–255 1444). Mon., Tues., Thurs., Fri., 10.30–5; Wed. 1.30–8. *Note*: An annual subscription to the BFI is currently £13.50, or £28.50 to include library membership. Library membership only is available at £25, or at £5 per day. There are a range of discounts to students, the unemployed and senior citizens.

Folklore

The Folklore Society, c/o University College, Gower Street, London WC1E 6BT (tel. 071–387 5894)

Genealogy and Heraldry

College of Arms, Queen Victoria Street, London EC4 4BT (tel. 071–248 2762). Mon.–Fri., 10–4; Sat. by appointment.
N.B. There are no public search rooms. Research is undertaken only by the Heralds and their staff, on a fee-paying basis (brief preliminary search is free).

Institute of Heraldic and Genealogical Studies Library, 79–82 Northgate, Canterbury, Kent CT1 1BA (tel. 0227 68664). Mon., Wed., Fri., 10–5, by appointment.

London Regional Genealogical Library of the Church of Jesus Christ of Latter-Day Saints (of Salt Lake City, Utah, USA), 64–68 Exhibition Road, London SW7 2PA (tel. 071–589 8561). Mon.–Fri., 9.30–9.30, Sat.; 9–1.

Religious Society of Friends, Friends House, Euston Road, London NW1 2BJ (tel. 071–387 3601). Tues.–Fri., 10–5; closed for one week before Spring Bank Holiday and one week at end of November. *Bona fide* researchers providing suitable introductions/letters of recommendation may use the Library on payment of a search fee, or searches will be carried out by staff at a fee.

Society of Genealogists Library, 14 Charterhouse Buildings, Goswell Road, London EC1M 7BA (tel. 071–251 8799). Tues., Fri., Sat., 10–6; Wed., Thurs., 10–8; closed on Mondays. Non-members pay search fees (currently £2.50 for one hour; £6.00 for half day ($3\frac{1}{2}$ hours); £8.00 for full day). Closed for one week in February and one week in October.

Geography and Maps

British Library Reference Division, Department of Printed Books, Map Library, British Museum (King Edward Building), London WC1B 3DG (tel. 071–323 7700/7703). Mon.–Sat., 10–4.30 or from 9.30 with reader's pass; closed for the week following the last complete week in October. Moving to St Pancras in 1996.

Royal Geographical Society, Kensington Gore, London SW7 2AR (tel. 071–589 5466). Mon.–Fri., 10–5. Library open to *bona fide* researchers by arrangement; map room open to general public.

Government and Official Information

British Library Reference Division, Department of Printed Books, Official Publications and Social Sciences Library, Great Russell Street, London WC1B 3DG (tel. 071–323 7536). Admission by reader's ticket. Mon., Fri., Sat., 9.30–4.45, closed for the week following the last complete week in October. Moving to St Pancras in 1993.

Central Office of Information, Hercules Road, Westminster Bridge Road, London SE1 7DU (tel. 071–928 2345). Telephone or written enquiries only.

Foreign & Commonwealth Library (tel. 071–271 3000). Is moving during 1992 to main FCO building in Whitehall, where restricted space will mean it will be open to *bona fide* researchers only, by appointment.

Oriental and India Office Collections (formerly India Office Library), Orbit House, 197 Blackfriars Road, London SE1 8NG (tel. 071–412 7873). Mon.–Fri., 9.30–5.45; Sat., 9.30–1. Moving to St Pancras in 1996.

Public Record Office, Ruskin Avenue, Kew, Richmond, Surrey TW9 4DU (tel. 081–876 3444) and Chancery Lane, London WC2A 1LR (same tel. no.). Admission by reader's ticket. Mon.– Fri., 9.30–5; closed first two weeks in October.

See also under '*Parliament*'.

International Affairs

Royal Institute of International Affairs Library, Chatham House, 10 St James's Square, London SW1Y 4LE (tel. 071–957 5700). Open to non-members by arrangement with the librarian. *Note*: The press cuttings collection for period 1940–71 has been transferred to British Newspaper Library, Colindale (indexes at Chatham House).

Law

Use of the law libraries in London is limited to members of the legal profession, but *bona fide* researchers may be able to obtain information by telephone or written enquiry. For other law libraries, see the *Aslib Directory*.

Inner Temple Library, Inner Temple, London EC4Y 7DA (tel. 071–353 2959/8761)

Institute of Advanced Legal Studies, University of London, 17 Russell Square, London WC1B 5DR (tel. 071–637 1731)

The Law Society, 113 Chancery Lane, London WC2A 1NB (tel. 071–242 1222). (Holds records of solicitors from 1907, also LEXIS index to newspaper law reports.)

Lincoln's Inn Library, Lincoln's Inn, London WC2A 3TN (tel. 071–242 4371)

Middle Temple Library, Middle Temple Lane, London EC4Y 9BT (tel. 071–353 4303)

Royal Courts of Justice Library, Strand, London WC2A 2LL (tel. 071–936 6000)

London

Corporation of London Records Office, P.O. Box 270, Guildhall, London EC2P 2EJ (tel. 071–260 1251 or 071–606 3030, ext. 1251). Mon.–Fri., 9.30–4.45.

Greater London Record Office and History Library, 40 Northampton Road, London EC1R 0HB (tel. 071–606 3030, ext. 3820). Tues.–Fri., 9.30–4.45; Tues. to 7.30 by appointment. Closed last two weeks in October.

Guildhall Library, Aldermanbury, London EC2P 2EJ (tel. 071–260 1862/3). Mon.–Sat., 9.30–4.45.

Westminster City Archives, Victoria Library, 160 Buckingham Palace Road, London SW1W 9UD (tel. 071–798 2180). Mon.–Fri., 9.30–7; Sat., 9.30–1, 2–5.

N.B. A number of London borough public libraries hold sizeable local history collections. Consult current edition of *Record Repositories in Great Britain*, HMSO, London.

Medicine

Marylebone Public Library Medical Library (Westminster City Libraries), Marylebone Road, London NW1 5PS (tel. 071–798 1037). Mon.–Fri., 9.30–7; Sat., 9.30–5. Reference and lending facilities (tickets from other public libraries may be used).

Royal College of Physicians of London Library, 11 St Andrew's Place, London NW1 4LE (tel. 071–935 1174). Mon.–Fri., 10–5. *Bona fide* researchers not members of the profession may use the reference facilities only.

Royal College of Surgeons of England Library, 35–43 Lincoln's Inn Fields, London WC2A 3PN (tel. 071–405 3474). Admission by introduction from a graduate of the College. Mon.–Fri., 10–6. Closed in August.

Wellcome Institute for the History of Medicine Library, The Wellcome Building, 200 Euston Road, London NW1 2BQ (tel. 071–383 4414). Mon.–Fri., 9.45–5.15; Tues.–Thurs. to 7.15.

For further information see the latest edition of *Directory of Medical and Health Care Libraries in the British Isles*, Library Association, London.

Military

Liddell Hart Centre for Military Archives, King's College, Strand, London WC2R 2LS (tel. 071–873 2187/2015). Mon.–Fri., 9.30–

5.30 (term); 9.30–4.30 (vacation), by written application. N.B. 20th-century records only.

Ministry of Defence Library, Service HQ, 3–5 Great Scotland Yard, London SW1A 2HW (tel. 071–218 4445). Telephone or written enquiries only.

National Army Museum, Department of Archives, Photographs, Film and Sound, Royal Hospital Road, London SW3 4HT (tel. 071–730 0717). Admission by reader's ticket. Tues.–Sat., 10–4.30. Now handles research enquiries for Society for Army Historical Research.

Public Record Office, Ruskin Avenue, Kew, Richmond, Surrey TW9 4DU (tel. 081–876 3444) and Chancery Lane, London WC2A 1LR (same tel. no.). Admission by reader's ticket. Mon.–Fri., 9.30–5; closed for two weeks in October.

See also under '*World Wars I and II*'.

Music

British Library Music Reading Area, Great Russell Street, London WC1B 3DG (tel. 071–636 1544, ext. 4207, or enquiries 071–323 7528). Mon.–Fri., 9.30–4.45; Sat., ask at Manuscripts Students' Room. Will be moving to St Pancras in 1993.

Royal College of Music Reference Library, Prince Consort Road, London SW7 2BS (tel. 071–589 3643). Admission by reader's ticket. Mon.–Fri., 10–5; closed late July to early September, also for two weeks at Christmas and at Easter.

Royal Opera House Archives, Covent Garden, London WC2E 7QA (tel. 071–240 1200, ext. 235). Mon.–Fri., 10–1, 2–6. *Bona fide* researchers, on written application.

Vaughan Williams Memorial Library, English Folk Dance and Song Society, Cecil Sharp House, 2 Regent's Park Road, London NW1 7AY (tel. 071–485 2206). By appointment.

Natural History

British Museum (Natural History) Library, Cromwell Road, London SW7 5BD (tel. 071–938 9191). Mon.–Fri., 10–4.30.

Royal Botanic Gardens Library and Archives, Kew, Richmond, Surrey, TW9 3AE (tel. 081–940 1171). Mon.–Thurs., 9–4.30; Fri., 9–5. Prior application to consult the archives is necessary.

Naval

National Maritime Museum Library, Romney Road, Greenwich, London SE10 9NF (tel. 081–858 4422, ext. 274). Tues.–Fri., 10–4 (Mondays open to reader's ticket holders only).

Research for Writers

Royal Naval Historical Library, at Ministry of Defence HQ Library, see under '*Military*' on page 187.

Newspapers and Periodicals

British Library Newspaper Library, Colindale Avenue, London NW9 5HE (tel. 071–323 7353). Admission by reader's ticket. Mon.–Sat., 10–4.45; closed for the week following the last complete week in October.

British Library Reference Division, Department of Printed Books, Great Russell Street, London WC1B 3DG, for periodicals (monthly or quarterly), to be seen in the main Reading Room (tel. 071–323 7676) or North Library Gallery (tel. 071–323 7767). Mon., Fri., Sat., 9–5; Tues., Wed., Thurs., 9–9; closed for the week following the last complete week in October. Will be moving to St Pancras 1993–6.

Parliament

House of Lords Record Office, House of Lords, Palace of Westminster, London SW1A 0AA (tel. 071–219 3074). Mon.–Fri., 9.30–5. Intending searchers should write to the Clerk of the Records in advance, giving at least one week's notice and details of the nature of their research and/or specific documents they wish to consult.

See also under '*Government and Official Information*'.

Politics (20th-century)

British Library of Political and Economic Science (London School of Economics), 10 Portugal Street, London WC2A 2HD (tel. 071–955 7223), by appointment.

Churchill Archives Centre, Churchill College, Cambridge CB3 0DS (tel. 0223 336087). Mon.–Fri., 9.30–12.30, 1.30–5, by appointment with the Archivist. N.B. Certain collections are subject to special conditions of access.

Printing and Publishing

St Bride Printing Library, Bride Lane, London EC4Y 8EQ (tel. 071–353 4660). Mon.–Fri., 9.30–5.30.

Recorded Sound

National Sound Archive, 29 Exhibition Road, Kensington, London SW7 2AS (tel. 071–589 6603). Mon.–Fri., 10–5, with late opening Thurs., to 9. Listening service by appointment 3–4 days in advance. Northern listening service at British Library Document Supply Centre, Boston Spa, W. Yorks (tel. 0937 843434). Charged listening service at North Devon Library Services HQ, Barnstaple, Devon.

Religion

Catholic Central Library, 47 Francis Street, London SW1P 1QR (tel. 071–834 6128). Non-members for reference and research only. Mon.–Fri., 10.30–6.30; Sat., 10.30–4.30.

Church House Record Centre, Dean's Yard, London SW1P 3NZ (tel. 071–222 9011). Mon.–Fri., 10–5, by appointment.

Dr Williams's Library, 14 Gordon Square, London WC1H 0AG (tel. 071–387 3727). Mon., Wed., Fri., 10–5; Tues., Thurs., 10–6.30; closed first half of August. Admission by recommendation; subscription rate for borrowers (details on application to Librarian).

Jewish Museum and Central Library, Woburn House, Upper Woburn Place, London WC1H 0EP (tel. 071–388 4525). Write to the Curator for information.

Lambeth Palace Library, London SE1 7JU (tel. 071–928 6222). *Bona fide* students, others by special permission. Mon.–Fri., 10–5. Closed for ten days at Christmas and at Easter.

Methodist Archives and Research Centre, formerly at Epworth House, London, are now housed at the John Rylands University Library of Manchester, Deansgate, Manchester M3 3EH (tel. 061–834 5343). Mon.–Fri., 10–5.30; Sat., 10–1.

Religious Society of Friends (Quakers) Library, Friends House, Euston Road, London NW1 2BJ (tel. 071–387 3601). Tues.–Fri., 10–5. Closed one week before Spring Bank Holiday and one week at end of November. Letter of introduction required for non-members.

Sion College, Victoria Embankment, London EC4Y 0DN (tel. 071–353 7983). Mon.–Fri., 10–5. Annual subscription rates and temporary membership available.

See also under 'Cathedral Archives and Libraries'.

Recommended title: *Keyguide to Information Sources on World Religions*, compiled by Jean Holm, Mansell, London, 1991

Royal Archives

By special permission of the Keeper of the Queen's Archives, Windsor Castle, Berks. Apply in writing.

Science and Technology

British Library Science Reference and Information Service: 25 Southampton Buildings, Chancery Lane, London WC2A 1AW (tel. 071–323 7494/6), Mon.–Fri., 9.30–9; Sat., 10–1. Also at 9 Kean Street, London WC2B 4AT (tel. 071–323 7288), Mon.–Fri., 9.30–5.30. Moving to St Pancras in 1993.

City of Westminster Central Reference Library, Ground Floor, 35 St Martin's Street, London WC2H 7HP (tel. 071–798 2034). Mon.–Fri., 10–7; Sat., 10–5.

Imperial College of Science and Technology Archives, Sherfield Building, Imperial College, London SW7 2AZ (tel. 071–589 5111, ext. 3022). Mon.–Fri., 10–12, 2–5, by appointment. Letter of introduction required.

Royal Society of London Library, 6 Carlton House Terrace, London SW1Y 5AG (tel. 071–839 5561). Mon.–Fri., 10–5. Admission on introduction by a Fellow: *bona fide* researchers on written application.

Science Museum Library, Exhibition Road, London SW7 5NH (tel. 071–938 8200). Mon.–Fri., 10–5.30.

See also the Highgate Literary and Scientific Institution, listed under 'Private Subscription Libraries'.

Science Fiction

Science Fiction Foundation Research Library, Polytechnic of East London, Longbridge Road, Dagenham, Essex RM8 2AS (tel. 081–590 7222, ext. 2177). By appointment.

Theatre

Mander and Mitchenson Theatre Collection, The Mansion, Beckenham Place Park, Beckenham BR3 2BP (tel. 081–658 7725). Open to *bona fide* researchers by appointment.

Society for Theatre Research, c/o Theatre Museum, 1e Tavistock Street, Covent Garden, London WC2E 7PA. Written enquiries only.

Theatre Museum, 1e Tavistock Street, London WC2E 7PA (tel. 071–836 7891). Tues.–Fri., 10.30–1, 2–4.30, strictly by appointment. Entrance to the Study Room is not the Museum entrance, but round the corner in Tavistock Street at basement level, approached by a ramp. The collection includes that of the Enthoven Collection, previously at the Victoria & Albert Museum, and the library of the former British Theatre Association.

Recommended books:

A Directory of Theatre Research, ed. Diana Howard, published by the Society for Theatre Research/Library Association, London, 2nd ed., 1986; new edition in preparation

The London Stage, a series published by Scarecrow, Metuchen, N.J., consisting of a day-by-day calendar of plays produced at the major London theatres in the period 1890–1939; 12 vols to date, continuing

Transport

Chartered Institute of Transport Library, 80 Portland Place, London W1N 4DP (tel. 071–636 9952). *Bona fide* researchers may use the reference facilities. Mon.–Fri., 10–5.

London Transport Museum Library, Covent Garden, London WC2E 7BB (tel. 071–379 6344). Mon.–Fri., 10–5.

National Tramway Museum, Crich, Matlock, Derbyshire DE4 5DP (tel. 0773 852565). Mon.–Fri., 9–5.

United Nations

United Nations Information Centre Library, Ship House, 20 Buckingham Gate, London SW1E 6LB (tel. 071–630 1981). Mon., Wed., Thurs., 10–1, 2–5.

Weather

National Meteorological Library, London Road, Bracknell, Berks RG12 2SZ (tel. 0344 85 420242). *Bona fide* researchers admitted, preferably by appointment; otherwise written enquiries. Mon.–Fri., 8.30–4.30.

Wills

Borthwick Institute of Historical Research (York University), St Anthony's Hall, Peaseholme Green, York YO1 2PW (tel. 0904 642315). Mon.–Fri., 9.30–12.50, 2–4.50, by appointment; closed for one week at Easter and part of Christmas vacation (PCY wills).

Principal Registry of the Family Division, Somerset House, Strand, London WC2R 1LP (tel. 071–936 6960). Mon.–Fri., 10–4.30 (wills and administrations since 1858).

Public Record Office, Chancery Lane, London, WC2A 1LR (tel. 081–876 3444). Admission by reader's ticket. Mon.–Fri., 9.30–5; closed two weeks in October (PCC wills).

Women's Studies

Fawcett Library, City of London Polytechnic, Old Castle Street, London E1 7NT (tel. 071–247 5826). Term-time, Mon., 11–8.30, Wed.–Fri., 10–5; vacation, Mon., Wed., Fri., 10–5. Annual subscription or one-day pass for non-members.

Feminist Library, 5 Westminster Bridge Road, London SE1 (tel. 071–928 7789). Tues., 11–8; Sat., Sun., 2–5.

Recommended title: *Personal Writings by Women to 1900: A Bibliography of American and British Writers*, compiled by G. Davis and B.A. Joyce, Mansell, London, 1989. Autobiographies, diaries, letters, travelogues alphabetically by author, with chronology (from 1475) and subject index.

World Wars I and II

Churchill Archives Centre, Churchill College, Cambridge CB3 0DS (tel. 0223 336087). Mon.–Fri., 9–12.30, 1.30–5, by appointment with the Archivist. Letter of introduction required. (Papers of military and naval commanders, politicians and scientists; certain collections subject to special conditions of access).

Imperial War Museum Library, Lambeth Road, London SE1 6HZ (tel. 071–416 5000). Mon.–Fri., 10–5, preferably by appointment. Closed last two full weeks in October.

Wiener Library, Institute of Contemporary History, 4 Devonshire Street, London W1N 2BH (tel. 071–636 7247/8). Letter of introduction required. Subscription payable for extensive research, but short-term use of reference facilities free. Mon.–Fri., 10–5.30. N.B. The collection of books was mostly transferred to Tel Aviv University in 1980, but the bulk of the material has been retained on microfilm in London.

APPENDIX II

Reference Books for the Writer

Good reference books are expensive, and the average writer cannot afford to compete with a library in keeping his personal collection fully up to date. He would be foolish even to try. What he buys, therefore, must be related to his own pocket, mobility and access to a well-stocked reference library, as well as to the special nature of his work.

Some basic suggestions for a writer's bookshelf are listed below. It is recommended that a plan for systematic renewal should be worked out, whereby you replace the essential yearbooks annually and other books in rotation. Those which are discarded may be sold to a secondhand book-dealer and the proceeds put towards the purchase of new editions. Excellent reference works may often be picked up in secondhand bookshops for a fraction of their original cost and are a good buy for those not engaged on highly topical work; the information they contain can be supplemented or updated by the occasional visit to the library or, in case of urgent need, by a telephone call to the reference librarian. Remainder dealers also frequently sell reference books at substantial discounts, and you should also keep an eye open for special offers advertised by book clubs. Paperbacks are by no means to be scorned: although naturally they will not stand up to as much handling as hard-covers, you will not be so reluctant to discard them when revised editions become available – nor, in the meantime, will you feel guilty about giving them the full 'working tool' treatment, annotating and marking them as your research proceeds.

At the end of a major project you may decide to dispose of a number of books in order to create shelf space for a new set related to your next work, and here again the secondhand bookseller with whom you are in the habit of dealing will undoubtedly give you a fair price. Depending on shelf space, do not however be *too* ruthless! (How to locate specialist booksellers will be found on page 33, and details of bookfinding services on page 41).

Suggested Basic Reference Library for the Writer

The essential items are:

1 A good English dictionary.

   The Oxford English Dictionary (OED), 2nd edition, 20 volumes, 1989, is obviously ideal, but probably beyond the pocket (and shelf-space) of the average writer for home use. A compact edition of the original edition, with supplement, was issued (together with reading glass) in 1987. For most purposes *The Shorter Oxford English Dictionary* (2 vols, 3rd ed. 1973) or the *Concise Oxford Dictionary* (8th ed., 1990) will be adequate. *Webster's Third New International Dictionary* (1981) concentrates on current usage, but is also expensive. Recommended single-volume dictionaries include *Chambers' English Dictionary* (7th ed., 1988), *Collins' English Dictionary* (1991) and *Webster's New Collegiate Dictionary* (1983). For those who like to keep a smaller dictionary handy for quick reference, the *Oxford Paperback Dictionary* (3rd ed., 1988) or the *Penguin English Dictionary* (1986) are excellent. Already mentioned in chapter 10 is the *Oxford Writers' Dictionary* (1990); this has replaced the earlier *Oxford Dictionary for Writers and Editors*.

2 An encyclopedic dictionary.

   Up-to-date editions include the *Cassell Encyclopedic Dictionary* (1990), *Collins' Concise Dictionary Plus* (1990) and the *Oxford Encyclopedic Dictionary* (1991).

3 An up-to-date biographical dictionary.

   Who's Who, if you can afford it. Look out for the new, three-volume *Concise Dictionary of National Biography*, which is in preparation. The best inexpensive buy is *Chambers' Biographical Dictionary* (1990, paperback rev. ed., 1991). Another recent paperback is the *Hutchinson Dictionary of Biography* (1990).

4 A good atlas, plus, if possible, a world gazetteer.

   The Times Atlas of the World (rev ed., 1991) is the best, but there is a cheaper version, *The Times Concise Atlas of the World* (rev. ed. 1991). Other up-to-date recommended titles are the *Philip's Atlas of the World* (1991), *Philip's Concise World Atlas* (1991) and *Philip's International World Atlas* (1991) – the latter is also a gazetteer. *The Statesman's Year Book World Gazetteer*, edited by John Paxton and now in its fourth edition (1991), is the best of its kind.

   N.B. Atlases are brought up to date every few years, and it is wise to buy the latest edition of the best you can afford. If in doubt, take the advice of a firm like Stanford's, 12–14 Long Acre, London WC2E 9LP (tel. 071–836 1321).

5 A road atlas/gazetteer of the British Isles.
The Ordnance Survey Touring Atlas of Great Britain (4th rev. ed., 1990), the *A-Z Great Britain Road Atlas* (1988; paperback version, 1990) and the *AA Great Britain Road Atlas* (19th rev. ed., 1990) are all excellent.

6 An encyclopedia.
Here the choice depends very much on your needs and on the money you have to spend. Choose the best you can afford. *The New Encyclopedia Britannica*, in thirty volumes (15th ed., 1979) is a good investment, but probably not worthwhile unless you live a great distance from a reference library. If, on the other hand, you ever have the chance to acquire a secondhand set of the 9th (the so-called 'scholars' edition) or the 11th *Britannica* (with supplements, the most extensive), do so. There are several other good encyclopedias on the market; *Chambers', Everyman's, Macmillan* are all excellent. (It pays to shop – or rather browse – around before parting with a substantial sum.) Good value so far as single-volume encyclopedias are concerned are *The Cambridge Encyclopedia* (1990) and *The Longman Encyclopedia* (1989).

7 A dictionary of quotations (or more than one).
Standard works are *The Oxford Book of Quotations* (3rd ed., 1980), *The Oxford Book of Modern Quotations* (1991) and *Bartlett's Familiar Quotations* (15th ed., 1985). For quick reference there are the *New Penguin Dictionary of Quotations* (1991) and the *New Penguin Dictionary of Modern Quotations* (1991). *The Concise Oxford Dictionary of Quotations* (2nd ed., 1981), in paperback, is available as a boxed set with *The Concise Oxford Dictionary of Proverbs* (1982). In recent years there have been many different compilations on subjects ranging from biographical quotations to war quotations, too numerous to list here. Buy the one that most reflects your writing interest.

8 A dictionary of dates.
The most up to date are the *Encyclopedia of Dates and Events*, published by Headway (1991) and the *Pan Book of Dates* (1990). Other recommended compilations are *Everyman's Dictionary of Dates* (7th ed., 1985), *Chambers' Dictionary of Dates* (1983), and the *Teach Yourself Encyclopedia of Dates and Events* (1979). James Trager's *The People's Chronology* (Heinemann, 1979) contains a good deal of information not often found in more conventional dictionaries of dates. A much earlier work, which occasionally may be picked up secondhand

at modest cost, is *Haydn's Dictionary of Dates and Universal Information* (1910); this also contains dates and items of interest that have had to be dropped from recent works.

9 A concise world history and/or chronology of historical events. William L. Langer's *An Encyclopedia of World History* (5th ed., Harrap, 1973) is out of print and unlikely to be reissued. There is a two-volume illustrated edition published in the United States under the title *The New Illustrated Encyclopedia of World History* (Abrams, New York, 1975). As this is one of the best reference tools, look for it secondhand. Useful for quick reference are S.H. Steinberg's *Historical Tables 58 BC – AD 1990* (Macmillan, 1991) and *The Wall Chart of World History* (Studio, 1991).

10 A thesaurus.
    A new edition of *Roget's Thesaurus of English Words and Phrases*, edited and brought up to date by E.M. Kirkpatrick, was published by Longman in 1987; it is available in hard- or paperback. Another modern compilation is *The Oxford Thesaurus*, edited by Laurence Urdang (Oxford University Press, 1991).

11 *Fowler's Modern English Usage*, revised by Sir Ernest Gowers (Oxford University Press, 2nd ed., 1965). This can be purchased in paperback as a boxed set together with *The Oxford Paperback Dictionary*.

12 *Brewer's Dictionary of Phrase and Fable*, 14th ed., Cassell, London, 1989; concise edition, 1991

13 *The Writers' & Artists' Yearbook*, published annually by A & C Black, London. Every writer should possess a current edition. This is one reference book that should be renewed each year.

14 One or more other directories reflecting the writer's chief interests: *The Cassell and Publishers' Association Directory of Publishing*; *Benn's Media Directory*; *Willings' Press Guide*. The radio and television writer will want the current *Guide to the BBC* and the *Radio Authority Pocket Book*.

●

The above titles will form a first-class nucleus reference library, which can be built up over the years according to the dictates of the writer's bank balance and his work requirements. Some further suggestions are:

Britain: An Official Handbook, published annually by HMSO, London
The Cambridge Historical Encyclopedia of Great Britain and

Ireland, ed. Christopher Haigh, Cambridge University Press, Cambridge, 1985

Concise Guide to Reference Material, ed. A.J. Walford, Library Association, London, 1981; new edition in preparation

Debrett's Correct Form, compiled by Patrick Montague-Smith, Debrett's Peerage/Country Life/Futura, London, paperback rev. ed., 1979

Debrett's Peerage & Baronetage, new ed., Debrett's Peerage/Macmillan, London, 1990

Europa World Year Book, published annually by Europa, London

Hollis Press & Public Relations Annual, published annually by Hollis Directories, Sunbury-on-Thames, Middx

International Authors' & Writers' Who's Who, published every few years by International Biographical Centre, Cambridge (12th ed., 1991)

International Who's Who, published annually by Europa, London

Oxford Companion to English Literature, 5th ed., ed. M. Drabble, Oxford University Press, 1985

Pears Cyclopaedia, 100th ed., Pelham, London, 1991

Record Repositories in Great Britain, HMSO, London; updated every few years (latest edition 1991)

The Shorter New Cambridge Bibliography of English Literature, ed. G. Watson, Cambridge University Press, Cambridge, 1981

The Statesman's Year Book, published annually by Macmillan, London

Whitaker's Almanack, published annually by Whitaker, London

Who Was Who, 8 vols to date, covering the years 1897–1990, plus cumulative index volume, A & C Black, London

The Writer's Handbook, ed. Barry Turner, published annually by Macmillan, London

Index

division of holdings
between Chancery Lane
and Kew, 51
*Guide to the Contents of
the Public Record Office*,
59
ordering procedures, xii, 51
publications, 51, 52, 105,
127
reader's tickets, 51
see also Ireland, Public
Record Offices; Scottish
Record Office

Quaker records, 122–3, 128,
189
quotations
dictionaries of, 48, 195
from copyright material,
11, 26–7

Radio Authority, 53
record agents, 117, 120, 137
record offices, *see* county
record offices; Ireland,
Public Record Offices;
Public Record Office
(London); Scottish
Record Office
recorded material, 53–5,
106–7, 188–9
reference books, suggested
nucleus library of, 194–7
reference libraries (UK), 34,
179–80
reference material, guides to,
37–8, 59, 141–2
religious records, 179, 189
Religious Society of Friends,
122–3, 189
reprographic facilities, *see*
photocopying
research costs, 9–11, 96–7,
123, 139–40

research methods, 6–7, 9,
21–31, 107–8
researcher, the writer as, xi,
1–8
researchers, freelance, 10,
108, 136–7, 139–40, 143
see also genealogists;
picture researchers;
record agents
Roman Catholic records, 123
Rowse, Dr A.L., *quoted*, 7
Royal Archives, 189
Royal Botanic Gardens
Library, 22, 34, 187
Royal Commission on
Historical Manuscripts, 20,
50, 98, 169
Royal Institute of
International Affairs
Library, 46–7, 185
Russia, 155–6

St Catherine's House
(London), 121, 122
St George Saunders, Joan,
quoted, 7
Scandinavian sources,
153–4
school records, 104
science and technology, 46,
68, 190
science fiction, 87, 190
Science Museum Library, 34,
190
Science Reference and
Information Service, British
Library, 36, 39, 46,
67–8, 190
Scotland
General Register Office,
121, 169
National Library of
Scotland, 34, 51, 168

Personal Notes